Renaissance Literature and Postcolonial Studies

THE UNIVERSITY OF
WINCHESTER

Postcolonial Literary Studies

Series Editors: David Johnson, The Open University and Ania Loomba, University of Pennsylvania

Published titles:
Medieval Literature and Postcolonial Studies, Lisa Lampert-Weissig
Renaissance Literature and Postcolonial Studies, Shankar Raman
Eighteenth-century British Literature and Postcolonial Studies,
    Suvir Kaul
Victorian Literature and Postcolonial Studies, Patrick Brantlinger
Postwar British Literature and Postcolonial Studies, Graham MacPhee

Forthcoming titles:
Romantic Literature and Postcolonial Studies, Elizabeth A. Bohls
Modernist Literature and Postcolonial Studies, Rajeev Patke

Visit the Postcolonial Literary Studies website at
www.euppublishing.com/series/epls

Renaissance Literature and Postcolonial Studies

Shankar Raman

Edinburgh University Press

Edinburgh University Press Ltd
22 George Square, Edinburgh

www.euppublishing.com

Typeset in 10.5/13 Sabon
by Servis Filmsetting Ltd, Stockport, Cheshire, and
printed and bound in Great Britain by
CPI Antony Rowe, Chippenham and Eastbourne

A CIP record for this book is available from the British Library

ISBN 978 0 7486 3683 9 (hardback)
ISBN 978 0 7486 3684 6 (paperback)

Contents

Series Editors' Preface

Postcolonial Literary Studies foregrounds the colonial and neo-colonial contexts of literary and cultural texts, and demonstrates how these texts help to understand past and present histories of empires. The books in the series relate key literary and cultural texts both to their historical and geographical moments, and to contemporary issues of neo-colonialism and global inequality. In addition to introducing the diverse body of postcolonial criticism, theory and scholarship in literary studies, the series engages with relevant debates on postcolonialism in other disciplines – history, geography, critical theory, political studies, economics and philosophy. The books in the series exemplify how postcolonial studies can re-configure the major periods and areas of literary studies. Each book provides a comprehensive survey of the existing field of scholarship and debate with a time line, a literature survey, discussion of key critical, theoretical, historical and political debates, case studies providing exemplary critical readings of key literary texts, and guides to further reading. At the same time, each book is also an original critical intervention in its own right. In much the same way that feminism has re-defined how all literary texts are analysed, our ultimate aim is that this series will contribute to all texts in literary studies being read with an awareness of their colonial and neo-colonial resonances.

DJ and AL

List of Illustrations

Acknowledgements

Sins of omission and commission weigh heavily on a book such as this, given the variety of topics, texts and cultures it engages. That I have not omitted and committed more than I have is due to readers who responded to the manuscript with characteristic care and generousity: in particular, Mary Fuller, Diana Henderson, and the editors of this series (David Johnson and Ania Loomba) helped refine its claims and expression, catch errors, and direct me to new sources.

At different points en route, others contributed their energies to the book as well, sometimes unbeknownst to them: Lynne Jones and Noel Jackson played the role of 'intelligent reader outside the field', Wolfgang Struck introduced me to Olearius, and Maureen Quilligan spurred my interest in de Bry. The Folger Shakespeare Library provided access to many of the primary sources dealt with here, as well as a stimulating environment in which to write; I am especially grateful to Carol Brobeck, Gail Paster, David Schalkwyk and the staff at the Folger for making me feel so comfortable during my fellowship there. Throughout, I drew on the support and encouragement of people close to me: my parents, Lianne, Tara, Jumbi, Ruma, Esha, Mihir, Maya, and Uma, all chipped in the ways that only they could. An additional thanks must go to Jackie Jones of Edinburgh University Press and the series editors not only for bringing me into this project but for their patience and forbearance. I can only hope that the final product validates their faith.

Some of my case studies draw on material published elsewhere, albeit much altered for this volume: Palgrave Macmillan generously permitted me to make use of essays on Gil Vicente and Luis Vaz de Camões; the *Journal of Medieval and Early Modern Studies* has recently published a much longer piece on the de Bry compendia of travel narratives; and my reading of Donne is based on an article that originally appeared in *Criticism*. The full bibliographical details for these may be found in the Works Cited list.

Timeline

Note: The timeline begins with some context-setting events pre-dating the voyages to the New World and India, which have come to signal the beginning of early modern colonialism.

Date	Historical Events	Literary and Other Texts
1368–1644	Ming Dynasty in China founded by Zhu Yuanzhang.	
1405	Death of Timur-I Lang (Tamerlaine) ends threat of military invasion of China from east.	
1405–33	Zheng He's naval expeditions to Indian Ocean, reaching east coast of Africa.	
c. 1415 onwards	Portugal begins Atlantic explorations under Prince Henry the Navigator (1394–1460).	
1434	Portuguese reach Cape Bojador, leading to involvement in sub-Saharan African gold and slave trades.	
1453	Constantinople falls to the Ottoman Turks, signalling end of Byzantine Christian Empire.	
1479–1516	Reign of Ferdinand of Aragon and Isabella of Castille in Spain.	

c. 1480	Spanish Inquisition begins investigating heresy among Jewish converts to Christianity.
1482	João II establishes Casa da Mina e Tratos de Guiné to manage Portuguese West-African trade.
1487	• King João II sends Pedro da Covilhã on overland expedition to India and East Africa. • Portuguese Bartolomeu Dias reaches Cape of Good Hope.
1492	• Spanish Conquest of Granada completes *Reconquista*, the crusades to recover Iberian peninsula from the Muslims, and expels Jews. • Genoese explorer Columbus departs on voyage leading to discovery of the New World. • Turkish emperor Bajazeth II invades Hungary.
1493	Papal Bull 'Inter cetera divina' divides New World between Spain and Portugal, entrusting them with evangelising natives.
1494	Treaty of Tordesillas divides New World between Spain and Portugal.
1496–1521	Reign of Manuel I ('The Great'), important period of Portugal's development as overseas power.
1497	Portugal expels Jews.
1498	Vasco da Gama's fleet reaches India.
1499–1500	Amerigo Vespucci and Alonso de Ojeda's voyage from Spain to South America and mouth of Amazon river.

Columbus' famous letter reporting the discovery of the New World.

By 1500	Hindu Vijaynagar empire established, holding sway through local military chiefs over much of southern India.	
1500	• Portuguese Pedro Alvarez Cabral's discovery of Brazil. • Portuguese develop the caravel, a small armed ship capable of dominating larger vessels as well as carrying substantial cargo. • Casa da Índia e da Guiné established to manage Portuguese Asian and African trade.	Pero Vaz de Caminha's 'Letter to King Manuel I' on Portuguese discovery of Brazil.
1502	Vasco da Gama establishes Portuguese colony at Cochin, India.	
1503	• Casa de Contratácion established to regulate Spanish overseas trade. • First arrival of gold in Spain from Mexico; beginning of Spanish emigration to Americas.	
1505	Portuguese occupy Tangier and Agadir on North African coast.	
1508	Egyptian-Indian fleet defeats Portuguese squadron at Chaul.	First Spanish printing of chivalric romance *Amadis de Gaul*.
1509	• Francisco de Almeida destroys Egyptian-Indian fleet at Diu, revenging his defeat the previous year. • Henry VIII ascends English throne (r. 1509–47).	• Gil Vicente, *Auto da Índia*.
1509–11	Spain seizes Oran, Bougie and Tripoli from Muslims on North African coast.	
1510	• Portuguese acquire Goa as headquarters in India.	

	• Almeida and 11 of his captains killed by Khoikhoi in Table Bay (South Africa), in retaliation for raiding local villages.	
1511–30		Peter Martyr d' Anghiera, *Decadas del nuevo mundo*.
1511	Afonso de Albuquerque reaches Amboyna and captures Malacca, centre of Asian spice trade. Later brings back large returns in trade from India, leading to Lisbon displacing Venice as entrepôt for Asian goods.	
1513		Gil Vicente, *A Exortação da Guerra*, a play encouraging Portugal's campaigns in North Africa.
1515–47	François I's reign in France.	
1516	Charles I's reign in Spain begins (r. 1516–56).	Ludovico Ariosto, *Orlando Furioso* (complete edition in 1532).
1517	Turks take Cairo; Arabia comes under Turkish suzerainty after Mecca's surrender to Selim I.	Gil Vicente, *Auto da Barca do Inferno*.
1519	• Charles I takes title of Emperor Charles V, Netherlands and Austria being joined with Spain to form the Hapsburg Empire. • Hernando Cortés enters Tenochtitlan, capital of Mexico, and is received by Montezuma, leading to conquest of Mexico and fall of Aztec empire.	

1519–22	Portuguese Fernão de Magelhães [Magellan] circumnavigates globe.	
1520–66	Ottoman Sultan Suleiman I's reign ('The Magnificent').	
1521	Ottomans capture Belgrade.	*Kitab-I Bahriye* (Book of the Sea), navigational book by Ottoman Admiral Piri Reis.
1521–47	João III's reign in Portugal, which establishes Portuguese inquisition (1536) and continues expansionist policies of predecessor, Manuel I.	
1522	• Ottoman conquest of Rhodes. • Slave uprising on Spanish island of Hispaniola.	
1522–67	Consolidation of Ming empire in China and beginning of contacts between Chinese elites and Jesuits.	
1524–76	Shah Tahmasp I's reign in the Safavid empire of Iran.	
1526	• Defeat and death of Hungarian king Louis II at Battle of Mohács; John Zapolya accepts Ottoman suzerainty. • Babar, descendant of Timur-I Lang, wins decisive battle of Panipat over Ibrahim Shah Lodi, and founds Mughal Empire in North India. • Congo king Mbemba Nzinga complains to João II about Portuguese merchants selling his people as slaves to work in São Tomé plantations.	

1528		Anonymous Nahuatl account by Aztecs of Tlateloloco about Spanish conquest.
1528–9	Ottoman siege of Vienna, which fails to take the city.	
1529	Treaty of Zaragoza [Saragossa] between Spain and Portugal establishes eastern meridian demarcating their overseas empires.	
1530		Peter Martyr d'Anghiera, *De orbe novo*.
1531	Frenchman Nicolas Villegagnon discovers site of Rio de Janeiro.	
1532	Francisco Pizarro's expedition from Panama to Peru, leading to execution of the Inca a year later.	• Francisco de Vitoria, *De Indis et iure belli relectiones*, on government of colonies and international law. • François Rabelais, *Pantagruel*.
1534	Frenchman Jacques Cartier's first voyage to North America.	François Rabelais, *Gargantua*.
1535	• Charles V of Spain's expedition to Tunis, part of campaign against Ottoman Turks. • Jacques Cartier's second voyage, leading to Lawrence River and Quebec.	
1536	• The Arauco war between Spanish and Mapuche people begins, a conflict that lasts three centuries. • First revolt in Cuba by imported African slaves at gold mine of Jobabó.	

1537		Magnificent miniatures illustrating Iranian national epic, the *Shah Nama* (Book of Kings), presented by Safavid ruler to Ottoman Selim II in 1568.
1537–40	Turco-Venetian War, resulting in Venice surrendering last possessions in Morea to Ottomans.	
1538	• Turkish expedition to India seizes Aden from Portugal (recovered by Portuguese in 1548). • Second Cuban uprising of imported slaves supported by local insurgents.	
1540	Pope officially approves Ignatius of Loyola's Society of Jesus (aka the Jesuits).	
1541	Fourth Ottoman campaign, leading to annexation of Hungary.	
1542	• Ireland made a Kingdom, setting off England's arduous colonisation of island. • After a two-month battle with Iroquois Indians, Cartier abandons fort of Charlesbourg-Royal, reoccupied by Roberval shortly thereafter.	Alvar Nuñez Cabeza de Vaca, *La Relacíon* (later called *Naufragios*), account of disastrous Spanish expedition in Florida.
c. 1543	First Portuguese contacts with Japan, leading to introduction of musket, which transforms Japanese warfare.	
1545	• Discovery of silver mines in Potosí (in what was then Peru). • Safavid capture of Kandahar from Mughals.	Publication in Paris of *Brief Recit et succincte narration* [on Cartier's second voyage].

1545–63	Council of Trent, major reform council condemning Protestant heresies and lending support to Counter-Reformation.
1546	Discovery of silver in Zacatecas, Mexico.
1548	Charles V of Spain annexes 17 provinces of the Netherlands.
1549–51	Jesuit Francis Xavier introduces Christianity into Japan; doctrinal intolerance of Jesuits leads to conflicts with nobility.
1551	Sir Thomas More, *Utopia* (English edn).
1552	• Bartolomé de las Casas, *Brévisima relacíon de la destruccíon de las Indias* (written c. 1542). • João de Barros, first volume of *Décadas da Ásia*, history of Portuguese expansion, subsequent volumes published through 1615, and then continued by Diogo do Couto.
1552–6	Ivan IV of Russia ('the Terrible') conquers Kazakhstan and Astrakhan from the Tartars, giving Russia control of the entire Volga and opening way for expansion east and southeast.
1553	Englishman Richard Chancellor reaches Moscow via White Sea.

1554	Portuguese defeat Ottoman fleet off Hormuz.	López de Gómara, *Historia de las Indias*, description of Hérnan Cortés' conquest of Aztec empire.
1555	• English given trading rights by Russia. • Nicolas Villegagnon's expedition establishes French base in Brazil.	Richard Eden, *Decades of the Newe Worlde or West India* (translated from Peter Martyr's *Decadas* and other texts).
1556	• Abdication of Charles V, Netherlands and Spain pass to his son Philip II (r. 1556–98). • Akhbar ascends to Mughal throne (r.1556–1605).	Micael de Caraval and Luis Hurtado de Toledo, *Auto de las Cortes de la Muerte*, one of the earliest Spanish plays on the conquest and its aftermath.
1557	• Portuguese establish permanent settlement in Macau, off Chinese coast. • Sebastian I of Portugal (r. 1557–78) ascends throne under regency of mother, Joanna of Austria.	André Thévet, *Les Singularitez de la France Antarctique*.
1558–1603	Elizabeth I's reign in England.	
1560–74	Charles IX's reign in France, starting as a ten-year old under his mother's regency.	
1562–98	Religious Wars in France, following persecution of Huguenots (French Protestants).	
1562	• John Hawkins initiates English participation in trans-Atlantic slave trade by taking a load of 300 slaves from Sierra Leone. • Jean Ribault and René de Laudonnière arrive on Florida coast.	

1563		• *The Whole and True Discoverye of Terra Florida,* English version of Jean Ribault's first voyage. • António Galvão, *Tratado dos Descobrimentos* [Treatise on Discoveries]. • John Foxe, *Acts and Monuments* (1st ed.).
1564		Bernadino de Sahagún, *Coloquios y doctrina cristiana*, a dialogue, perhaps fictional, between Nauhatl elders and Christian missionaries.
1565	• Ottoman siege of Malta. • Coalition of Ahmadnagar, Golconda, and Bijapur Badar defeats Vijaynagar at Talikota, leading to break up of Vijaynagar empire into autonomous principates. • Conflict between Spaniard Menendez and Ribault, leads to massacre of French in Carolina.	Girolamo Benzoni, *Historia del Mondo Nuevo*.
1566	Ottoman Selim II ascends throne (r. 1566–74).	Nicolas Le Challeux, *Discours de l'histoire de la Floride*.
1567–1648	The revolt of the Netherlands agains Spanish rule.	
1567	Philip II sends Duke of Alva to suppress revolt in Netherlands; tribunal (the 'Council of Blood') investigates rebellion and heresy, leading to execution of thousands and open rebellion against Spain.	

1569–71	Revolt of Moriscos (Christian converts from Islam) in Spain, brutally suppressed, leading to expulsion of Moriscos in 1609.	
1569		• Alonso de Ercilla y Zuñiga, *La Araucana* (first part). • Bernadino de Sahagún, *Historia general de las cosas de Nueva España*, monumental description of Aztec life, written in Nauhatl.
1570	• Ottoman Turks attack Cyprus, leading to Venetian Republic abandoning island in 1573 and agreeing to pay indemnity. • Nagasaki opened by local lord to foreign trade, becoming largest Japanese port for foreign commerce.	• Abraham Ortelius, *Theatrum Orbis Terrarum*, important early modern atlas. • John Foxe, *Acts and Monuments* (enlarged 2nd ed.). • François de Belleforest, *L'Histoire universelle du monde*.
1571	• Battle of Lepanto, where a naval fleet of Holy League (Spain, Venice, and Papacy) defeats Ottoman navy. Not a decisive victory, since Turks rebuild navy to ravage coast of Italy soon after, seizing Tunis in 1574. • Crimean Tartars attack and sack Moscow.	
1572	St Bartholomew's Day Massacre (23–4 August): murder of Admiral Coligny and massacre of Protestants in Paris and province after Henry of Bourbon's marriage to Margaret of Valois.	• Luís Vaz de Camões, *Os Lusíadas*, epic on Vasco da Gama's voyage to India. • André Thévet, *Cosmographie Universelle*.

1572–3	Mughal emperor Akhbar's defeat of Rajputs gives access to sea ports and new revenues.	
1572–6	Northern provinces of Netherlands expel Spanish garrisons.	
1574	• Reign of Henri III in France begins (r. 1574–89). • Reign of Ottoman Sultan Murad II begins (d. 1589), who initiates war with Safavid empire of Iran in 1576.	
1575		Torquato Tasso, *Gerusalemme Liberata*, epic poem about the Crusades.
1576	• Spanish plunder Antwerp, the most important trading port on Europe's Atlantic coast. • Englishman Martin Frobisher reaches what is today Frobisher Bay in Canada. • Mughal conquest of Bengal from the Afghans.	• Jean Bodin, *Six Books of Commonwealth*, arguing for religious tolerance and defending sovereign monarchy. • Humphrey Gilbert, *Discourse of a Discoverie for a new passage to Cataia.*
1577	Sir Francis Drake begins circumnavigation of world via Cape Horn, returning to England in 1580.	• Raphael Holinshed, *Chronicles of England, Scotland and Ireland.* • Richard Eden, *History of Travel in the East and West Indies.*
1578	• Death of King Sebastian, along with Abd-Malik (King of Fez) and the pretender to throne of Fez, at Battle of Al Kasr Al-Kabir, where Moors defeat Portuguese and mercernary troops. • Defeat of Russians by Sweden at Wenden.	• Jean de Léry, *Histoire d'un Voyage faict en la Terre du Brésil.* • Alonso de Ercilla y Zuñiga, *La Araucana* (second part).

1579	Union of Utrecht by seven northern provinces of Netherlands.	• Sir Thomas North's translation of Plutarch's *Lives*. • Urbain Chauveton, *Histoire nouvelle du Nouveau Monde*, based on Benzoni's earlier history.
1580	• Philip II takes over Portuguese throne after death of Cardinal Henry. First Portugal and then its overseas dominions come under Spanish sway. • Commercial Treaty between Ottomans and English, granting latter privileges formerly limited to France and Venice. English extraterritorial rights expanded by successive renewals of treaty in 1603, 1606, 1626, 1641, 1662, and 1675.	Death of Luís Vaz de Camões.
1580–95		Michel de Montaigne, *Essais*.
1581	• Northern provinces of Netherlands declare independence from Spain. • Levant or Turkey Company created by royal charter, with monopoly over English-Ottoman trade.	• Robert Wilson, *The Three Ladies of London*. • Fray Diego Durán, *The History of the Indies of New Spain*, valuable source for information about pre-conquest Mexico.
1582	Russia makes peace with Poland and Spain; Ivan IV forced to accept loss of land.	Richard Hakluyt, *Divers Voyages touching the Discoverie of America*.
1583		John Foxe, *Acts and Monuments* (enlarged 4th ed.).

1584	• Maurice of Nassau, son of William of Orange, assumes Stadtholdership of Dutch Republic. England begins to aid the Dutch. • Theodor I succeeds Ivan IV in Russia, followed by Boris Godunov in 1598, leading to the so-called Time of Troubles. • Sir Walter Raleigh's discovery and annexation of Virginia.	
1585	Spanish capture Antwerp.	• Juan Gonzalez de Mendoza, *Historia de las cosas mas notables, ritos y constumbres del gran reyno de la China,* first major Western work on Chinese history. • Lucas Janszoon Waghearen, *Spiegel der Zeevaart*, important navigational text.
1586		William Camden, *Britannia.*
1587	• Sir Francis Drake defeats Spanish fleet at Cadiz. • English colony established at Roanoke Island (North Carolina), mysteriously disappears by the time the next ships return (hence, 'the Lost Colony'). • Toyotomi Hideyoshi (1536–98) banishes Portuguese missionaries from Japan.	Christopher Marlowe, *Tamburlaine the Great I.*
1588	War with Spain and destruction of Spanish Armada in storm.	• George Peele, *Turkish Mahomet and Hiren the Fair Greek.*

		• Christopher Marlowe, *Tamburlaine the Great II.*
		• Thomas Hariot, *A briefe and true report of the new found land of Virginia.*
1588–1629	Shah Abbas's reign on Safavid throne, leads to rise of Safavid state and centralisation of authority.	
1589	Henri IV takes up French throne, Catholic party refuses to recognise him.	• Richard Hakluyt, *Principall Navigations, Voyages and Discoveries of the English Nation.*
		• Alonso de Ercilla y Zuñiga, *La Araucana* (third part).
		• Richard Wilson, *The Three Lords and Three Ladies of London* (c. 1588–9).
1590		• Edmund Spenser, *The Faerie Queene* (1–3).
		• Christopher Marlowe, *The Jew of Malta.*
		• José de Acosta, *Historia Natural y Moral de las Indias.*
		• Theodore de Bry, *America I* [engraved edition of Thomas Hariot's 1588 *A briefe and true report*].
		• William Shakespeare, *Titus Andronicus* (early 1590s).
1590–1628		Theodore de Bry, *India Occidentalis* or *America* (13 vols) and *India Orientalis* (12 vols);

numerous editions of German and Latin translations of travel narratives, with engravings by de Bry and his successors.

1591		• Sir Philip Sidney, *Astrophil and Stella*. • Robert Greene, *Orlando Furioso*.
1592		• Thomas Kyd, *The Spanish Tragedy* (written between 1582 and 1592). • Thomas Kyd's *Soliman and Perseda* entered in Stationer's Register. • Anon., *Selimus*. • Anon., *Tamar Cham* (Parts 1 and 2).
1594	Lisbon closed to English and Dutch traders, giving them incentive to establish direct trade with East.	• George Peele, *The Battle of Alcazar*. • Fulke Greville, *Mustapha*.
1595	First Dutch fleet to the East Indies, a disastrous voyage under the command of Cornelius Houtman.	
1596		• William Shakespeare, *The Merchant of Venice* (approximate date). • Edmund Spenser, *The Faerie Queene* (Parts 4–6). • Anthony Munday, *Amadis de Gaul* (translation of the well-circulated Spanish chivalric romance).

		• Jan Huygen van Linschoten, *Itinerario* (English translation entitled *John Huighen van Linschoten his Discourses of Voyages to ye Easte & Weste Indies* appears in 1598).
		• Sir Walter Raleigh, *The Discoverie of Guiana*.
		• Pedro de Oña, *Arauco domado* (Arauco Tamed), epic poem exalting Spanish heroism in conquest of Chile.
		• Thomas Lodge, *A Margarite of America*.
		• George Chapman, *De Guiana, carmen epicum*.
1597	Hideyoshi executes a number of Jesuits, Franciscans and Japanese Christians.	• Anon, *Verhael van de Reyse* [Account of the Voyage], earliest account of first Dutch voyage to the East Indies.
1598	• French civil war ends with Edict of Nantes, giving Huguenots equal political rights with Catholics, but not freedom of religious worship. • Shah Abbas moves Safavid capital to Isphahan; arrival in Iran of English merchant adventurers Anthony and Robert Sherley. • Philip III ascends Spanish Throne (r. 1598–1621)	• Lope de Vega, *La Dragontea* (fanciful versified account of Drake's adventures). • 1598–1600: Richard Hakluyt, *The Principal Navigations, Voyages, Traffiques and Discoveries of the English Nation* (expanded 2nd ed.). • William Haughton, *Englishmen for my Money, or a Woman will Have her Will*.

1599		• Willem Lodewycksz., *D'Eeerste Boeck* [The First Book], account of the troubled Dutch expedition to the East Indies. • Mustafa Ali ibn Ahman ibn Abdulla, *Kunh ul-Ahbar* [The Essence of History]. • Edward Wright, *Certaine Errors in Navigation*. • Anon., *Mully Mollocco*.
1600	Chartering of English East India Company, first voyages to Spice Islands.	Thomas Heywood, *The Fair Maid of the West*, Part One (c. 1600–3).
1601	Matteo Ricci and the first Jesuit mission to be admitted to Peking.	• John Wheeler, *A Treatise of Commerce*. • Bento Teixeira Pinto, *Prosopopeya*, first Brazilian epic.
1602	• Dutch East India Company (VOC) granted monopoly on Dutch trade east of Cape of Good Hope. • Spanish traders arrive in eastern Japan.	
1603	• James I (r. 1603–25) succeeds Elizabeth upon her death. • Ottoman Sultan Ahmed I ascends throne (r. 1603–17). • John Mildenhall, East India Company representative, arrives at Agra but fails to secure trade concessions from Mughals (until 1608).	• Richard Knolles, *General Historie of the Turks*. • William Shakespeare, *Antony and Cleopatra* (c. 1603–07) and *Othello* (c. 1603–4).

1604		• Lope de Vega's *Comedias* (25 volumes) published.
1605	• Mughal emperor Jehangir (r. 1605–27) succeeds Akhbar.	• Inca Garcilaso de la Vega (1539–1616), *La Florida del Inca* [The Florida of the Inca], account of Hernando de Soto's expedition. • Anon., *The Famous History of the Life and Death of Captain Thomas Stukeley*.
1606	English Virginia Company chartered, sends 120 colonists to Virginia.	• Marc Lescarbot, *Théâtre de Neptune* (1606, published 1609), written to celebrate return of Jean Poutrincourt to Port Royal Bay (Canada). • Henrico Martinez, *Reportorio de los tiempos y historia natural de Nueva España I* [Chronicles of the Times and Natural History of New Spain].
1607	Jamestown founded, the first successful English colony on North American mainland.	• John Day, William Rowley and John Wilkins, *The Travels of the Three English Brothers*, a play on the voyage of the Sherley brothers to Persia. • Tahir Muhammed, *Rauzat ut-Tahirin* [The Garden of the Immaculate], a world history by a Mughal historian.

• Ben Jonson, *The Masque of Blackness* (first performed in 1605).
• Anthony Nixon, *The Three English Brothers. Sir T. Sherley His Travels, Sir H. Sherley His Embassage to the Christian Princes, Master R. Sherley His Wars ag. The Turkes.*

1609	• Dutch establish trading post in Hirado, Japan. • North African pirate corsairs begin to attacking English ships, capturing about 500 by 1616. • Shipwreck of *The Sea Venture* in the Bermudas. • Moriscos expelled from Spain.	• Inca Garcilosa de la Vega, *Comentario Reales do las Incas* [History of the Conquest of Peru]. • Hugo Grotius, *Mare Liberum*, key text in laying basis of international law. • Bartolomé Leonardo de Argensola, *Conquista de las Islas Molucas* [Conquest of the Moluccan Islands].
1609–21	Twelve Years Truce temporarily halts conflict between Spain and Dutch Republic, essentially establishing independence of latter.	
1610	• Henri IV's assassination; Louis XIII (r. 1610–43) accedes to throne at age nine under regency of mother, Marie de Medici. • John Guy leads expedition to colonise Newfoundland.	• Gaspar Pérez de Villagrá (1555–1620), *Historia de la Nueva México*, [History of New Mexico] epic poem on the colonisation of Mexico.

		• John Mason, *The Turk*
		• William Shakespeare, *Cymbeline*.
1611	Establishment of Plantation of Ulster in Ireland, forfeited to English Crown by Tyrone's rebellion.	William Shakespeare, *The Tempest*.
1612	• England gains trading rights in Surat after defeating Portuguese fleet. • Persecution of Christianity grows in Japan.	• Michael Drayton, *Polyolbion* (Part 1). • Samuel Purchas, *Hakluytus Posthumus*. • Sir John Davies, *The True Causes why Ireland was not Entirely Subdued*. • Richard Daborne, *A Christian Turn'd Turk*.
1613	Michael Romanov elected to Russian throne (reigns through 1645), sees restoration of order and establishment of serfdom.	• Lope de Vega, *Fuenteovejuna*. • Samuel Purchas, *Purchas His Pilgrimes; or Relations of the World and the Religions observed in all Ages*. • Thomas Middleton, *The Triumphs of Truth*. • George Chapman, *The Memorable Masque of the two honourable houses or Innes of Court; the Middle Temple and Lyncolnes Inn* (dating uncertain). • Guamán Poma de Ayala, *Nueva Corónica y Buen Gobierno* [New Chronicle and Good Government], revisionist account by Peruvian of conquest, written in a mixture of Quechua and Spanish (dating uncertain).

1614	Pocahontas marries John Rolfe.	• Sir Walter Raleigh, *History of the World*. • George Chapman begins translation of Homer's *Odyssey*. • Lope de Vega's *El Nuevo Mundo descubierto por Cristóbal Colón* (The New World Discovered by Christopher Columbus) printed, probably composed between 1598 and 1603.
1615		*De Christiana expeditione apud sinas* [Of the Christian expedition among the Chinese], an expanded Latin translation of Jesuit Matteo Ricci's account of his residence in China from 1583 to 1610.
1615–19	Sir Thomas Roe's embassy to Mughal court, also fails to secure treaty for English.	
1617	English East India Company establishes trading houses in Shiraz and Isphahan.	• Thomas Middleton, *The Triumphs of Honour and Industry*. • Thomas Goffe, *The Raging Turk*.
1618	• Beginning of Thirty Years' War, growing into a religious war between Protestants and Catholics across Europe, followed by Swedish and French struggle against Hapsburgs. • Sir Walter Raleigh executed.	• Thomas Coriate, *Traveller for the English Wits: Greetings from the Court of the Great Mogul* and *Mr. Thomas Coriate to his Friends in England sendeth greeting*. • John Fletcher, *The Knight of Malta*.

1619		Thomas Goffe, *The Courageous Turk*.
1620	Plymouth Colony established with arrival of Mayflower pilgrims at Cape Cod.	• John Fletcher, *The Island Princess* (c. 1620–1).
1621	• Spain resumes war with Netherlands. • Dutch West India Company chartered with monopoly of trade in African and American waters. Dutch East India Company receives trading rights from Safavid Shah Abbas. • Philip IV succeeds in Spain (reigns to 1665).	• Francis Bacon, *New Atlantis*. • Thomas Mun, *A Discourse of Trade from England unto the East Indies*.
1622	Powhatan forces attack Virginia Colony, killing 347 settlers.	Thomas Middleton, *The Triumphs of Honour and Virtue*.
1623	• Massacre of English by Dutch at Amboyna, forcing English to abandon trade in Siam, Japan, and East Indies. • Ottoman Sultan Murad IV's reign begins (through 1640).	
1624	Spanish driven from Japan, intercourse with Phillipines stopped.	John Smith, *The Generall Historie of Virginia, New-England and the Summer Isles*.
1625	• Death of James I, succeeded by Charles I (executed in 1649 after end of Civil War). • Dutch settle Manhattan.	• Ben Jonson, *A Staple of News*. • Hugo Grotius, *De jure pacis et bellis*. • Lope de Vega, *Arauco domado* (Arauco Tamed) (alternative dating 1598–1603), play on Chilean uprising in mid-sixteenth century.

		• Lope de Vega, *El Brasil restuido* [Brazil Restored], play about the Iberian retaking of Bay of All Saints from the Dutch.
1626		Tirso de Molina, *Todo es dar una cosa* (Much of a Muchness), written between 1626 and 1632, first of a trilogy of plays on Pizarro's conquest of Peru.
1628–57	Reign of Mughal emperor Shah Jahan, imprisoned and deposed by Aurangzeb in 1657.	
1629		Richard Brome, *The Northern Lass*.
1630		• Philip Massinger, *The Renegado* (first performed in 1624). • John Smith, *The True Travels, Adventures and Observations of Captain John Smith*.
1630s	Peasant rebellions and ethnic strife in China, leading to rebel band under Li Zicheng capturing Beijing and last Ming emperor committing suicide. Rise of Manchus in northern China.	
1631		Thomas Heywood's *The Fair Maid of the West*, Part 2 (written as sequel to revival of Part 1).

1632		• John Selden, *Mare Clausum*, a response to Grotius's theories on international law and trade. • Bernal Diaz del Castilo (1492–1585), *Historia Verdadera de la conquista de la Nueva España* [True History of the Conquest of New Spain], written some time after 1568 to refute Gómara's earlier *Historia*).
1633		Edmund Spenser, *A View of the Present State of Ireland* (written in 1590s).
1635		• William Davenant, *The Temple of Love*. • Henry Glapthorne, *The Hollander*. • Tirso de Molina, *Amazons in the Indies*, part of trilogy on Spanish in Peru.
1636	Japanese forbidden to go abroad and those abroad not allowed re-entry.	Henry Blount, *A Voyage into the Levant*.
1637		• Thomas Morton, *New England Canaan*, an attack on Puritan religious intolerance. • Domingo Francisco Chimalpáhin Cuauhtlehuanitzin, *Eight Relations and the Memorial of Colhuacan*, a world history written in Nauhatl.

1638	• Ottoman reconquest of Baghdad from the Safavids. • Japanese proscription on building large ships, as well as expulsion of Portuguese traders. Leaves only Dutch at Hirado and Chinese at Nagasaki as Japan's contacts to outside world.	William Davenant, *Madagascar and Other Poems.*
1639	• Expulsion of all Portuguese from Japan. • Site of Madras granted to English.	
1640	Portuguese revolt against Spanish rule, leading to João of Braganza being elected to Portuguese throne.	Richard Brome, *The Antipodes* (first performed in 1636).
1641	• Massacre of Protestants in Ulster, Ireland. • Capture of Malacca by Dutch, leading to their domination of East Indies.	
1642–6	English Civil War.	
1643		Roger Williams, *Key into the Language of America.*
1644	Qing dynasty commences in China with entrance of Manchu forces into Beijing and defeat of rebel forces of Li Zicheng.	
1646		Willem Bontekoe, *Journalen van de Gedenckwaerdige Reijsen van Willem Ijsbrantz. Bontekoe 1618–1625* [Journals of the Memorable Voyages of Willem Bontekoe], popular account of East Indies by a Dutch VOC employee.

1647		Adam Olearius, *Beschreibung der muscowitischen und persischen Reise* [Description of the Russian and Persian Journey] (expanded edition in 1656).
1648	Treaty of Westphalia formally recognises independence of the Dutch Republic.	
1649	Execution of Charles I in England, leading to Commonwealth under Oliver Cromwell.	
1651	English Navigation Act forbidding import of goods except in English vessels or those of the producing country.	Pedro Calderón de la Barca, *La Aurora en Copacabana* [The Dawn in Copacabana] (approx. date), nostalgic revisitation of Spain's imperial glories.
1652–4	First Anglo-Dutch War resulting from English Navigation Act of 1651.	Andrew Marvell's 'Bermudas' (probably composed after July 1653).
1656	Venetian destruction of Ottoman fleet at mouth of the Dardanelles.	• James Harrington, *Oceana*. • William Davenant, *The Siege of Rhodes* (Part 1).
1656–9	War between England and Spain after English capture Jamaica and treasure ships at Cadiz.	
1657		• Andrew Marvell, 'On the Victory Obtained by Blake over the Spaniards in the Bay of Santa Cruz in the Island of Tenerife, 1657'.

		• Richard Ligon, *A True and Exact History of the Island of Barbadoes.*
1657–61	Dutch war with Portugal over conflicting interests in Brazil.	
1658	• Mughal emperor Aurangzeb ascends throne (r. 1658–1707), shifts away from relative religious tolerance of his predecessors. • Dutch expel Portuguese from Ceylon (present-day Sri Lanka).	William Davenant, *The Cruelty of the Spaniards in Peru.*
1659		• William Davenant, *The History of Sir Francis Drake.* • Richard Brome, *The English Moor or The Mock Marriage* (first performed in 1637).
1660	Restoration of English monarchy, Charles II takes throne.	
1661	Treaty between England and Portugal and marriage of Charles II to the Infanta Catherine of Braganza. English receive as dowry Tangier, Bombay and two million crowns.	
1663		William Davenant, *The Siege of Rhodes* (Part 2; first performed in 1658–9).
1664	British seize New Amsterdam (New York) and appropriate Dutch stations on African coast.	

1665	Second Anglo-Dutch War begins.	Andrew Marvell, 'The Character of Holland' (anonymously published, thought to be composed in 1652–3).
1666		John Dryden, *Annus Mirabilis*.
1667		John Milton, *Paradise Lost*.
1668	Spain formally grants Portugal its independence.	Aphra Behn, *Oroonoko*.
1670		
1672	Third Anglo-Dutch War.	• John Dryden, *Conquest of Granada*. • Andrew Marvell's 'The Character of Holland' reprinted.
1673		Franciso Nuñez de Pineda (1607–82), *Cautiverio Feliz y rázon individual de las guerras dilatadas der reino de Chile* [Happy Captivity and Personal Account of the long Wars of the kingdom of Chile], account of campaigns against and his captivity by the Mapuche people of Chile. • John Dryden, *Amboyna*.
1676		John Dryden, *Aurangzebe*.
1681		Posthumous Folio edition of Andrew Marvell's poems.

Chapter 1

Exploring the Terrain

Two interwoven threads guide this book: we have always been postcolonial; we shall never be fully postcolonial. The literatures of the European Renaissance offer fertile ground to explore these seemingly contradictory hypotheses. A great deal hinges, of course, upon how we construe the 'post' in postcolonial and connect it to the already complex notion of the 'colonial' (see Appiah 1991).

In one sense, postcoloniality today might simply describe a historical situation: the fact of living now, after the rise and fall of the European colonial empires that emerged during the Renaissance, controlling at their heyday around four-fifths of the world. There is no doubt that early European ventures eastward and westward inaugurated a new kind of colonialism, not least in scale and scope: from a variety of starting points, and enmeshed with the movement from feudal to capitalist economies, a truly global enterprise coalesced, one that Immanuel Wallerstein aptly calls 'the modern world-system' (1974). Echoes of this passage still resound in contemporary forms of globalisation and current debates on race and immigration – to name just two domains upon which early modern colonialism has left an indelible imprint.

This history also suggests the need for a broader, more ecumenical sense of 'postcolonial', signalling even more complex relations between past and present: for the experiences of colonisation and decolonisation make visible structures of power, categories of thought and patterns of behaviour that extend beyond their early modern manifestation. The suggestion that we have always been postcolonial thus takes its impetus from a recognition of continuities and inheritances permeating spaces and times that might at first glance seem divergent, discrete. Ultimately, being postcolonial today brings into view comparable 'postcolonialities' – and 'anti-colonialities' – in other times and places.

But what of the converse assertion, that we shall never be fully postcolonial? If being so were merely a narrow matter of identifying dates that marked the beginnings and ends of historical periods, then it would be absurd to suggest that we shall never be postcolonial. In an obvious sense, we already are (or wish to be). However, as the writings of Frantz Fanon powerfully show, neither the end of colonial periods nor decolonisation itself necessarily overturns ways of thinking and behaving, let alone institutional structures, put in place through colonial rule. After all, even being schooled in a coloniser's language has far-reaching implications: 'To speak', Fanon tells us, 'means above all to assume a culture, to support the weight of a civilization' (1967: 17–18).

Fanon's claim is double-edged. On the one hand, it underscores the extent to which strictures originating in European colonialism have created our present, making it impossible to dissolve them entirely. Certainly, European colonialism no longer functions as it used to, but nonetheless its consequences endure, mutating and surviving; the world has been re-shaped irreversibly. The transformations occasioned by European colonialism have been so cataclysmic that our languages, actions, institutions, values, and to a degree our desires have irrevocably taken up their impress. Let me speak of myself: as a non-Christian Indian male from a middle-class family, schooled in my formative years in a Jesuit educational institution whose medium of instruction was English, I find it well-nigh impossible even to imagine what my world would be like, who 'I' might be, without my native fluency in a language not my mother tongue, without my inhabiting a cultural world primarily shaped by European writers and thinkers – even as I have come to recognise the deep, abiding connections between these languages and texts I hold dear and the depredations of colonialism.

On the other hand, Fanon recognises that language is not simply a prison-house but equally a site of possibility, of collective intervention through which our consciousnesses can be changed, our conditions of existence altered. We do indeed come 'after' colonialism. Though shaped by colonial pasts, we are not fully determined by them, nor is colonialism the sole feature defining the varied histories of what were once Europe's colonies. If the world cannot be unmade, it can at least (perhaps) be remade, producing constellations that, while growing out of colonial pasts, go beyond them and show the heavens more just. There is a sense, then, in which one might not want to be fully postcolonial, if that means putting our history behind us; we might want, rather, to reflect upon that journey and change what it means to be (or always be becoming) postcolonial.

Renaissance Anti-colonialisms

[A] crew of pirates are driven by a storm they know not whither; at length a boy discovers land from the topmast; they go on shore to rob and plunder; they see an harmless people, are entertained with kindness, they give the country a new name, they take formal possession of it for their king, they set up a rotten plank or a stone or two for a memorial, they murder two or three dozen of the natives, bring away a couple more by force for a sample, return home, and get their pardon. Here commences a new dominion acquired with a title by *divine right*. Ships are sent with the first opportunity, the natives driven out or destroyed, their princes tortured to discover their gold, a free license given to all acts of inhumanity and lust, the earth reeking with the blood of its inhabitants: and this execrable crew of butchers employed in so pious an exhibition, is a *modern colony* sent to convert and civilize an idolatrous and barbarous people. (Jonathan Swift, *Gulliver's Travels*)

From its inception, early modern colonialism contained anti-colonial elements that would subsequently be taken up by postcolonial critiques, suggesting that the colonial and the postcolonial are always interwoven formations. The early history of Spanish atrocities in the New World has often been recounted. Seeking to satisfy their hunger for precious metals along with the power these promised, the conquistadors sought to subjugate the Amerindian populations they encountered, compelling them to labour in mines and on plantations for a profit that would accrue to the colonisers alone. Central to Spain's justification of its actions was the insistence, buttressed by a vast array of legal wisdom and classical learning, upon the inhumanity of the New World inhabitants. The Spanish refusal to accept Aztec oral and pictographic narratives as history, because these did not conform to the Renaissance ideal of alphabetic literacy, was itself a form of colonisation: it colonised the Aztecs' very memory (Mignolo 1995: 140ff.). To lack alphabetic writing was tantamount to lacking reason and thus to a failure to be human.

Yet Spain was also the European nation that worried most insistently about the morality of its horrific actions in the New World, even as it pursued them. Against the odds, and the current of the dominant culture, rose the voice of the Dominican priest Bartolomé de las Casas, whose tenure in Hispaniola had brought him face to face with the barbarity of conquest. It is a wonder, remark Michael Hardt and Antonio Negri, that las Casas,

who was part of the Spanish mission, could separate himself enough from the common stream of opinion to insist on the humanity of the Amerindians and contest the brutality of the Spanish rulers. His protest arises from a simple principle: *humankind is one and equal.* (2000: 116)

This assertion of radical equality illuminates the inseparability of colonialism from anti-colonial critique: the same humanist context that Spain relied on to validate its behaviour enabled also the explicit refutation of its colonial practices.

At a debate in Valladolid in 1550, las Casas challenged the view of legal theorist Juan Sepúlveda that the Indians' innate savagery justified conquest and enslavement (see Todorov 1984: 146–82). Las Casas distinguished different senses of the barbarian available through Aristotle's *Politics* and *Ethics*, in particular between peoples who lacked a written language and those who were 'slaves by nature since they have no natural government, no political institutions . . . and are not subject to anyone' (1974: 33). While the Indians may lack the former, they did not, las Casas argued, lack the latter. Consequently, they fulfilled the criteria for being considered and treated as human beings: 'They are not ignorant, inhuman, or bestial. Rather, long before they had heard the word Spaniard they had properly organised states, wisely ordered by excellent laws, religion, and custom' (42). Importantly, both las Casas and his adversaries drew on Aristotelian sources to argue their conclusions, and did not disagree that the right to resist conquest belonged to all humans; their divergence concerned who counted as properly human. If for Sepúlveda and his ilk the Amerindians were, in Aristotelian terms, 'natural slaves' (see Pagden 1982: 27–56), las Casas instead saw them as already civilised, and, as perfectible human beings, equal with the Spaniards because they too could be brought to follow the true path of Christianity: 'the nature of men is the same and all are called by Christ in the same way' (1974: 271). This universalism, which denied any essential difference between the Spanish and those who were to suffer their yoke, remained a constant undertow pulling against the dominant colonialist discourse. Punctuating Iberian expansion into the New World is thus a resistance to the celebration of Spain's prowess, one that both underscores the value of what is being destroyed and legitimates opposition.

The Spanish nobleman Alonso de Ercilla's remarkable epic *La Araucana*, published in three parts from 1569 to 1589, offers a pertinent example. Yet another witness to many of the events upon which he based his heroic poem, Ercilla resided for about seventeen months in what is modern-day Chile and participated in Governor Don García Hurtado de Mendoza's campaign to quell insurrections by the Mapuche Indians or the Araucano, whose war against the colonialists would ultimately span three centuries. Even as his epic celebrates Spanish conquest, it 'tilt[s] . . . its sympathies', David Quint writes, 'to the Araucanian chiefs and their desperate struggle' (1993: 159). The 1569 prologue to the *Araucana* is quite explicit about its defence of the Indians:

> And if it appears to some that I show myself somewhat inclined to the side of the Araucanians, treating their affairs [*cosas*] and valiant deeds more extensively than is required for barbarians, should we wish to consider their education, customs, modes and exercise of warfare, we will see that many have not surpassed them, and that there are few who have with such constancy and firmness defended their lands against such fierce enemies as are the Spanish . . . [E]ncircled by three Spanish towns and two fortresses . . . with pure valour and stubborn determination they have redeemed and sustained their liberty, shedding in sacrifice so much blood, theirs as well as of the Spaniards, that one may say truthfully that there are few places not stained with it and peopled with bones . . . All of these things I have wished to cite as proof and token of the great valour of these people, worthy of greater praise than I can give them with my verses. (1993: 69–70; my translation)

While it is not their being (potentially) Christians that lifts the Araucanians to the status of the Spaniards here, their bravery and valour, along with the marks of civilisation evident in their 'educations, customs, modes, and exercises of warfare', achieves that parity. The proof comes in their willingness to 'redeem' and 'sustain' their liberty, leading to martial actions that indeed produce an all-too-material equality with the coloniser in commingling blood and depositing bones.

As is also true of las Casas' writings, the anti-colonial strain in Ercilla's poem is complicated and contradictory. Responding to the assertion that the Indians were by nature inferior beings and thus fitted for exploitation, Ercilla defends them instead as 'warrior aristocrats, men of honour, who would rather die than fall under a foreign domination that would also occasion their fall in social caste' (Quint 1993: 174). This picture hardly matched the realities of Araucanian life – they were primarily nomadic herdsmen, though with some settled agricultural practices. However, Ercilla reinvents the natives via a royalist-aligned ideology, seeing in them the traces of a feudal nobility already on the decline in Spain (and indeed Europe as a whole). Thus, Indian resistance to the Spanish acquires, as Quint persuasively argues, 'a peculiarly conservative cast: it becomes a displaced version of the struggle between crown and nobility in Spain, and the reflection of the divided class allegiances of the poet, who is at once the prototypical new royal

servant and the nostalgic aristocrat yearning for an earlier class identity'
(175).

What ultimately tips the poet's sympathies towards the Indians –
despite the fact that their rebellion is directed not only against their
immediate oppressors, but thereby also against Spain – is his deep revul-
sion at the consequences of the *encomienda* system put in place by the
colonial settlers – and which they fought tooth and nail to maintain,
even given royal injunctions to the contrary. An *encomienda* was essentially a group of villages under the control of a Spanish colonist, who in
theory also took upon himself the burden of defending the inhabitants
and seeing to their religious instruction. In return, the villagers were
required to offer their labour for a certain period to the *encomendero*,
either free or at a fixed, nominal wage. What emerged in practice was
brutal enslavement, with the natives worked to death in gold and silver
mines, and unable to maintain their families by keeping their fields in
cultivation (see Parry 1940). Las Casas would claim that in eight years
ninety per cent of the indigenous population had been exterminated
through starvation and maltreatment. Despite his conflicted ideological attachments, Ercilla, too, found the violent reality of colonial rule
unpalatable and fundamentally unjustifiable:

> The great spilling of blood has been . . .
> that which all in all has destroyed
> the fruit expected from this land;
> because they [the Spanish] have in an inhuman way exceeded the laws and
>   limits of war,
> committing in their invasions [*entradas*] and conquests
> enormous cruelties never seen before.
>
> (Ercilla 1993: 32.4, 840; my translation)

Ercilla's epic refuses triumphalism, and its principled refusal to countenance the violence of the colonisers 'not only allows for the poem's
genuinely divided, inconsistent sympathies, for the poet really does go
from one side to the other', but also 'permits those sympathies to be
based on other criteria than power, and it thus permits a critique of
ideology' (Quint 1993: 178). In the midst of the colonial epic, then, a
genuine anti-colonial resistance arises.

The leavening of colonial ideologies with counter-valences that would
now be affiliated with the postcolonial need not take the form of explicit
critique or resistance. A telling instance from Stephen Greenblatt's
Marvelous Possessions suggests a different sense of how colonial formations harbour in themselves potentialities around which anti-colonial

responses might later coalesce. The episode in question concerns the voyage with which, rightly or wrongly, early modern colonialism is seen to originate: Columbus's 'discovery' of the New World. The event is commemorated by a much-studied document, the Genoese explorer's letter to Luis de Santangel celebrating the 'grand victory with which Our Lord has crowned my voyage'. The triumphal missive describes the thirty-three day voyage from the Canary Islands culminating in the discovery of 'very many islands filled with people innumerable'. All these, Columbus has

> taken possession for their highnesses [the King and Queen of Spain], by proclamation made and with the royal standard unfurled, and no opposition was offered to me [y no me fué contradicho]. To the first island which I found, I gave the name *San Salvador*, in remembrance of the Divine Majesty, Who has marvellously bestowed all this; the Indians call it 'Guanahani'. To the second, I gave the name *Isla de Santa María de Concepción*; to the third, *Fernandina*; . . . and so to each one I gave a new name. (1930: 1.2)

Greenblatt's reading of this document is rich and nuanced, but I want to focus only on Columbus's odd remark that in taking possession 'no opposition was offered' to him, or, as the original Spanish phrasing puts it, 'I was not contradicted'.

The phrase's oddity lies, Greenblatt points out, in its utter inapplicability. It would be felicitous in a European context since it establishes the legality of the Spanish claim to 'the newly discovered lands by the "voluntary choice" of the original inhabitants' (58), but it makes little sense here because the natives to whom it is presumably directed cannot even understand the speech act by which Columbus takes possession of their lands, let alone dispute it. While Columbus's letter implies a reasonably straightforward communication with the Amerindians, this could hardly be true. Given that the explorer's aim was to reach India, the one interpreter on board the ships, Luís de Torres, had been chosen 'because he spoke Hebrew, Aramaic and some Arabic; so there is no reason at all to think there was any initial communication at all' (Hulme 1986: 20), to say nothing of a discussion of the legality of Spanish usurpation.

So, why does Columbus even claim to have offered the natives the possibility of contradicting him? The answer is that the ritual performance of possession is not ultimately directed at the natives at all: Columbus's actions 'are performed entirely *for a world elsewhere*' (Greenblatt 1991: 56). If the natives must be regarded as capable of opposing him, this is because 'Columbus is observing a form' recognisable to other Europeans capable of challenging Spain's claims, and 'that form evidently calls for the possibility of a contradiction, a counter-declaration to the one by which possession is claimed' (59). Hence,

> *Why* there was no objection is of no consequence; all that matters is that there was none. The formalism of Columbus' proclamation derives not only from the fact that it represents the scrupulous observance of a preconceived form . . . but also from its complete indifference to the consciousness of the other. The words are a closed system, closed in such a way as to silence those whose objections might challenge or negate the proclamation, which formally, but only formally, envisages the possibility of contradiction. (59–60)

The emptiness of formal acknowledgement reveals itself in the reality that followed hard upon the heels of such declarations: the violence of Spain's encounter with the Indians, missionary expansion, enslavement and genocide. Even had other European powers objected – and they did – the Spanish crown was not likely to yield its territorial possessions in the New World on legal grounds alone. And there is no denying the pure formality of a colonial performance that almost cynically deprives populations of rights and lives.

And yet forms do matter, as does language, however inadequate these seem when confronted by brute realities of power and domination. For, inhering in the very form of European legal discourse is a recognition that things could be otherwise, that there may be values and exigencies beyond might alone. And though it is important, Greenblatt writes,

> to recognize the practical emptiness of this acknowledgment . . . there seems to me nothing to be gained from a contemptuous dismissal of the discourse in which the acknowledgement is embedded. Where else do we get our own ragged sense that there is something other than force, our own craving for justice? (64–5)

It is precisely this kind of textual resistance to his expansive claim, a resistance buried deep in the very language through which it is asserted, that Columbus has to overcome.

While the Genoese explorer and the Spanish conquistadors and settlers who followed in his wake overrode in practice the juridical equality ascribed to the natives, the possibility it opens up could not be fully foreclosed. At the turn of the eighteenth century, roughly 300 years after Columbus's declaration, the black slave Toussaint L'Ouverture headed the first successful uprising against slavery in the French colony of Sainte-Domingue (modern-day Haiti), taking his revolutionary inspiration in part from the language of formal equality that the French

Revolution had made available again. If liberty, equality and fraternity were indeed universal human rights, then all inhabitants of the colony – be they black, white or mixed – had to be treated as full members of the new French republic. Toussaint's report to the French Directoire in 1797 insisted that the declaration of freedom could not be reversed. 'Do you think', demanded the ex-slave,

> that men who have enjoyed the blessing of liberty will calmly see it snatched away? . . . But no, the same hand that has broken our chains will not enslave us anew. France will not revoke her principles, she will not withdraw from us the greatest of her benefits. (quoted in Hart and Negri 2000: 117)

Toussaint expresses here the activation, towards anti-colonial ends, of potentialities he sees buried within the language of the colonising power. If potentiality remains no more than that in the moment of Columbus's encounter with Amerindian natives, it nonetheless marks a site of future resistance, actualised when material circumstances change.

I have focused thus far on acts of critique, resistance and imagination that become visible through a careful reading of European texts, often interpreting them against their grain. This type of engagement with colonial discourses reflects a dominant strand in postcolonial studies, and indeed characterises much of this book as well. Such approaches, in collaboration with gender studies, have transformed how we read texts and expanded immeasurably the horizon of texts considered worth reading at all. If nothing else, we have learnt to adjust our sense of what counted as 'literature' to early modern sensibilities, which did not recognise sharp divides between literary and non-literary texts. Travel narratives and other historical documents surrounding colonialism have thereby shown themselves to reward the close hermeneutic attention characteristic of literary studies. Nonetheless, such readings run certain risks. However well-meaning, their terms of analyses often assume or support the tendency to see the histories of the peoples and lands that fell under the sway of European colonialism primarily through the lens of their colonial pasts, as if colonial history were the only history that mattered (see Loomba 1998: 17–18 and McClintock in Williams and Chrisman 1994: 295). Other peoples' pasts recede, all leading to a universal postcolonial present.

Following the pioneering work of historians such as D. B. Quinn and literary scholars such as Greenblatt and Hulme, much of the first phase of colonial/postcolonial enquiry into the early modern period focused on the Americas. Thus, the intellectual and material structures out of which Columbus's 'mistake' arose have been exhaustively studied (see, for example, Hulme 1986; Todorov 1984; and Wey-Gómez 2008) to reveal the paradoxes underlying Columbus's multi-layered journal of the 1492–3 expedition. Certainly, there is no denying the importance of what Joan Linton calls 'the romance of the New World' (1998). Nevertheless, modes of English and Spanish colonial activity in the New World have as a result sometimes turned into the models for colonialism *tout court*. Consequently, a number of scholars (including myself) have expanded the ambit to consider different, and in particular more mercantile, forms of colonialism visible when we look eastward (see Mishra and Hodge's distinction between settler and non-settler countries in Williams and Chrisman 1994). Indeed, Hulme's rich discussion of Columbus's New World discovery already recognises the extent to which this voyage did not inaugurate early modern colonialism *ab novo*, but was fabricated out of existing presumptions – often recognisably proto-colonial – deriving from Europe's relationship to the Arab world as well as kingdoms and states in the East. These continued to shape the consequences of that fateful journey west. Columbus was, after all, in search of a new sea-route to India, and the discovery of America an accidental by-product.

Although Columbus's voyage was to have

> such a devastating and long-lasting effect on both Europe and America, and is still celebrated as one of the outstanding achievements of humanity, the record itself tells of misunderstandings, failures and disappointments. The greatest of these – that he had not reached Asia – was too overwhelming for Columbus ever to accept. (Hulme 1986: 19–20)

The historically prior journey to the New World turns out to depend upon anterior preoccupations with Old worlds east of Europe (see Archer 2001). Their persistence appears in Columbus's repeated attempts to convince himself that he had in fact arrived in the domains of the Grand Khan (the putative emperor of Cathay or China) despite mounting evidence to the contrary. As Hulme shows, two antecedent frameworks, each with a long pedigree, are especially prominent: 'a discourse of Oriental civilization and a discourse of savagery'. Each of these was identifiable by 'the presence of key words: in one case "gold," "Cathay," "Grand Khan," "intelligent soldiers," "large buildings," "merchant ships"; in the other "gold," "savagery," "monstrosity," "anthropophagy"'. And each of these semantic networks can be traced back to two foundational texts that precede the New World discovery: Marco Polo's account of his travels in China and Herodotus' *Histories* (Hulme 1986: 20–1).

My next section will consider the impress of earlier colonial formations upon those developing in the early modern era. Such sedimenta-
tions open onto another important sense in which we can see colonial
formations as already postcolonial – though not as critique or resistance
but as complicity. First, however, let me emphasise the necessity of
recovering alternative locations from which to view colonial pasts. For
there were indeed other possibilities.

The trajectories brought to light by colonial/postcolonial studies were
never inevitable (see Abu-Lughod 1991), and a continuing task for postcolonial criticism remains the consideration, often speculative, of how
things might have been (and still could be) otherwise. Attention to texts
from outside the European world can help reorient our sense of terms
that we often take for granted. One of the most famous non-European
travellers of the medieval world was Ibn Khaldun (1332–1406), whose
wanderings led to a monumental history of the world, the *Kitab al-Ibar*.
The Arabic word for history, *kitab*, also means book, suggesting the
significance of the written for Khaldun. But his evocation of written
literacy depends upon an understanding of history significantly different from the range of European conceptions derived from Greek and
Roman authors (such as Herodotus, Thucydides, Cicero and Tacitus).
Khaldun's preface states:

> The inner meaning of history [*kitab*] ... involves speculation and the
> attempt to get at the truth, subtle explanation of the causes and origins
> of existing things, and deep knowledge of the how and why of events.
> [History] therefore is firmly rooted in philosophy. It deserves to be
> accounted a branch of [philosophy]. (Cited in Mignolo 1995: 136)

In the colonial period, Mignolo argues, humanist historiography
moved from seeing history as an eyewitness record to understanding
it as 'a narrative of past events, which were saved from oblivion by
written records and transmitted to future generations by alphabetic narratives' (1995: 140). New World historians thus increasingly insisted
on understanding history as a collective memory of the past as chrono-
logical sequence, for which having letters was deemed essential. This
attitude treated New World natives as peoples without history – which
it became the task of the European to supply. Often absent from that
asymmetrical relationship was the kind of philosophical speculation that
Khaldun stresses, which demands entering into what appears foreign
or alien to uncover its internal causes and rhythms, to connect visible
existence to hidden essence. Instead, the very gap between observer and
observed, colonial historiographer and native, was naturalised, giving

the impression that western writing conveyed simply neutral facts about indigenous populations – whose 'truth' in turn belonged not to them but to those able to describe them. Of course, this was not always the case (see my discussion of Léry below), but it was, I think, predominantly so. And while postcolonial studies of early modern texts have often usefully revealed the stakes behind these rhetorical constructions of natives, they have not always successfully questioned the understanding of history implicit in the European emphasis on writing. To do so successfully we need to turn not only to texts outside the western tradition, such as Ibn Khaldun's, but to different kinds of evidence as well; for instance, by integrating into textual study non-textual material from ethnographical and archaeological investigations. Going beyond the European documentary record (see Subrahmanyam 2005) at least holds out hope for seeing and understanding written history differently, and thus these remnants of the past potentially function as alternative loci, signalling what postcolonialism might (or might not) yet become.

Imperial Translations

> But still, tell me, Tityrus, who is this god of yours?
> Meliboeus, I thought that that city they call Rome –
> I was such a fool – was just like that town of ours . . .
> I knew . . . ,
> But this city stands as far above the rest
> As the cypress outgrows the trailing hedgerows.
>
> (Virgil, Eclogue I)

> Now does Spain's fleet her spacious wings unfold,
> Leaves the New World and hastens for the old:
> But though the wind was fair, they slowly swum
> Freighted with acted guilt, and guilt to come:
> For this rich load, . . .
> The New World's wounded entrails they had tore,
> For wealth wherewith to wound the Old once more . . .
>
> (Andrew Marvell, 'On the Victory Obtained by Blake')

An important source for early modern English attitudes towards Ireland, William Fynes Moryson's *Itinerary* (1617), expresses, too, an understanding of English colonialism as a beneficial repetition. The Norman conquest repeats the earlier Roman colonisation of England, thereby putting in place a template for English colonial practice in his day:

> as the wise Romans . . . enlarged their conquests, so did they spread their language with their laws, and the divine service all in the Latin tongue,

and by their rewards and preferments invited men to speak it, [so] . . . also the Normans in England brought in the use of the French tongue in our Common Law. (quoted in Ferguson 2003: 96)

In this portion of his text criticising the Irish failure to learn English, Moryson paints the Norman invasion as, in Margaret Ferguson's words,

> a precursor of, and model for, England's own assumption of an imperial mantle. He offers a comforting version of the *translatio imperii* theory, according to which there is no competition for imperial dominion but rather an inexorable westward movement of power from one empire to its successor. Moryson implies that Protestant England will simply replace the ancient Romans, the medieval Church, and the Normans as colonizer of new territories. Maturing into empire from former colony, England will extend its cultural sway as if Spanish and Dutch . . . contenders for imperial power did not exist. (2003: 97)

Moryson's *Itinerary* points to a very different way in which postcoloniality inheres in – and is constitutive of – colonial discourses: neither as anti-colonial critique nor as site for alternative possibilities, but as repetition and complicity. Recalling England's own history of subjugation, Moryson commemorates that colonial past not as a legacy to combat but as one to be appropriated and furthered, providing the coordinates for present-day and future action. To be a colonial power is inseparable, in other words, from being postcolonial in the sense of having oneself been colonised in the past. England's particular history was, of course, unique to it. But all the European states that would compete in the early modern period over the right to empire had their own colonial histories leading back to Rome; and they were themselves created by processes of conquest, colonisation and cultural change during the middle ages (see Bartlett 1993).

England's specificity may be glimpsed in Moryson's evocation of the common law above, which does not fit neatly into his paradigm. Unlike most of Continental Europe, where traditional judicial practices had been absorbed – if not always smoothly – into systems fundamentally based on Roman law, the English situation was one where the common law, projected as the immemorial or primordial law of the land (see Pocock 1957: 30–55), remained in conflict with aspects of Roman jurisprudence brought in through Church and nobility, as well as through the demands of mercantile exchange. Thus, what Moryson possessively calls 'our' common law seems one of those kernels that resisted the waves of colonisation to which the island had been subject. Nevertheless, the logic of Moryson's rhetorical extension of empire was a familiar one:

national expansion beyond existing dominions took as pattern and ideal the example of Rome. As we shall see below, not only for England, but for other European polities as well, 'the Roman past was . . . not simply *a* past but *the* past' (Hunter 1977: 95).

This reliance of early modern colonial discourses on reconstructions of an antecedent classical heritage is captured in the persistence of the trope referred to by Ferguson (above): *translatio imperii*, that is, the translation or transferral of empire. The phrase has a long, convoluted history (see Goez 1958). Its widespread adoption in the period grew out of the conjunction of medieval historiography with biblical exegesis, particularly of the Old Testament prophecy in which Nebuchadnezzar's dream of a golden empire, followed by ones of silver, bronze and iron, was interpreted as a divinely authorised succession of temporal rule: from the Babylonians, to the Persians, the Greeks and finally to the Romans. The final stage, a divided empire of iron and clay, was taken to mark the division of the Roman empire itself into eastern and western dominions, setting the stage for the final transcendence of history itself with the Last Judgement.

Munich's Alte Pinakothek collection includes a celebrated painting by the German artist Albrecht Altdorfer, part of a series executed in 1529. It depicts vividly one of the foundational moments in the transfer of empire: the decisive Battle of Issus in 333 BC between the armies of the Macedonian conqueror Alexander the Great and the Persian monarch Darius. The large canvas is dominated by its cosmic background in which sun and darkness, light and shadow, clash, expressing the magnitude of what was at stake in the foregrounded battle. According to Reinhart Kosellek, a contemporary Christian viewer would see in this luminous painting

> the transition from the second to the third world empire, which was [to be] followed by the fourth and last empire, that of the Roman Imperium . . . The battle, through which the decline of the Persian emperor was to occur, was not just any battle, but one of the few events between the beginning and the end of the world which also prefigured the fall of the Holy Roman Empire. (1979: 17; my translation)

The relevance of this rich allegory to the early modern present is revealed in two curious details. First, the painting anachronistically inscribes, on flags held by commanders, the numbers of casualties that would be suffered by a particular military unit, but it nonetheless omits one crucial number: the date of the battle itself. For Altdorfer, we might say, the battle is always being fought and won, history frozen through its repetition. Even more pertinent is another anachronism: the Persians in the painting are dressed from top to toe like the Turks who in 1529 (the very year of the painting) had been beaten back after a failed siege of Vienna. The ancient battle is thus understood as the mirror of a contemporary conflict upon which Europe's integrity depends. The painting may look ahead to an eschatological terminus, the culminating moment of the final battle between Christ and the Antichrist, but that Day of Judgement is yet to come. In the present, the Roman empire persists in European states that are its last defenders against the infidels. The mantle of empire, once worn by the Macedonians and then the Romans, has passed westward to its Christian inheritors.

The English currency of this idea is confirmed by its unexpected appearance in a Shakespearean comedy whose connections with empire long remained unnoticed. In *A Midsummer Night's Dream*, describing to Puck the origins of the flower whose effects drive the play's dramatic action, Oberon recounts the time he saw Cupid's failed attempt to shoot with his arrow 'a fair vestal throned in the west' (II.i.158). The fiery 'love-shaft' was 'quench'd in the chaste beams of the watery moon, / And the imperial vot'ress passed on, / In maiden meditation, fancy-free' (II.i.162–4). The lines encode a praise for the virgin Queen Elizabeth, who is 'rhetorically tied to empire by allusions to the westering movement of authority in the *translatio imperii*' (James 1997: 22; see also Bate 1993: 139–40). Referring to her as an 'imperial vot'ress' lightly evokes a further dimension of the play's engagement with early modern colonialism, since the phrase associates her with the play's other 'vot'ress', the fairy queen Titania's companion, who gives birth to the Indian boy around whom the narrative revolves (see Raman 2002: 239–79). Thus does the English stage seek to associate the legacy of Rome with England's ongoing imperial ventures.

Shakespeare's admittedly oblique strategy derives from a widely disseminated mythology of Britain's origins that itself grew out of Virgil's own mythologisation of Rome's birth. According to this story, imperial rule under Virgil's patron Augustus Caesar drew its legitimation from foundations ostensibly laid by Trojan War survivors. Nor was the use of this mythology restricted to England: '[t]he Troy legend, canonized to ease Rome's painful transition from republican to triumviral and finally imperial government under Augustus Caesar, became a privileged topos for nationalistic endeavours in early modern Europe' (James 1997: 14). The English imperial variation can be traced back to Geoffrey of Monmouth's influential *History of the Kings of Britain* (c. 1136), which recorded the myth that Brutus – grandson of Aeneas, the founder of

Rome – had founded Britain, sailing to the island from Rome to establish Troynovant [New Troy], later renamed London. Early modern English chronicle histories repeatedly cite this myth. Richard Grafton's *A Chronicle at Large and Meere History of the Affayres of England* (1569), for instance, announces that his history of the realm begins '[w]hen Brute . . . first entred this Island and named it Briteyne' (31). Even sceptical accounts such as Raphael Holinshed's *Chronicles* (1577) or William Camden's *Britannia* (1610) regularly included the story, as did more celebratory writers such as Michael Drayton or John Stow (see Kahn 1997: 3). The English derivation from Rome was buttressed by Henry VII's claim to be descended from a half-British Emperor Constantine, who had ostensibly 'united British kingship with Roman emperorship' (Koebner 1953: 3; cited in MacDougall 1982: 17), and by the history of Julius Caesar's occupation of Britain (to which Moryson refers, above): 'to a great extent, Rome was familiarized for the English by being represented in terms of its past kinship with Britain and as a model for England's present and future' (Kahn 1997: 4; see also Garbero 2009). Indeed, the popularity of the Roman play in Shakespeare's era indicates, as Clifford Ronan puts it, that '[a]s an age of colonization and empire was launched, England found in Rome a glass where the island could behold its own image simultaneously civilized and barbarous, powerful and hollow' (1995: 7).

It is in this vein that the English polymath John Dee urges Queen Elizabeth to go beyond England's current confines truly to establish a 'British Empire' – a phrase he is generally accredited with coining – by building up a standing and fully-equipped navy of sixty or more ships to ensure that British merchants could roam the world freely. Dee's sustained attention to English imperial pretensions in the 1570s and 1580s came at a vital period in English overseas exploration, and his close connections to – and influence upon – Martin Frobisher and Humphrey Gilbert, who undertook their adventures in new-found lands in this period, has been well documented (see Sherman 1995: 164–6 and 173–5, and Macmillan 2001: 3). In unpublished manuscripts presented to Queen Elizabeth, the Secretary of State Francis Walsingham and the Lord Treasurer William Cecil, Dee laid out an extensive legal case based both on Roman-derived civil law and on classical and contemporary historical/geographical evidence (see Cormack 1997: 124–8) to support the argument for English sovereignty over the lands and peoples that England's voyagers might encounter. Among the 'earliest, boldest, and most ingenious advocates' for the British empire (Sherman 1995: 148), Dee's writings sought to picture it as it 'hath bene: Yea, as it, yet, is: or, rather, as it may, & (of right) ought to be' (1577: A2r). This contorted sentence shows Dee 'struggl[ing] with the appropriate *tense* of the imperial outlook; and he reminds us that it was as much retrospective as prospective' (Sherman 1995: 151).

Not only did Dee develop the important criterion – later amplified in Richard Hakluyt's manuscript *Discourse on Western Planting* (1584) – of claiming territory by actual occupation of newly discovered lands (rather than by mere discovery, as the Spanish and Portuguese had done), but he marshalled the resources of British chronicle histories to 'prove' Elizabeth's entitlement to conquered regions in the northwest. In 'Of Famous and Rich Discoveries' (c. 1577–8), he returned to the legend of the Trojan Brutus

> and his lineal descendant the sixth-century Welsh King Arthur, who conquered thirty northern kingdoms and supposedly planted colonies in those islands and regions. Especially because Queen Elizabeth was herself of Welsh descent she was deemed to be a direct descendant of Arthur and was, therefore, entitled to all his conquered territories. (MacMillan 2001: 8; see also Sherman 1995: 187–9)

Drawing heavily on Geoffrey of Monmouth's *History* – as well as chronicles by John Bale, John Harding, and Humphrey Llwyd – Dee sought to bolster the Roman and Welsh origins of the Queen's claim against such early sixteenth-century writers as Polydore Vergil, who had claimed that Arthur's history was no more than a romantic fabrication. Catherine Belsey notes that it was in the wake of Dee's writings that Elizabeth began visually to portray herself as a ruler of more than Britain alone, asserting a broader imperial claim in the 'Sieve' portraits of 1579–80 by being depicted alongside a luminous globe (2008: 110).

Medieval and early modern Europe inherited the Roman legacy of *imperium* in a threefold manner, David Armitage shows: the word 'denoted independent authority; it described a territorial unit; and it offered an historical foundation for claims to both the authority and the territory ruled by the Roman emperors' (2000: 30). These different meanings were already intertwined in Augustus' 'spatial, temporal, and political' assertion of Rome's claim to universal dominion (Nicolet 1991: 15–56). To this we need to add Ferguson's pertinent observations that the word empire signalled from the outset 'a site of contested meaning rather than an empirical phenomenon whose precise features are specifiable', and that the legacy of Rome's claim to 'dominion without temporal or spatial end' – *imperium sine fine*, as Virgil's *Aeneid* famously asserts – was especially subject to contestation in the early modern period (2003: 18–19). Indeed, Heather James argues, 'the Achilles heel of the Troy legend is, finally, its long, tortuous history'. For even as the history of its transmission rooted it deeper in the soil of European culture, that history also dispersed it across different nations, each of which sought to translate the myth into terms applicable to it. Rather than one monolithic legend, then, what emerged were multiple stories, competing for primacy by raising their own myths upon Virgilian foundations: 'France had its Francus, son of Priam; Denmark claimed Danus; Ireland, Hiberus; Saxony, Saxo' (James 1997: 15; see also 22–3).

If Rome offered a pattern for early modern empire-building, that pattern was itself variously inscribed in the diverse European attempts to expand beyond the boundaries of individual nation-states. Remarkably, even the Turkish empire regarded itself as the legitimate inheritor of Rome's legacy: for example, Suleiman the Magnificent 'sought consciously and deliberately to vie with the Holy Roman Emperor and the Pope as imperial successor to the Roman empire as well as to link himself with the civilizations of Greece, Persia, and Arabia' (Goffman 2002: 107). In this 'radically alternative version of the traditional *translatio imperii*', the Turkish ruler 'maintained that he alone continued to embody the might and traditions of imperial Rome, which he . . . saw as having come down to him through the Byzantine Empire' (Hopkins 2008: 57).

But Rome's mantle fitted certain countries better than others. While the English and the French sought to increase their status by developing commercial and military alliances with the Ottomans in the 1580s (see Vitkus 2003: 59), the Spanish (and, to a lesser degree, Portuguese) precedent remained paramount. When Charles V was named Holy Roman Emperor in 1519, 'the Empire was united with the Spanish Monarchy under his rule to become the most far-flung monarchy the world had ever known'. Though not comprehending all of Europe, it included domains in the New World of which even the Romans had been ignorant. 'This was the nearest the post-classical world would come to seeing a truly world-wide monarchy, and hence the closest approximation to universal *imperium* since the last days of the *Imperium Romanum* itself' (Armitage 2000: 32; see also Yates 1975: 1–28). Consequently, early modern England, France and the Netherlands were postcolonial not just as (potential) heirs to the Roman imperium, but because they were post-Iberian, their colonial endeavours shaped by possibilities and limits that Spain and Portugal had already established.

Northern European belatedness is symptomatically revealed by the often-noted paucity of grand narratives surrounding colonial conquest:

while travel narratives are abundant, very little in the literary culture of these nations approaches the wealth of texts generated by the Spaniards, from Bernal Díaz del Castillo and Francisco López de Gómara's accounts of the conquest of Mexico, to Garcilosa de la Vega's tale of the Incas, to Ercilla's epic poem on Araucanas and Lope de Vega's new world plays (see Shannon 1989). '[W]hat is there in English literature that can compare to the letters of Hernán Cortés or the "true history" of Bernal Díaz?', the historian D. A. Brading asks. 'Where, in all the long centuries of European imperialism, was there a scene to equal the public debate staged at Valladolid between Juan Ginés de Sepulveda and Las Casas?' (1991: 1). These questions are clearly rhetorical, but if absence there was, it was not 'because of a defect in the historical sensibilities of some of these nations' (Pagden 1995: 66), but because events in French or British America generally did not compare in scale to Spanish accomplishments. It is less that the English or French failed to claim the Roman mantle than that their claims could not be made entirely plausible during the first stages of European expansion. William Strachey attempted to draw a parallel – as Moryson had done in Ireland's case – between the English in America and the Roman generals who had invaded ancient Britain and 'reduced the conquered parts of our barbarous Island into provinces and established in them colonies of old soldiers building castles and towns in every corner, teaching us even to know the powerful discourse of divine reason' (1953: 24). But the vexed early history of English New World settlements gave the lie to this description – at least until the English stopped trying to settle among the native population and sought to eradicate them instead. (Indeed, Strachey is writing roughly a decade prior to an inflectional event of just this sort: the 1622 massacre of Virginia colony settlers, following the breakdown in relationships with the Powhatans who had been maltreated by the English.) By contrast, the Spanish had been committed from the outset to occupation and usurpation, their policy shaped both by a forcible claim to be the primary contender for Rome's inheritance and by a history of internal conquest that had expelled the Moors from the Iberian peninsula.

As Jonathan Hart has argued, the French and English responses to their most important colonial precursor were contradictory, the ambivalence clearly visible in 'a double and often simultaneous movement in . . . [their] writings about Spain and the New World – emulation and condemnation' (2000: 3). While in later years both France and England would develop different colonial models, building up bases for trade and, increasingly, agricultural production, the primary focus in the sixteenth century was to do what Spain had somehow managed to do:

discover and appropriate a seemingly unending supply of gold and silver. The Frenchman Jacques Cartier's first expedition to the North Atlantic in 1534 had as its objective the discovery of 'certain islands and countries where it is said that a great quantity of gold and other precious things is to be found' (in Biggar 1993: 117). In this he echoed Columbus: the single term shared by the semantic networks that Hulme identifies in Columbus's *Diario* (see above) is, after all, gold. The English expeditions led by Frobisher to Newfoundland in the 1570s – in which the Queen herself invested – were also driven by the desire for precious metals; like Cartier's, these voyages too would return instead with pyrites, fool's gold, rather than the thing itself. The most spectacular English case was that of Sir Walter Raleigh, a 'would be *conquistador*[] ... openly contemptuous of commerce and agriculture as possible objectives of empire' (Pagden 1995: 67). Spain's power was not derived, Raleigh trenchantly wrote, from 'the trade of sacks of Seville oranges, nor from aught else that Spain, Portugal or any of his other provinces produce. It is his Indian Gold that ... endangereth and disturbeth all the nations of Europe' (Raleigh 1848: xiv). Indeed, Raleigh's failure to return home with the riches he promised his sovereign would ultimately result in his execution (see Fuller 1991: 42).

Nor did this emulation go unnoticed by the Spaniards, as a remark by the cardinal of Seville on mid-century French colonial policy in the wake of Cartier's voyage testifies:

> Their motive is that they think ... that these provinces are rich in gold and silver, and they hope to do as we have done; however, in my judgment they deceive themselves because, if there are no fisheries, this whole coast as far as Florida is entirely unfruitful. In consequence of which they would be lost, or at best would make a short excursion, having lost a few men and the greater part of all they took from France. (in Biggar 1930: 325–6; my translation)

The cardinal was right. The French failed to find gold and diamonds in what would come to be called New France. But the possibility and desire remained powerful for much of the sixteenth century, even in the face of repeated failure. Mary Fuller's excellent study of Raleigh's *Discoverie of the Large, Rich and Bewtiful Empire of Guiana* shows how that desire itself becomes the ultimate referent of the English explorer's narrative. Purportedly about the discovery of a land more opulent than Spanish Peru, Raleigh's story ends up being one about 'not discovering Guiana' (1991: 55), for like the promised land itself, which Raleigh himself never saw, the gold functions as an absent centre towards which both text and voyage are always drawn but can never reach. And indeed, Raleigh does not in a sense want to reach the desired end, as is suggested by its repeated deferral in his narrative. What drives the colonial enterprise through and beyond Raleigh is the fantasy itself. Pagden echoes the economist Joseph Schumpeter in asserting that 'nearly every European empire began as the formal ideological expression of . . . the purely instinctual inclination towards war and conquest' (1995: 63). If so, that inclination drew sustenance from fantasies like Raleigh's: there in the distance, just beyond where we have reached now, something glimmers, and even if we do not reach it this time, next time we will. But even such dreams needed some connection to the actual. And for French and English alike, the Spanish conquests provided a necessary touch of the real, holding open the possibility that they too in turn would inherit, as the Spanish had, the legacy of Rome. Prefacing the travel narrative by Raleigh's lieutenant, Lawrence Kemys, is a laudatory poem by George Chapman, which adapts the famous opening of Virgil's epic to fit the avaricious dreams engendered by Spanish success: 'Riches and conquest, and renown I sing' (Kemys 1596: A1v).

But if northern European nations saw Spain as a model to imitate, their post-Iberian emulations were equally – and increasingly – shaped by a pressure to differentiate themselves as well. In short, the pattern of Spain's colonial successes was taken up by subsequent entrants into the colonial fray both positively and negatively. As Pagden perceptively notes (1995: 68), Chapman follows his Virgilian opening with a qualification: 'Riches with honour, conquest without blood' (Kemys 1596: A1v). While the ends of French and English pretensions to empire initially mirrored Spain's, their means were not always consonant – or, at least, so they claimed. From the 1560s onwards, especially in the wake of rising religious conflicts within Europe between Catholics and Protestants – which contributed to the 1565 Spanish massacre of French Huguenots in Florida, the Spanish invasion of the Netherlands and the Spanish Armada – a potent anti-Spanish rhetoric burgeoned in both France and England, partly to further their ambitions of establishing permanent settlements in the New World. In this context, the *translatio imperii* trope took on yet another life through the translation into English and French of Spanish texts about the Americas.

Las Casas' condemnations of his compatriots' actions in the 1552–3 *Argumentum apologiae* or *Defense of the Indians* and the 1552 *Brevisima Relacíon de la Destruccíon de las Indias* [*A Short Account of the Destruction of the Indies*] thus came to support a different colonial function as well, helping to give rise to the so-called Black Legend – namely, the assertion of Spain's unique brutality in the lands it claimed as colonial possessions (see Greer et al. 2008 for a reconsideration of this important trope). Transmitted widely in the 1570s and 1580s, his texts would be seized upon and translated by the English, the French and the Dutch, to justify their own mode of entrance into the colonial arena on the basis of their difference from the Spanish. The stage for the dissemination of las Casas' writings had already been set by earlier French accounts of their attempts to settle in Florida. Among the most important, was Nicolas Le Challeux's *Discours de l'Histoire de la Floride* (1566), whose extended title emphasised its anti-Spanish contents: 'containing', the title continued, 'the treason of the Spaniards, against the subjects of the King, in the year 1565. Written in truth by those who remain, A thing so lamentable to hear, that was premeditatedly and cruelly executed by the said Spaniards: Against the authority of our Sire, the King, to the loss and injury of all this kingdom' (my translation; see also Hart 2000: 71). The text itself described Jean Ribault's fourth voyage, which culminated in conflict with a Spanish expedition led by Don Pedro de Menéndez. The Spanish commander was apparently responsible not only for killing the women and children in the fort which the French had established in Florida, but managed to convince Ribault and his men to surrender before massacring most of them. Le Challeux, who numbered among the few survivors, recounts that the Spanish sought to dismember the bodies, and 'plucking out the eyes of the dead, they stuck them on the ends of daggers, and then with cries, howls, and revelry, they threw them against our French people (1566: 34; my translation).

Atrocities committed against European competitors in the Americas were coupled with Spain's burgeoning military aggression within Europe. The Dutch revolt against Philip II's attempts to prosecute Protestants and centralise government and taxes had led to an invasion of the Netherlands by a Spanish army commanded by the Duke of Alva, triggering what is often called the Eighty Years' War for Dutch independence (1568–1648). While the Spanish overran the southern Netherlands fairly quickly, the seven northern provinces were to prove intractable, formally declaring their independence from the Spanish king in 1581. This religious and political war provided the backdrop for the revival of anti-Spanish propaganda, and in particular the translation of colonial texts which offered descriptions – whether justificatory or condemnatory – of how Spain treated the indigenous peoples of the New World. An English translation of las Casas' *Brevisima Relacíon* under the title *The Spanish Colonie* appeared in 1583, with a preface encouraging support for the Dutch rebellion, while in France the same text was translated 'in various guises and under different titles' from 1579 onwards (Hart 2000: 103).

The French and English failure to discover precious metals in the Indies led them to emphasise maritime prowess and the development of North American commercial colonies of settlement. At the same time, 'the abandonment of the search for gold and silver by France and Britain quickly changed into a form of triumphalism' (Pagden 1995: 68). And indeed in many ways the desire for gold that led the Spanish to the New World was also to prove their undoing. One important consequence of Spain's success – as Adam Smith and Montesquieu later insisted – was that the 'over-dependence of the metropolis upon the single staple produced by the colonies had resulted in the suppression of political independence, of the kind enjoyed by British colonists, and ... this combination had had the effect of forcing the metropolitan economy into decline, while preventing growth, either human or economic, within the colonies themselves' (Pagden 1995: 70). For the flood of specie into Spain without the concomitant development of productive domestic uses for it led to massive inflation that crippled its economy from the late-sixteenth century onwards. In fact, much of the money did not remain in Spain at all, flowing out all too quickly to financiers in order to pay for its expanded military ambitions within Europe, in particular for wars following the Dutch revolt. If the New World had enabled Spain's claims to be Rome's successor, that fortuitous discovery would ultimately trigger instead the further translation of empire away from the Iberian peninsula to its northern European competitors.

Having failed to emulate Spain, the English assertion of their difference from Spain would rest in good measure on the conception of a maritime British empire. While naval dominance would not become a reality until the nineteenth century, the possibility of thus redefining England's colonial status was articulated at length by John Dee (see above), and the myth persisted in part because it helped distinguish the British empire from ancient empires, such as Rome's, as well as contemporary ones, such as Spain's. 'This enduring and encouraging myth' asserted that

> [a]n empire of the seas would not be prey to the overextension and military dictatorship which had hastened the collapse of the Roman Empire, nor would it bring the tyranny, depopulation and impoverishment which had hastened the decline of Spain. The British empire of the seas was both historically novel and comparatively benign; it could therefore escape the

compulsions that destroyed all previous land-based, and hence obviously military, empires. In short, it could be an empire for liberty. (Armitage 2000: 100–1)

Though insisting upon England's specific colonial difference, this emerging idea was nonetheless overlaid upon an enduring association between English expansionist efforts and the Roman conception of a colony, an association that had been forged in particular through the ongoing 'internal colonisation' of Ireland. As D. B. Quinn (1966) and Nicholas Canny (1988) have amply demonstrated, Ireland would serve as testing ground for English colonial policy in the New World (I return to Ireland in more detail below, in the Debates chapter). Writing to William Cecil in 1565, Sir Thomas Smith, an influential player in English attempts to pacify Ireland, expressed his opinion that

> it needeth nothing more than to have colonies. To augment our tongue, our laws, and our religion in that Isle, which three be the true bands of the commonwealth whereby the Romans conquered and kept for a long time a great part of the world.

Crucially, colonisation was linked here – again, following the Roman model – with civilisation, so that Smith would name Rome, Carthage and Venice as precedents for his and his son's abortive expeditions to Ireland 'to make the same civill and peopled with naturall Englishe men borne' (quoted in Armitage 2000: 48–9), endeavours premised upon seizing land forcibly from the native Irish and cultivating these 'in parcels by the English *coloni*, with the help of those Irish *churls* who could be persuaded to join the English' (Armitage 2000: 49).

In its emphasis on civilisation (and its implicit counterpart, barbarism), Smith's language points to yet another pervasive legacy of the ancient world that complexly unites the early modern nations competing for empire, and marks as well the extent to which early modern conceptions re-deployed ideological patterns derived from earlier colonialisms. As we have seen, both Sepúlveda's defence of Spain's treatment of native Americans and las Casas' condemnation reached back to Aristotle, in particular to the Greek philosopher's discussion of the category of 'natural slaves'. English depictions of Irish inhabitants were no less likely to insist upon the irremediable savagery of the natives in order to legitimate colonial violence (see Carroll and King 2003: 66–74). Despite persistent claims that the English were different from the Spanish, the articulation of national mission by even a central figure like Richard Hakluyt was fundamentally shaped by the same humanist absorption of classical civil philosophy. Hakluyt's manuscript, 'Discourse on Western

Planting' (a key text for understanding Elizabethan colonial ideology), was presented to Sir Francis Walsingham along with a Latin synopsis of Aristotle's *Politics*. The connections between these two works ran deep, and Hakluyt's praise for the Aristotelian ideal of the *polis* echoed in his advice on how England should operate in the New World. The conjunction of these two texts provided a template for England's American ventures:

> if England were to be a *civitas perfecta* and its citizens capable of living the *vita beata* [blessed life], they like the citizens of the Aristotelian *polis*, would need to be supplied with virtue, a physical sufficiency and an abundance of fortune ... One way to supply that, and to found a new commonwealth, would be through the 'natural' activity of founding villages or *coloniae*, composed of families. (Armitage 2000: 74)

This sense of why 'planting' Englishmen in the West was essential fed into the assessment of the native Americans as well, portrayed by Hakluyt as both 'savages' and 'infidels'. The double characterisation was crucial since it asserted the inseparability of England's civilising mission from its religious one: 'without civilisation, and hence induction into the classically-defined conception of life in the *polis* or the *civitas*, Christianity could not be implanted' (Armitage 2000: 76). Thus, Hakluyt writes to Walter Raleigh that 'nothing more glorious or honourable can be handed down to the future than to tame the barbarian, to bring back the savage and the pagan to the fellowship of civil existence and to induce reverence for the Holy Spirit into atheists and others distant from God' (Hakluyt 1587: av-v; Armitage's translation). No doubt, the English route to this end repeatedly claimed a difference from the Spanish in desiring to gain – to cite Chapman's phrase again – 'Riches with honour, conquest without blood'. But, like Spain's, England's empire too was built upon a shared colonial armature inherited from the ancients, in which the conceptual opposition between civilised self and barbarous other was central. And its transformation of both New and Old worlds on this basis was to be at least as thoroughgoing – and often as brutal – as Spain's.

Cannibals

> *Como Era Gostoso o Meu Francês* [How Tasty was My Little Frenchman] (The title of a 1971 film by the Brazilian director Nelson Pereira dos Santos)

It was through the figure of the cannibal that early modern Europe most insistently addressed the nature of the peoples it encountered.

Consequently, the cultural category of cannibalism or anthropophagy persistently accompanied European discourses of civility and barbarism, becoming especially important in the wake of numerous travel accounts that detailed encounters with tribes who purportedly engaged in the act. Eating the flesh of one's fellow human beings marked a fall from humanity, expressing a fundamental cognitive and social failure to maintain the distinctions upon which civilisation itself was seen to depend. The very word 'cannibal' was a Renaissance invention, emerging from Columbus's inaugural voyage; it points not to an unambiguous phenomenon but to a complex web of associations, interweaving inherited presuppositions about the Indians Columbus expected to encounter with misunderstandings about the Indians he did encounter (or heard about) (see Hulme 1986: 16–22). The term soon became widespread in Europe, and accusations of cannibalism ubiquitous in texts and images produced during this period. They served an array of ideological functions, usually asserting the superiority of Christian Europe as well as legitimating violence against the indigenous inhabitants of lands to which the European colonisers laid claim. And yet the notion of the cannibal remained remarkably fluid. Its deployment was far from static, ranging from the demonstration of the innate savagery of native populations to – perhaps surprisingly – a robust defence of their practices as well as a critique of European attitudes and behaviours.

An important text by the Milanese Girolamo Benzoni, who spent fifteen years in Central and South America, diagnoses the use to which the Spanish put the trope. His 1565 *Historia del Mondo Nuovo*, published in Venice about nine years after his return, offered hostile descriptions of the conquests of Mexico and Peru, which were eagerly lapped up in Europe, where a number of editions and translations quickly followed the book's initial appearance. Benzoni's *Historia* forcefully catalogued the characteristics putatively attributed to American Indians by the Dominicans in order to persuade King Ferdinand that these 'brutish races . . . deserved to be sold as slaves, rather than be allowed to live at liberty'. Prominent among these was the claim that the Indians 'eat human flesh, and also the flesh of some extremely dirty animals'. The Spanish colonisers adduced this and other evidence affirming 'that no nation more wicked or wretched can be found under heaven' (in Burton and Loomba 2007: 52–3) in order to justify their ill-treatment of the natives rebelling against being forced to extract under miserable conditions the rich metals and precious stones coveted by the Spanish.

Along with las Casas' condemnation of Spanish colonial practices in the New World, Benzoni's text helped establish the anti-Spanish Black

Legend. This negative image was promulgated yet further through Theodore de Bry's influential multi-volume compilation of travel narratives *India Occidentalis* or *America* (see Chapter 3), whose Latin and German translations of Benzoni's work paired them with high-quality engravings depicting some of the cruelties it described. The broadly Protestant (and indeed Calvinist) bias of the de Brys provided one reason for their eager dissemination of the cruelties perpetrated by Catholic Spain; they did not seek, however, to overturn the association of cannibalism with the New World. Quite the contrary, as the lurid cover illustration for this book shows. In addition to Benzoni's text, the *America* series reproduced two of the most important European eyewitness accounts of cannibalism in areas of Brazil where the Portuguese and French were trying to establish control: the German Hans Staden's *Warhaftige Historia und beschreibung eyner Landtshafft der Wilden, Nackten, Grimmigen Menschfresser Leuthen in der Newenwelt America glege* (1557: Marburg) [that is, *True History and Description of a Land of Wild, Naked, Savage, Man-munching People, Located in the New World, America*] and the French Huguenot priest Jean de Léry's *Histoire d'un Voyage faict en la Terre du Brésil* (Geneva: 1578) [*History of a Voyage made to the Land of Brazil*]. These two very different texts cannot be seamlessly absorbed into the normative ideological paradigm of civilisation versus barbarism. They reveal instead how responsive the idea of the cannibal was to other determinants.

The cover illustration showing the Tupinamba tribe at their cannibal barbecue is a seventeenth-century coloured version of an engraving from *America Tertia Pars*, first published in Frankfurt in 1592. The unclothed and bearded white figure standing with upraised arms behind the man-munching indigenes is Hans Staden, a German who took up service as a gunner for the Portuguese on a voyage to the island of São Amaro, off the Brazilian coast. According to his testimony, he was captured in 1551 by the Tupinamba – a tribe allied with the French, and enemies to the neighbouring Tupinikin, with whom the Portuguese had made alliance – and held captive for nine months, during which he was constantly threatened with being eaten. The engraving revels in the graphic horror of the act, showing native men and women gnawing greedily on human corporeal parts, even as another native fans the flames of the *boucan* or outdoor grill upon which the neatly dismembered bodies are arranged.

Following the image inward along the line indicated by the row of women's heads leads the eye to Staden himself, and in particular to his right forefinger pointing upwards to the heavens. In contrast, the palm of his left hand almost theatrically lays open for our view the horrors to which he bears witness. The engraving's combination of these two gestures is telling in the context of Staden's narrative. If the left hand makes the viewer a shared witness to the ultimate barbarism, the right directs us to the divine source of his (and, ideally, our) difference, maintaining the separation between civilised European and Brazilian savage – despite Staden's physical reduction to the status of native (as indicated by his nudity). Thanks to the fortitude supplied him by his religious faith, he may be witness, he may even be dinner, but he will not participate in the activities before him. The small detail of Staden's beard, for instance, not only constitutes a physical sign of his difference from the natives, but echoes his own act of resistance: the refusal to allow the Tupinamba to remove that beard. Soon after his capture, a native woman approaches him with

> a sliver made out of crystal fastened to a thing that looked like a bent branch, and she scraped off my eyebrows with this crystal. She also wanted to scrape off the beard around my mouth, but I would not suffer this and said she should kill me with my beard. Then they answered that they did not want to kill me yet and left me my beard. But a few days later, they cut it off with a pair of scissors, which [a] Frenchman had given to them. (Staden 2008: 56)

As with de Bry's engraving, Staden's narrative underscores the gap between the dictates of Christian civilisation and the abhorrent practices of the natives. Just as the captured European bears witness to the barbarous act, his upraised right hand calls upon his God to witness, and presumably punish, its perpetrators.

This opposition between Christian civility and native barbarism is no more than we would expect. And in such reports as Amerigo Vespucci's, the association between cannibalism and Brazilian natives has been fully cemented, leaving no doubt as to the natives' expulsion from the domain of the human:

> They eat little flesh unless it be human flesh, and your Magnificence must know that they are so inhuman as to transgress regarding this most bestial custom. For they eat all their enemies that they kill or take, as well females as males, with so much barbarity, that it is brutal thing to mention: how much more to see it, as has happened to me an infinite number of times. They were astonished at us when we told them that we did not eat our enemies. Your Magnificence may believe for certain, that they have many other barbarous customs. (1894: 11)

Rather than simply follow the 'bestial custom' of consuming human flesh, the natives Vespucci describes exceed even that, making no distinctions between female and male in the pursuit of their gustatory pleasures. This excess in turn establishes the certain belief that they have yet 'many other barbarous customs' – an extension which consequently needs no further justification. The absurd exaggeration – 'as has happened to me an infinite number of times' – recurs in different ways throughout early modern depictions of the New World.

Descriptions such as Vespucci's are equally revealing in what they fail to do: they ignore the ethnographical complexities visible in later accounts such as Staden's or Léry's, and reduce to a binary opposition the complex responses of European travellers to anthropophagy. For it is the very mobility of even so extreme a figure as the cannibal that reveals the diversity and variations inhering in early modern colonial encounters with alterity. That Staden eventually escaped being eaten is itself 'proof enough of the contingency of the ritual sacrifice for the Tupi' (editors' introduction in Staden 2008: xlv). So is the story of how he avoided what seemed an inevitable fate. Having spent almost two years at the Portuguese fort in Brazil, Staden had learnt enough of the Tupi language to be able to communicate with his captors – though this meant that their threats were only too comprehensible as well. Moreover, he knew that his survival depended less on the Tupi taste for human flesh than on the dynamics of colonial occupation, in particular the conflict between the French-allied Tupi and the Portuguese. (Even Vespucci's account betrays the fact that cannibalism was a ritual practice directed at enemies alone, rendering it all the more unlikely that the Tupi ate 'little flesh unless it be human'.) Consequently, Staden consistently sought to convince his captors that he, being German, ought not to be assimilated to their Portuguese enemies – he even accompanied the Tupi warriors on one of their war raids. The attempts to exempt himself from the list of their enemies staved off his demise for a while, but would probably not have sufficed had he not also been able to use the fact of an epidemic among the Tupi to pretend that he was a shamanic healer who could intercede with his god to save at least some of those afflicted.

Even this brief summary suggests how Staden's narrative conveys a rich sense of the varied contextual determinants of Tupi cannibalism. But perhaps as remarkable is the degree to which his account is directed towards ends quite different from Vespucci's reductive use of the civilised/savage opposition. Certainly, Staden does not doubt the divide between himself and the Tupi. That separation is generalised by the de Bry engraving, which even relocates the image to make it accompany Léry's account instead, thereby accentuating the cannibal theme more powerfully than Léry's own text does. But Staden's narrative is not overly concerned with emphasising the natives' barbarism. Rather, it seeks 'to produce a homily of redemption and faith in which Tupi cannibalism is but one the many tests and redemptive proofs the text offers' (Whitehead 2000: 732). In other words, this New World story is closer in impulse to the popular genre of saints' lives or to the Old Testament tale of Job, providing a vivid experience of the trials that faith demands. Furthermore, it is a story of salvation, of Staden's surviving these tribulations thanks to the intercession of his god. '[The] threat of bodily and spiritual dissolution through the visceral certainty of customary cannibalism is not the only test that Staden's god inflicts upon him, and other physical dangers – shipwreck, disease (both epidemic and dental), and the perfidy of the French – also loom large as moments in which evidence of Staden's god becomes manifest' (editors' introduction in Staden 2008: xxi).

The coupling between religious and colonial discourses takes an even more striking turn in Léry's *History*, which undertakes a remarkable reversal of cannibalism's usual implications. Published many years after his return to France, Léry's account derives from a brief period in the mid-sixteenth century when the French sought to establish a trading colony in the Bay of Guanabara (near present-day Rio de Janeiro and Niteroi). This foothold in what was hopefully named *France Antarctique* would not ultimately survive, but it has left us with one of the most fascinating texts to emerge from Europe's encounter with the Americas.

Describing his first sighting of Brazil, Léry's ship passes by a flatland inhabited by the Ouetaca, 'savages so wild and fierce that, just as they cannot live in peace with each other, they wage open warfare against all their neighbours as well as against strangers in general'. Reports of their sheer speed and ferocity lead him to observe that

> since these devilish Ouetaca remain invincible in this little region, and furthermore, like dogs and wolves, eat flesh raw, and because even their language is not understood by their neighbours, they are considered to be among the most barbarous, cruel, and dreaded nations that can be found in all the West Indies and the land of Brazil. (1990: 28–9)

Léry soon disembarks in the lands of the friendlier Tupinamba, but the dreaded Ouetaca's cannibalistic preferences remain fresh and raw in his mind during his encounter with Nicholas Durand de Villegagnon, the leader of the earlier French expedition to Brazil who was in charge of the colony.

Despite having written to Calvin for ministers to establish a Reformed mission among the Tupi, Villegagnon and his associate Cointa almost immediately enter into doctrinal disputes with the newly arrived Huguenots on the defining matter of transubstantiation. Here, at some length, is Léry's account of their relapse:

> For although [these two Frenchmen] rejected the transubstantiation of the Roman Church ... and although they did not approve of consubstantiation either, they were not content with what the ministers taught and proved by the Word of God, that the bread and wine were not really turned into the Body and Blood of our Lord ... Well, however that may be, said Villegagnon and Cointa, the words 'This is my Body; this is my Blood' cannot be taken other than to mean that the Body and the Blood of Jesus Christ are contained therein. What then if you ask: 'Then how did they mean it, since you said that you rejected the doctrines both of transubstantiation and consubstantiation?' I have no notion of what they meant, and I firmly believe that they didn't either; for when they were shown by other passages that these words and expressions are figures – that is, that Scripture is accustomed to calling the signs of the Sacraments by the names of things signified – although they could not provide any proof to the contrary, nonetheless they remained obstinate; to the point that, without knowing how it might be done, nevertheless they wanted not only to eat the flesh of Jesus Christ grossly rather than spiritually, but what was worse, like the savages named the Ouetaca ... they wanted to chew and swallow it raw. (1990: 41)

For Léry, their inability to distinguish between names and significations turns Christians of Villegagnon and Cointa's ilk not just into savages but the most barbarous of savages. As Frank Lestringant remarks, 'the catholics appear worse than the authentic anthropophages, since they eat the body and drink the blood of the living, incarnate God' (1990: 17; my translation). Despite Villegagnon's seeming acceptance of the Reformed faith, he fails to demarcate with requisite sharpness the original Christian body from its true copy or image; his ignorance of how to read signs draws him yet closer to the Ouetaca, whose barbarity partly consists in 'even their language' being incomprehensible to their neighbours. This professed Christian thus reveals himself as nothing other than a false copy, a simulacrum masquerading in the place of truth.

What is extraordinary about Léry's *History*, though, is not this (quite common) Protestant assimilation of Catholics to the cannibals, but how its attack on Catholicism repeatedly shifts emphasis to defend the behaviour of the natives. For there is a crucial difference between Villegagnon and the Ouetaca: savage and bloodthirsty the latter may be, but they do not pretend to be other than they are; unlike Villegagnon, they do not dissimulate. Léry's relative openness to the alien is power-fully communicated by his later description of cannibalism among the Tupinamba:

> When the flesh of a prisoner, or of several . . . is thus cooked, all those who have been present to see the slaughter performed gather again joy-fully around the boucans, on which they gaze with a furious and covetous eye, contemplating the pieces and members of their enemy. However many of them there are, each of them will, if possible, have his morsel. Not, however, (as far as one can judge) that they regard this as nourishment; for although all of them confess human flesh to be wonderfully good and delicate, nonetheless it is more out of vengeance than for the taste (except for what I specifically said concerning the old women, who find it such a delicacy); their chief intention is that by pursuing the dead and gnawing them right down to the bone, they will strike fear and terror into the hearts of the living. (127)

Horrifying as this description may appear to us, it is not without an ethnological mitigation: the Tupinamba act 'more out of vengeance than for the taste'; their extreme relish for human flesh – 'gnawing [their enemies] right down to the bone' – expresses a cultural reflex rather than a naturally savage appetite.

Indeed, by the chapter's end, Léry shifts from difference to resem-blance. He acknowledges that while he could amplify the myriad examples of savage cruelty, those already provided are 'enough to horrify you, indeed, to make your hair stand on end'. 'Nevertheless', he continues, 'so that those who read these horrible things . . . may also think more carefully about the things that go on every day over here [that is, in France], among us':

> if you consider in all candour what our big usurers do, sucking blood and marrow, and eating every one alive – widow, orphans, and other poor people, whose throats it would be better to cut once and for all, than to make them linger in misery – you will say that they are even more cruel than the savages I speak of . . . Such men . . . eat [people's] flesh, break their bones, and chop them in pieces as for the pot, and as flesh within the cauldron. (1990: 131)

While this comparison of the usurers' slow cruelty with the relative speed of cannibal revenge remains metaphorical, Léry soon makes the connection literal, reaching into the immediate present of the religious wars in France to recount how the 'bloody tragedy that began in Paris on the twenty-fourth of August 1572' led to atrocities revealing savagery at the very core of the French (and, by extension, European) self:

[T]he fat of human bodies (which, in ways more barbarous that those of the savages, were butchered at Lyon after being pulled out of the Saône) – was it not publicly sold to the highest bidder? The livers, hearts, and other parts of these bodies – were they not eaten by the furious murderers, of whom Hell itself stands in horror? (1990: 131)

The French religious wars expose European civility as no more than a veneer; its very forms of belief force to the surface an innate savagery. And so Léry memorably concludes his litany of French crimes by redirecting yet once more the guilt laid at the barbarians' door: 'So let us henceforth no longer abhor so very greatly the cruelty of the anthropophagous – that is, man-eating – savages' (1990: 133).

Léry's willingness to contest European preconceptions also hints at a central, if often evanescent, feature of the richest European travel accounts both west and east: the creation of a space that withholds condemnation, that registers plurality without immediately turning difference into opposition. Before these accounts organise and hierarchise the information they gather to produce classificatory knowledge, they first lay before their readers the experience of difference and plurality as itself a form of knowledge.

How deeply Léry enters the world of the Tupi is captured in his rapt response in the chapter entitled 'What may be called religion among the savages':

These ceremonies went on for nearly two hours, with five or six hundred men dancing and singing incessantly; such was their melody that – although they do not know what music is – those who have not heard them would never believe that they could make such harmony. At the beginning of this witches' sabbath, when I was in the women's house, I had been somewhat afraid; now I received in recompense such joy, hearing the measured harmonies of such a multitude, and especially in the cadence and refrain of the song, when at every verse all of them would let their voices trail, saying *Heu, heuaure, heura, heuraure, heura, heura, oueh* – I stood there transported with delight. Whenever I remember it, my heart trembles, and it seems their voices are still in my ears. (1990: 142 and 144)

Léry's peculiar assertion that the Tupi 'do not know what music is', even as he describes their 'measured harmonies', anticipates the paradoxical logic for which Jacques Derrida (1974: 101–40) excoriates the anthropologist Claude Levi-Strauss: the claim in *Tristes Tropiques* that the Brazilian savages do not possess writing, lacking even a word for it – even though they have words, it turns out, for painting, drawing, making wavy lines and so on. But what differentiates Léry is that he cannot help but being 'transported with delight', despite his nigh reflexive reservations about this 'witches' sabbath'. When he recalls that night, he does so not with Levi-Strauss' sentimental nostalgia for the lost purity of the savage, but via carnal (re)possession, feeling the moment anew in the trembling of his heart and ringing in his ears. The virtual is actualised within him. Michel de Certeau's nuanced reading of Léry's voyage emphasises how such episodes ultimately function to 'effect [Léry's] return to himself through the mediation of the other'. But it is important as well to hold on to what escapes this movement, for as de Certeau admits, 'something still remains over there, which the words of the text cannot convey; namely, the speech of the Tupis. It is part of the other that cannot be retrieved – it is an evanescent act that writing cannot convey' (1998: 213; see also Greenblatt 1991: 16–17). If Léry eventually transforms Tupi into an object that the European will translate, he registers too, in their speech without meaning a rift in time that will perpetually sunder him from himself, remind him of possibilities once held open – until the ravages of colonialism rendered them irretrievable.

This abiding connection between the Tupinamba and the Frenchman becomes explicit in Léry's recollection of the sorrow he felt upon leaving the New World:

> So that saying goodbye here to America, I confess for myself that although I have always loved my country and do even now, still, seeing the little – or next to none at all – of fidelity that is left here, and, what is worse, the disloyalties of people toward each other – in short, since our whole situation consists . . . only in dissimulation and words without effect – I often regret that I am not among the savages, in whom (as I have amply shown in this narrative) I have known more frankness than in many over here, who, for their condemnation, bear the title of 'Christian'. (1990: 198)

In this retroactive memorialisation of valediction, the relationship between the Christian self and the savage other comes full circle: rather than 'cannibal', it is the word 'Christian' that comes to designate what is false and abhorrent. The brutal realities of early modern France transform the Christian into a 'word[] without effect', an empty sign lacking its referent. By contrast, the Tupinamba are seen to express most purely the virtues of loyalty and fidelity. This inversion disturbs the very distinction between civilised and savage that the cannibal was meant to uphold. Instead, the world to which Léry has returned loses its own coherence in being revealed as nothing more than a simulation of civility.

The justly famous essay 'Of Cannibals', by Léry's contemporary

Michel de Montaigne, draws out with admirable clarity the lessons implicit here: through the unlikely figure of the cannibal it develops a robust defence of the very principle of cultural relativism, seeing in the behaviours of those who seem alien the force of different – but not therefore incoherent – cultural logics, the presence of different modes of civilisation rather than its utter absence. '[T]here is nothing barbarous and savage', Montaigne writes,

> in that nation [of Antarctic France], from what I have been told, except that each man calls barbarism whatever is not his own practice; for indeed it seems we have no other test of truth and reason than the example and pattern of the country we live in. *There* is always the perfect religion, the perfect government, the perfect and accomplished manners in all things. Those people are wild, just as we call wild the fruits that Nature has produced by herself and in her normal course, whereas really it is those that we have changed artificially and led astray from the common order, that we should rather call wild. (1958: 152)

Looking into the cannibal means also, Montaigne and Léry suggest, being forced to look into ourselves, and to see ourselves being looked at. In seeing their difference we face ours – and face, too, an unexpected likeness. 'We took advantage', says Montaigne in 'Of Coaches', 'of their ignorance and inexperience to incline them the more readily towards treachery, lewdness, avarice and every sort of inhumanity and cruelty, after the example and pattern of our ways' (1958: 695). For we have seen the enemy, and it is us.

Gender and Race

Despite its willingness to draw from the Tupinamba lessons that Europeans could learn, Léry's *History* significantly hits an ideological limit in the gendering of the savage. In his description of cannibalism cited earlier, an exception stands out. Modifying the claim that the Tupi consume human flesh 'more out of vengeance than for the taste', Léry parenthetically excludes one subgroup, reiterating his earlier observation 'concerning the old women, who find [human flesh] such a delicacy'. His openness to the otherness of the other stops here in an encounter that appears entirely unassimilable. Thus, the narrative obsessively returns to the perverse appetite of the old women, as for instance in their eagerly waiting to 'receive the fat that drips off along the posts of the big, high wooden grills . . . Licking their fingers, they say, "Ygatou", that is, "It's good"' (1990: 126).

The 'profusion of cannibal scenes' appended by the de Brys to Staden's and Léry's narratives captures their fascinated horror through an iconic detail that is part of the image reproduced as this book's cover illustration: the Indian woman with sagging breasts (Bucher 1981: 46–64; here, 46). This specific representation is distinctive in deviating from a range of engravings that depict the Tupi as graceful and well-proportioned, even when they are shown to be indulging in acts condemned by most Europeans. The illustration makes the contrast visible in the difference between the comely woman in the left foreground, decorously consuming a carefully-held arm, and the three older women with pendulous dugs, standing behind her, greedily licking their fingers. (A stylised version of de Bry's young woman would later be used in the poster for 1971 Brazilian film 'How Tasty was My Little Frenchman', signalling the durability of this image over the centuries.) The de Brys' own fixation on this moment derives from a tension between religious faith and historical reality, between their Calvinism and their investment in seeing 'the Indian as a martyr of Spanish tyranny' (see Bucher 1981: 84). For Calvinists, all humans were fallen, and the difference between the just and the damned depended on predestination, on God's decision to save some and condemn others. 'In a system where man appears as corrupt in his very nature, the distinction between different degrees of corruption allowed Protestant colonists . . . politically to take the highest place in the hierarchy of men and thus to justify the dispossession of the Indians, marked with the sign of the damned' (Bucher 1981: 84). The figure of the gluttonous female native enabled this religious stance to be reconciled with the countervailing need to attack Spanish Catholicism. Though the Tupi in general could be represented as victims of Spanish brutality, the presence within them of an ineradicable barbarity nonetheless justified their position within the hierarchy of corruption that was a consequence of the Fall.

It is no accident that the paradigmatic figure for the monstrous beast within is the woman (and, for de Bry and Léry, the old woman): it reveals how deeply early modern colonial discourses were built upon gendered assumptions and hierarchies prevalent all over Europe. The early modern witchcraft craze as well as the mixture of fascination and fear with which matriarchal communities were regarded – expressed above all through the mythical figure of the Amazon – provided ample fuel for European visions of America. Nor were these attitudes confined to the New World. The Dutchman Jan Huygen van Linschoten's well-distributed *Itinerario* (1598), a travel narrative of his journey to India (see Case Studies below), offers an example from the eastern arm of European expansion.

Like Léry, Linschoten is often remarkably open and non-judgemental about the mores of the various peoples he meets. The East provides him with no evidence of cannibalism, but he does describe at length – and often approvingly – the severity of Chinese justice along with such practices as sati. These do not generally arouse his ire, which tends to be reserved for the loose sexual mores of women, be they native, Portuguese or 'mestico' (that is, of mixed parentage). Thus, Linschoten often rails against the singleminded desire of women in India to cuckold their husbands. He begins with the isolation of the women – 'the Portingales, Mesticos, and Indian Christian women . . . are little seen abroad, but for the most part sit still within the house, and go but seldom forth, unless it be to Church or to visit their friends' (1598: 59) – before moving on to their husbands' jealousy, evident in the refusal 'to bring any man into their houses, how special a friend he might be, that shall see their wives and their daughters' (1598: 60). These domestic details are but prelude to the unbridled sexual appetite of these women, who are

> very luxurious and unchaste, for there are very few among them, although they be married, but they have besides their husbands one or two of those who are called soldiers, with whom they take their pleasures: which to effect, they use all the slights and practices they can devise, by sending out their slaves and bawds by night, and at extraordinary times over walls, hedges and ditches, how narrowly soever they are kept and looked to. They have likewise an herb . . . which beareth a seed, whereof bruising out the sap, they put it into a cup or other vessel, and give it to their husband, either in meat or drink, and presently therewith, the man is as though he were half out of his wits . . . and sometimes it taketh him sleeping, whereby he lieth like a dead man, so that in his presence they may do what they will, and take pleasure with their friends, and the husband never know of it. (1598: 60)

This is Linschoten's version of Léry's 'witches sabbath', the slipperiness of the East synecdochically transposed onto the sexual slipperiness of women, who evade male control despite all attempts to confine them. Even the occasional surfacing of Protestant faith takes place through female excess. Hence Linschoten's description of Portuguese Goa being a town as full of cloisters and churches as Lisbon is qualified by a single difference: 'only it wanteth Nuns, for the men cannot get the women to travel so far, where they should be so shut up, and forsake Venus, with whom (so that they may enjoy and fulfil their lusts) they had rather lose their lives, whereof they make small account' (1598: 52).

These instances suggest that discourses of gender and sexuality offered flexible schemata to render comprehensible and to naturalise modes of colonial domination – and sometimes even to contest them. As with cannibalism, there was no single way in which these representations were deployed. Rather, we continually encounter variations that merge inherited conceptual frames with specific contextual determinants. As Ferguson's nuanced work on literacy and empire shows (2003), the effects of gendering are subtle and complex, demanding careful analysis and historicisation.

Let us focus, though, on some of the more obvious manifestations. For the New World, Raleigh's eloquent description of Guiana provides an emblematic instance:

> To conclude, Guiana is a country that hath yet her maidenhead, never sacked, turned nor wrought, the face of the earth hath not been torn, nor the virtue and salt of its soil spent by manurance, the graves have not been opened for gold, the mines not broken with sledges, nor their images pulled down out of their temples. It has not been entered by any army of strength, and never conquered or possessed by any Christian prince. (1848: 115)

The sexualised image of the land as a woman waiting for, even desiring, her own deflowering underscores both the masculinist construction of colonial agency and the misogyny that was its ineluctable counterpart. The implicit image of the native inhabitants as wanderers, not truly having made the land upon which they move their own, feeds into the English insistence upon full possession rather than mere discovery. Such images were widespread in sixteenth- and seventeenth-century Europe, as a quick survey of costume books and maps confirms.

And yet even Raleigh's blunt metaphor is more layered than it first might seem. For, as we have seen, Guiana is also a land that Raleigh does not enter. His refusal to seize its maidenhead does not reflect only his inability to complete his colonial mission because of material circumstances. The representation of discovery and conquest 'as forms of sexual violence . . . allows him also to represent at the symbolic as well as the literal level the absence of rape, the withholding of male desire'. Such restraint reflects a different set of constraints, those imposed upon him by a woman, his sovereign Queen Elizabeth, whose own unmarried status underwrites an alliance between virgin queen and virgin land which 'relegates men to an instrumental status' (Fuller 1991: 58). Even as masculine sexuality constructs conquest in terms of rape, it acknowledges other imperatives that forestall the action, in deference to a female power whose dictates reverberate even at this distance from the mother country.

In India, and more generally the East, where even the fiction of having discovered unpossessed territories could not be sustained, the preferred modality was marriage. For example, the first English play to take 'India' as its setting, John Fletcher's *The Island Princess* (1620–1), encodes English attempts to find their own place in the sun in terms of a contest between colonial suitors for the hand of the eponymous bride-to-be. In effect, the native woman Quisara functions as the figure for the Spice Islands or the Moluccas, where English, Portuguese and Dutch were competing to establish trade monopolies (see Raman 2002; Neill 2000; and Nocentelli 2010). Marriage, posited as a voluntary choice premised upon mutual desire, thus provides the metaphor whereby a mercantile colonialism conceals the actual forms of masculinist violence through which it was to become a reality. Loomba has examined the ideological labour and the implicit violence expressed in this 'fantasy of an Eastern queen who willingly crosses religious and cultural boundaries' (2002b: 32), noting that the Bible provided an important precedent for such constructions of the East: through the story of Sheba 'arriving laden with gold at Solomon's court and willingly surrendering her enormous wealth in return for sexual gratification'. This episode 'initiated a long tradition of stories in which the desire of the native woman for the European man coded for the submission of colonised people' (1998: 153). The romance of John Rolfe and the other Indian princess Pocahontas shows that such modes of interpretation were not limited to the East, but moved geographically in accordance with the exigencies of colonial representation. And Gordon McMullan's interpretation (1994) of Fletcher's title character as a converted Pocahontas confirms the play's resonance with a range of different colonial settings.

John Dryden's propagandist play *Amboyna* (1673) brings together the tropes of marriage and rape to produce an intra-European distinction between the English and the Dutch at a time when these two nation states were in regular conflict. Written shortly after England formally declared war against the Dutch for the third time in twenty years, Dryden's play revives – in the hope of drumming up public support for a doubtful war – a half-century old flashpoint in the Anglo-Dutch rivalry over 'India': the so-called 'massacre' of roughly a dozen Englishmen by the Dutch in the minuscule island of Amboyna (now part of Indonesia). For Dryden, too, the native female body is the site upon which difference is inscribed: the commercial conflict between Harman Junior, the son of the Dutch governor at Amboyna, and Captain Gabriel Towerson, the English representative of the East India Company, takes concrete form in their claims to Ysabinda, 'an Indian Lady betroth'd to Towerson' (1994: 9). The character is itself Dryden's invention. The spate of pamphlets following the original event in 1623 makes it clear that the basic issues leading up to the killing concerned rival claims to these East Indian islands. The resident English at Amboyna were accused of plotting with the islanders to seize the Dutch fort, murder their governor and 'by the help of your Plantations near . . . keep it for your selves' (V.i.124–5). A confession extracted under torture from a local soldier working for the Dutch, who had enquired after the fort's strength, ostensibly revealed an English plot to join with other like-minded soldiers and make themselves masters of the island. Further questioning of English residents led to accusations against Towerson, and ultimately to the execution of a number of them. English responses were predictably vehement and outraged, denying both Dutch colonial jurisdiction as well as the intent imputed to Towerson.

In Dryden's hands, the difference between nation states is produced by counterposing, through the opposed claims to Ysabinda, English civility and legality against the brutality and illegality of Dutch colonialism. That Ysabinda is already 'contracted' to Towerson evokes in refracted form the colonial myth of the native freely yielding herself up to the coloniser. All that is left, as the play begins, is the symbolic confirmation of voluntary submission through marriage. But Towerson is 'condemn'd', as he later bemoans, 'to be the second man' (IV.v.31). Counselled by the Dutch Fiscal (whose name underscores the commercial ethos he embodies), Harman lures Ysabinda into the woods immediately after the wedding, ties her to a tree, and rapes her. For Dryden, the rape constitutes the culmination of the Dutch mercantile ethos, which is governed solely by self-interest and greed. The Fiscal, for instance, soundly admonishes Harman for his 'fits of conscience' after the rape, saying that these

> in another might be excusable; but, in you, a Dutchman, who are of a Race that are born Rebels and live everywhere on Rapine; Wou'd you degenerate and have remorse? . . . The Woman is an Amboyner, and what's less now Marry'd to an Englishman: Come, if there be a Hell, 'tis but for those that sin in Europe, not for us in Asia; Heathens have no Hell'. (IV.iv.50ff.)

The Dutch rebellion against the Spanish – generally supported by the English on religious grounds – is transformed fifty years later into an ambiguous sensibility expressed in all its people, leading them to barbaric acts which they assume to be normal. Not to commit these is in fact to 'degenerate'. Moreover, Dutch barbarity is emphasised by association with Asian mores – since the heathen lack the operative distinction between Heaven and Hell which marks Christian civilisation, the Dutch too surrender all claims to being civilised when they abide (even cynically) by pagan belief (see Raman 2002: 189–235).

Reprinted around the same time as Dryden's play, Andrew Marvell's poem 'The Character of Holland' likewise impugns the Dutch for their religious, economic and moral barbarism:

> Hence Amsterdam, Turk-Christian-Pagan-Jew,
> Staple of sects and mint of schism grew,
> That bank of conscience, where not one so strange
> Opinion but finds credit and exchange.
> . . .
> Was this Jus Belli & Pacis? Could this be
> Cause why their burgomaster of the sea
> Should raging hold his linstock to the mine,
> While, with feigned treaties, they invade by stealth
> Our sore new circumcised Commonwealth?

(lines 71ff.)

Such a fall from the standards of European civilisation is epitomised for Dryden in Ysabinda's rape. The violation of the 'Indian' woman's body differentiates European colonialism into nationally specific forms.

In *The Island Princess* and *Amboyna* the condition for marriage is religious conversion, suggesting the further importance within colonial representations of coordinating the myth of a mutual and loving trade with the only too real missionary imperatives that imbued colonial ventures. In this vein, an Indian Queen (also called 'for her odours and riches the Queen of Merchandise') in *The Triumphs of Honour and Virtue* (1622) – one of numerous pageants by Thomas Middleton to make use of proto-colonial themes and motifs – acknowledges before her London audience that the 'celestial knowledge' received through her conversion to Christianity is more than fair price for the 'gums and fragrant spices' she is able to supply to the English merchants. Her new-found knowledge 'settles such happiness' on her as to outweigh all 'the riches and sweetness of the east' (1964: 7.358–9). Here, too, the actual process of conversion is assumed: the colonised land has already accepted the gender and religion demanded of it by the coloniser. In Fletcher's play, though, the process is fraught. The one moment of true anxiety that breaks its otherwise generically predictable romance plot occurs when the young Portuguese adventurer, Armusia, is told that he must convert to Islam before he can marry Quisara. His violent outburst and refusal to do so – of a piece with Hans Staden's refusal to shave his beard – has the desired effect: of convincing Quisara herself to convert and leaving even the King of Ternate 'half-persuaded' by the power of Christian faith.

The flip side to this Christian steadfastness – itself a form of masculinist assertion – was the effeminisation of the Asian or Oriental male. In such plays as Philip Massinger's *The Renegado* (1624), the Christian woman's very presence induces a loss of identity in the Muslim male who desires her, producing a 'kind of gender-confusion . . . The Muslim man thus stands in for the *haec vir*, or effeminate man . . . regularly taken to task in Elizabethan "defenses" of women for his failure to "wear the breeches"' (Burton 2005: 112). The persistence in literary texts of an opposition between masculine English firmness and Oriental effeminacy expresses, though, a pervasive anxiety that the reality might be quite different. According to Burton, apostasy sermons and early modern travel accounts suggested 'that Englishmen not only yielded in arguments of a religious nature . . . [but] were often swayed by riches or by sexual enticements' (2005: 101). And, of course, forced conversion was rife among the Ottomans. As Leslie Pierce shows, the Turkish empire created an 'inverted racialization', 'a kind of imperial ethnicity, a ruling class comprising Christian slaves converted to Islam and trained in the arts of government' (in Greer et al. 2007: 27). Beyond this spectre of ex-Christians rising to powerful positions within Eastern societies, the thought that Christians might voluntarily convert was experienced as 'even more shocking because [it] marked a willing subjugation of masculinity and Christianity' (Burton 2005: 102).

Sustaining the nexus of marriage, rape and conversion that we have been examining is the burning issue of the ethnic/racial differences that confronted Europeans everywhere they travelled. The well-nigh paradigmatic text for English Renaissance studies to explore the difference that 'race' makes is Shakespeare's *Othello*, with its tale of a doomed marriage between the fair Venetian Desdemona and the eponymous general-cum-Moorish-convert. As he recounts it, Othello's identity has been deeply shaped by what were in fact rediscovered classical texts (see French 1934), medieval travelogues and romances, along with discovery narratives. His 'redemption' from slavery – his salvation denoting a newly won physical as well as religious freedom – carries him into the strange worlds that these texts unfold, peopled by 'the Cannibals that each other eat, / The Anthropophagi, and men whose heads / Do grow beneath their shoulders' (I.iii.161–3). And indeed it is as virtually a metonym for such strangeness that Othello attracts Desdemona, whose inclination towards all that is 'strange, . . . passing strange' (I.iii.178) in Othello ultimately leads her to love him for the 'dangers [he] had passed' (I.iii.185). Her willing submission to this alterity – 'subdued' as she is 'to the very quality of [her] lord', and 'seeing [his] visage in his mind'

(I.iii.268–70) – leads her tragically to walk into her bedchamber at the play's end to face a horrible fate.

If the marriage echoes – even as it partly inverts in terms of gender – the rhetoric of mutuality prevalent in how Europe sought to represent its relationship to foreign territories, this mutuality is best captured in Desdemona's corroboration before her father that 'she was half the wooer' (I.iii.196). But haunting the marriage are spectres of rape and unnatural liaisons that express themselves most emphatically through the complex registers of racial difference (see Neill 1989). As Karen Newman notes, 'the black Moor and the fair Desdemona are united in a marriage' that many of the other characters 'view as unthinkable' (1987: 144). Thus, Brabantio's disbelief that Desdemona could 'fall in love with what she fear'd to look on' (I.iii.113) leads him to accuse Othello of having 'wrought upon her' (I.iii.121) with witchcraft and forbidden 'mixtures powerful o'er the blood' (I.ii.119). The imputation of miscegenation informs both plot and language. Iago's manipulation of Othello depends upon the latter's having internalised an ambivalence regarding his own blackness, as well as his age and the degree to which he has successfully incorporated the Christian culture he now belongs to (see Greenblatt 1980). The image of an unnatural union, miscegenous and bestial, is famously used by Iago to arouse Brabantio in the play's opening scene: 'Even now, now, very now, an old black ram / Is tupping your white ewe' (I.i.94–5).

The complex overlaying of racial and gendered discourses in *Othello* is captured in the chiastic crossing of two axes. First, and most obvious in the quotations above, black and white. The discomfort occasioned by this juxtaposition is well demonstrated by the play's performance history, and in particular by Othello's 'whitening' in later centuries. That fear of miscegenation was an issue in the Renaissance as well may be seen in *The Island Princess*, where Quisara's exceptional fairness is linked to the 'curious whitening effect that conversion has on non-Christian women' (Burton 2005: 145; see also Hall 1995: 114). But this axis is paradoxically intersected by another involving what we might call the blackening of Desdemona, whereby the white Venetian is associated with the monstrous. A hint of this operation may be found in Othello's description of her avid response to his storytelling, which aligns her with the hungry cannibals of whom he speaks: 'This to hear / Would Desdemona seriously incline, / . . . and with a greedy ear / Devour up my discourse' (I.iii.163ff.). Femininity in the play 'is not opposed to blackness and monstrosity, as white is to black, but identified with the monstrous, an identification which makes the miscegenation doubly fearful'

(Newman 1987: 145). One might compare Desdemona's double ascription – representative of whiteness and fears of monstrosity – with how the de Bry engraving of the cannibal feast visually separates and connects the young native woman from the gluttonous older ones. The long, flowing tresses of the former do double duty in the image, re-purposed as the wild and uncontrolled genital hair of the old woman immediately behind her, who is thus rendered yet more threatening.

The fluid and often incoherent ways in which race and gender interact (as in *Othello*) has contributed in recent years to questioning of the applicability of 'race' as a category in studying early modern cultures. As David Nirenberg recounts, Michel Foucault's lecture at the Collège de France in 1976 asserted 'that racism was a uniquely modern phenomenon, the product of particular state formation and binary representations of society that did not exist before the seventeenth century' (in Greer et al. 2008: 71). Emily Bartels' reading of *Othello* endorses a similar stance in claiming that Africans and blackness had not as yet accrued the negative connotations that would attach to them later, so that Iago's invective is motivated less by racial concerns than personal ones (1997: 62). Drawing on Homi Bhabha's work (see 1994), she emphasises, as does Carol Neely (1995), not Othello's blackness but his hybridity, seeing in his double role (both Moor and Venetian) an expression of flexible positioning along ethnic lines – a flexibility through which he acquires agency and power. One implication here is that hybridity (understood as constitutive of early modern European conceptions of self and identity) preempts the use of 'race' as an analytical category. Another implication, stressed in Loomba's critique of Bartels, is that hybridity is thereby '*counterposed* to blackness' as 'agency [is] to the force of European domination' (in Loomba and Orkin 1998: 150). The evocation of hybridity in postcolonial studies has often been problematic: 'as a descriptive catch-all term', it fails 'to discriminate between the diverse modalities of hybridity, for example, forced assimilation, internalized self-rejection, political cooptation, social conformism, cultural mimicry, and creative transcendence' (Shohat 1992: 110). And Loomba therefore objects that the celebration of hybridity as resistance or agency 'fuzzily import[s] . . . a certain kind of post-structuralist postcolonial' thinking, and ultimately tends to 'flatten and decontextualize the Shakespearean text' (1998: 150–1).

But the question still left hanging is whether we can fruitfully use 'race' in studying early modern texts. Or, as Nirenberg poses it, '[c]an people writing before the development of modern evolutionary theories be said to think in terms of "race"?' (in Greer et al. 2008: 72). This formulation acknowledges that modern conceptions of race, no matter how diverse or incoherent they are, have been fundamentally shaped by biological discourses originating in the eighteenth and nineteenth centuries. This scientific inheritance underpinned the German National Socialists' justification of anti-semitism through explicitly racial ideologies, which in turn led to race being discredited 'as a mode of discourse in the biological and social sciences (though not in popular usage)' (72) in the wake of the Second World War. The issue for colonial and postcolonial studies, however, is not whether racial ideas have an empirical validity but whether race is an appropriate category for analysing the mental universes and actions of people living and writing in earlier periods. Absent a theory of genetics to lend even the illusion of scientificity to biological determinisms, pre-modern systems of discrimination were, if anything, even more fluid and labile than later conceptions; explanations for ethnic – and gender – differences ranged from climatological and cosmographical (see, for example, Floyd-Wilson 2006; Burton and Loomba 2007: 22–3) to biblical to pedagogical to cultural and environmental. Thus, Robert Bartlett insists that 'while the [medieval] language of race – gens, natio, "blood", "stock", etc. – is biological, its medieval reality was almost entirely cultural' (1993: 197; see also Bartlett 2001: 39–56). In other words, even if tinged with the language of biology, pre-modern descriptions of difference cannot be properly called racial.

However, this separation of culture from biology is not particularly convincing because the assumption behind it – that there is a truly biological racism against which pre-modern discriminations can be measured and exonerated – is simply untenable: 'What does it mean to say that although a premodern ideology was expressed in biological terms, it was not racial because the differences it reinforced were not biological? . . . All racisms are attempts to ground discriminations, whether social, economic, or religious, in biology and reproduction' (Nirenberg in Greer et al. 2008: 74). The history of the Romance word 'raza' (whence the English 'race'), for instance, stretches well back into pre-modern times, becoming in fifteenth-century Spain 'part of a complex of interchangeable terms', including 'casta' [caste] or 'linaje' [lineage] 'that linked both behaviour and appearance to nature and reproduction'. While all these terms were contested, they nonetheless point to a language 'saturated, then as now, with resonance to what contemporaries held to be 'common sense' knowledge about the reproductive systems of the natural world' (77–8). Such commonsensical knowledge is vitally important, as Stuart Hall has argued. While far from coherent, it is nonetheless

the terrain of conceptions and categories on which the practical consciousness of the masses of the people is actually formed. It is ... the ground
which new conceptions of the world must take into account, contest and
transform, if they are to ... become historically effective. (1986: 20)

The case of Spain should not be taken to mean that 'race' *did* exist
in pre-modern cultures: its semantic networks do not justify projecting
modern 'race' and racism back to the earlier period. It is a mislead-
ing view 'that because racism is everywhere a deeply anti-human and
anti-social practice, that it is therefore everywhere *the same* – either in
its forms, its relations to other structures and processes, or its effects'
(Hall 1986: 23). Rather, Nirenberg's scepticism more limitedly counters
claims that 'race' *did not* exist before the modern period: these are mis-
leading and reductive because they short-circuit the process of comparison and discovery by referring to the mirage of a 'true' biological racism.

With terms such as race and gender, then, we are faced with a
paradox: we cannot live with them, nor can we live without them.
For we cannot simply let these notions of difference go by, as if their
variability and incoherence justifies dismissing them as purely fictional
constructs (see Gates 1986: 6). As Nirenberg puts it, '[r]ace demands a
history, both because it is a subject both urgent and vast and because its
own logic is so closely akin to that of the disciplines ... with which we
study the persistence of humanity in time' (86). The rhetorics of race and
gender are pieces of a culture's toolkit, mobile and adaptable responses
to fix and stabilise an underlying fluidity, combating an anxiety that
there only differences, multiplicities – and no identities. For these very
reasons, however, histories of race need to be understood not as describing reality nor prescribing a future, but 'as provocations to comparison',
for there is 'energy to be drawn from the collision of such polemics with
our particles of history, and new elements of both past and present to
be found in the wreckage' (87). Precisely in the disjunction between our
presents and pasts does their connectedness also appear, in a manner
that throws both past and present into question. And it is perhaps in just
such provisional, limited and strategic ways that 'race', 'gender', and
'ethnicity' reveal their utility for the reading of colonial texts.

Difference and Repetition

In an incisive essay on historicism and Irish postcolonial studies, David
Lloyd counsels us to think of the designations 'colonial' and 'postcolonial' as involving 'not mere empirical judgement but the consideration

of historical human subjects and their social relations as subjects and objects' (in Carroll and King 2003: 51). Drawing inspiration from Marx's *Grundrisse*, he proposes that we understand the term 'colonial' – and, by extension, 'postcolonial' – as a '"rational abstraction" rather than a transhistorical concept. That is, as a concept that can only function, like "labour" and "exchange", a posteriori, at the point when the phenomena it designates and unifies have emerged in their material actuality' (52). Thus, to borrow his example, India becomes a British colony in actuality only in the wake of the 1857 mutiny, when the British governmental apparatus puts itself in place of the material practices of the East India Company, and Britain's decisions and concerns dominate the interactions between the two countries. But this moment also enables a retroactive understanding of the East India Company as a 'phase of colonialism, even though the word itself may not have been used' (52). The material instantiation of colonialism as state activity enables us to abstract, to forge, the concept in such a way that we begin to recognise it, even in anterior periods. We can now understand colonialism as an integrated phenomenon, operating across a range of institutions and discourses.

Colonialism's inner dynamic – distinctive of European engagement with the lands they came for a time to possess – required

> the utter transformation of the colonised culture: the eradication of its structures of feeling, the subjection of its population to the colonisers' notions of legality, and the displacement of indigenous forms of religion, labour, patriarchy, and rule by those of colonial modernity. (47)

This driving impulse, clearly identifiable in retrospect, may seem natural to any empire, but is hardly so. Compare, for instance, Columbus's act of staking Spanish possession in the New World with the actions of the heavily armed Chinese fleet of Zheng He (1375–1435), grand eunuch and admiral in the early Ming dynasty. In 1431–3 Zheng He sailed the considerable distance from Nanjing to the Straits of Hormuz (at the entrance to the Persian Gulf) simply to display power, to show Chinese superiority as the unexercised *potential* for conquest. The fleet stopped briefly at some Asian ports, trading peaceably with native merchants before returning home. There were no battles fought, no claims staked. Even the avowedly expansionist Ottoman and Mughal empires were often characterised by a remarkable degree of inclusiveness towards peoples and territories that came under their sway: the Ottoman empire was 'notable for its devotion to keeping all of its pieces – all of its subject peoples – on the game board' (Pierce in Greer et al. 2008: 32).

Hardt and Negri attribute this European distinctiveness to what they call, borrowing a phrase from Gilles Deleuze, 'the discovery of the plane of immanence', that is to say, 'an affirmation of the powers of *this* world': between 1200 and 1600 '[h]umans declared themselves masters of their own lives, producers of cities and history, and inventors of heavens' (2000: 70–1). A consequence of this self-assertion was that 'human knowledge became a doing, a practice of transforming nature' (72), an attitude pithily captured in Sir Francis Bacon's claim in *The Great Instauration* to have opened 'an entirely different way . . . to the human understanding . . . in order that the mind may exercise its jurisdiction [*suo jure*] over the nature of things' (1854: 3.334). The implications of Bacon's attitude both for Europe and for the colonial sphere were to be immense.

However, even if this description reveals what is shared in European practices and was replicated across the numerous colonies belonging to individual imperial powers, it would be a mistake to treat colonialism and postcolonialism as being defined by one particular set of characteristics. They are, in Lloyd's terms, temporal rather than ideal concepts, marked by 'gradual shifts and accumulations of meanings' (in Carroll and King 2003: 51). Earlier, I touched upon the postcolonial potential visible in las Casas' insistence on humankind's equality. But his own anti-colonialism cannot be separated from its obverse: of his missionary vocation being implicated in the very colonial practices he attacks. 'In fact, Las Casas can think equality only in terms of sameness . . . He recognises that humankind is one, but cannot see that it is simultaneously also many' (Hardt and Negri 2000: 116). The multiplicity of peoples and places confronting early modern colonial ventures reveals a repeated dispersion and pluralisation of the very idea of the colonial, so that it becomes impossible to assert the sameness of different colonial moments, even as we schematically recognise the ubiquity of a global process. A striking example offered by Lloyd concerns the difference between the so-called colonial periods in US history and, say, British history. In the case of the former, the term refers not to the colonisation of the Americas and treatment of its indigenous peoples but

> to the relations between a white settler population and England as the dominant and regulative power. "Independence" then refers not to the process of decolonisation, as understood by indigenous populations, but to the establishment of an autonomous but no less European and imperial state by the settlers. (in Carroll and King 2003: 51)

Abraham Lincoln's own strong support for colonisation in the years leading up to the Civil War advocated the exportation of American slaves not only back to the lands from which they had been snatched but to the Caribbean and South America, so that they could freely colonise those regions. They would, in short, repeat – with a difference – what early modern Europe had achieved.

There is indeed no repetition without a difference. And in showing the mobility of tropes and representational structures deployed by early modern colonialism, I have tried to remain true to this dialectic, to attend to what Lloyd calls 'the differential'. 'There are', he writes, 'no identical colonial situations', and crucial to postcolonial studies is therefore a focus on 'the remarkably diverse ways' in which colonialism's 'rationalising drive is deflected by the particularities of each colonial culture' (in Carroll and King 2003: 47). Only a differential approach can steer between the Scylla and Charybdis of reductive abstraction ('all colonialisms are the same') and mere cataloguing of differences ('each colonialism is singular'). It allows lessons learned through investigating one site to be richly productive when analysing another, without demanding that the two domains exhibit complete congruence. For even a politics of difference can hardly be celebrated for its own sake alone. After all, the texts of early modern colonialism provide ample evidence that they recognised – and exploited – difference: in their hierarchical ordering of civilisations (see, for example, Figure 4, the frontispiece to de Bry's *India Orientalis II*); in how they sought to calibrate political and mercantile policies to further particular interests; in how they manipulated differences in order to establish domains of sovereignty and rule. And much the same could be said of the postmodern and postcolonial insistence on a politics of difference as well. As Hardt and Negri point out, 'the ideology of the world market has always been the anti-foundational and anti-essential discourse par excellence. Circulation, mobility, diversity, and mixture are its very conditions of possibility' (2000: 150).

These affiliations between contemporary postcolonial thought and what it critiques are neither accidental nor avoidable. They emerge most forcefully when – despite its own inclinations – critique gets entangled with notions of historical progress and development. While postcolonial studies has generally set itself against the linear time of 'progress' (a secularised version of the human perfectibility espoused by las Casas), the term itself 'is haunted by the figure of linear "development" that it sets out to dismantle. Metaphorically, the term . . . marks history as a series of stages along an epochal road from "the pre-colonial", to "the colonial", to "the post-colonial"' (McClintock 1992: 85). This may be so, but at its most effective postcolonial attention to the differential does more than this, for it also draws attention to alternatives, to what does not fit. At these junctures, it offers a mode of analysis or a perspective that, in Ferguson's words, 'seeks to understand life-worlds different from our own and also to allow ways in which those worlds might *not* have developed into modern societies as we in the West conceive them' (2003: 3). And such incommensurabilities often lurk even in the most colonial of texts. It falls to postcolonial studies to re-kindle these moments, breathing fire into them, so that by their light we may read – and act – differently in the future. For we shall never be – entirely – postcolonial.

Chapter 2

Debates

Texts and Contexts

> What should we do but sing his praise
> That led us through the watery maze,
> Unto an isle so long unknown,
> And yet far kinder than our own?

(Andrew Marvell, 'Bermudas')

What is a colonial text? An answer to this query is presupposed in the debate – remarkably, still alive – over the extent to which Shakespeare's late play *The Tempest* is such a text. The play's association with New World colonisation is an old one; it has been linked to the activities of the Virginia Company ever since the early nineteenth century, when Edmond Malone proposed the relevance of a number of pamphlets on Sir William Somers's 1609 voyage to Virginia, during which his ship, the Sea Venture, was wrecked on Bermuda (see Malone 1808). However, the nature of that relevance has been much debated in the twentieth century. Two of the best-known editors of the play offer sharply contrasting assessments. Writing in 1954, Frank Kermode's introduction to the Arden edition categorically asserts 'that there is nothing in *The Tempest* fundamental to its structure of ideas which could not have existed had America remained undiscovered' (xxv). Roughly a generation later, Stephen Orgel's Oxford text would be equally forthright in seeing '[t]he significance of the literature of exploration ... as both deeper and less problematic than has generally been argued', thus allying itself with critics for whom 'travel narratives provided Shakespeare not with sources but with models, both for the behaviour of New-World natives and for European responses to them' (Orgel 1987: 33).

What applies forcefully for *The Tempest* is no less true for other early modern texts, many of which often owe their 're-discovery' to the rise of colonial and postcolonial studies. Fletcher's *The Island Princess* or the Thomas Stukeley plays (see Edelman 2005), to cite two instances, have entered scholarly discourse and even the broader cultural sphere over the past few decades because of the increased attention paid to the relationships between colonialism and literary production. After centuries of neglect, they have been written about and re-issued in new critical editions. In 2002 the Royal Shakespeare Company staged *The Island Princess* as part of an ongoing commitment to revive rarely performed Elizabethan and Jacobean plays. Gordon McMullan's dramaturgical introduction for that production sketches the impact of colonial/postcolonial scholarship on its staging, as well as on the decision to revive it at all.

Of course, given Shakespeare's canonical status, it is not surprising that re-interpretations of his *oeuvre* have dominated the colonial turn; in addition to *The Tempest*, *Othello*, *Antony and Cleopatra* and *The Merchant of Venice* (to name just a few) have been richly transformed by the disclosure of their connections to early modern colonialism, and by their appropriations in postcolonial contexts (see, for example, Cartelli 1999 and De Sousa 1999). (The fact that these are *plays* also raises the question of the impact of postcolonial studies upon the performance of early modern dramatic works. This chapter does not deal with that question, focusing instead on textual appropriations. For *The Tempest*'s performance history, see the overview in Henderson 2003: 228–32.)

So, is *The Tempest* a colonial text? As we shall see, the importance of *The Tempest* for thinking about colonialism and postcolonialism derives in no small measure from its having acquired near-canonical status as the text upon which to stage that very question.

Tempestuous Histories

Before, between and beyond the Arden and Oxford editions of *The Tempest* lies an impressive array of interpretations shaped by decolonisation and the rise of postcolonial studies that has established something akin to a new orthodoxy: colonialism is understood as not just *a* but *the* discursive context through which the play acquires its meaning. Because a critical trajectory often becomes most clearly visible in retrospect, a recent reaction against this orthodoxy offers a good starting point. In *Shakespeare after Theory*, David Kastan argues that the current dominance of colonial/postcolonial readings of *The Tempest* is misplaced since European dynastic politics 'marks the play . . . more insistently than does the history of the new world'. This European history 'allows a reader to make sense of more in the text . . . that would seem arbitrary or inexplicable' (1999: 196). Kastan's is not the reductive claim that 'European court politics must replace new world colonialism as the "dominant discursive con-text" that reveals the meaning of *The Tempest*' (195). He is willing to grant the validity of colonial/ postcolonial readings so long as we are clear that they respond to an 'interpretive desire to locate the play in *our* historical moment'. Such readings disclose not how history marks the play's inception but rather how the play has 'absorb[ed] history' (196) in our own time, when the politics and aftermath of decolonisation have become especially urgent.

The distinction drawn here is important (if problematic) because it brings to the fore different ways in which a work might be understood to be a colonial text. Kastan's formulation implies a clean, temporal separation between what *The Tempest* was (for Shakespeare and his contemporaries, for example) and what it is (for us in our postcolonial worlds). Thus, his argument primarily criticises readings that assert the centrality of *early modern* colonialism to the play's concerns; it is directed in particular against what a recent edition calls the 'Americanization of *The Tempest*' (Vaughan and Vaughan 1999: 100). 'If one's interpretive desire', Kastan writes,

> is to reinsert the play into . . . the space of its diegetic setting as well as the performative space of its earliest productions . . . we should look more closely at the old world than the new, at the wedding of Elizabeth and Frederick rather than of Pocahontas and John Rolfe, at James' own writings rather than the writings from Jamestown. (Kastan 1999: 196)

As early as 1898, Sidney Lee's biography of Shakespeare, which saw in Caliban the representation of an American Indian, had claimed that *The Tempest* was in some fundamental way about America. The assertion was enthusiastically seconded by a range of British and North American scholars in the first half of the twentieth century, who 'persuaded themselves and most (apparently) of their generation that *The Tempest* had an essentially American setting, predominantly American themes, and, at least in Caliban, a truly American character'. This consensus went hand in hand with an understanding of Prospero as a largely positive force, seeking against all odds to raise the savage Caliban to civility: '[h]e was the benign imperialist, the conduit of language, learning, refinement and religion – the uplifter of "uncivilized man"' (Vaughan and Vaughan 1999: 102). It took a number of important critical interventions in the 1970s – particularly, Leslie Fiedler's treatment of the play as a colonialist myth (1972), along with Stephen Greenblatt's 'Learning to Curse' (1976) and Charles Frey's 'The Tempest and the New World' (1979) – to reverse the values implicit in this paradigm. These established in more complex ways not only the play's reliance upon the Virginia material, but the deeper resonance with its larger colonial surround. As we shall see below, such reassessment was sparked in some measure by Caribbean and Latin American appropriations of Shakespeare's play in the 1950s and 1960s, which 'recast Caliban as the emblem of South and Central American peoples and substituted Prospero as the imperialist, arrogant United States' (Vaughan and Vaughan 1999: 102).

In the Anglo-American context, particularisations of The Tempest in terms of England's attempts establish a foothold in the New World adopted more broadly postcolonial and politically urgent forms in the 1980s. Francis Barker and Peter Hulme's landmark essay (1985) treated the play as an exemplary case to pursue a wide-ranging discussion of the proper relationship between a text and its historical contexts. They argued forcefully for a 'properly political intertextuality' which 'would attend to successive inscriptions [in Kastan's terms, how a text absorbs history] without abandoning that no longer privileged but still crucially important first inscription of the text' (194). For The Tempest that first inscription is its relationship to 'the ensemble of fictional and lived practices, which for convenience we will simply refer to . . . as "English colonialism"' (198). Focusing on the strange moment of disturbance when Prospero appears to lose control over the masque he is staging for Ferdinand and Miranda, they asserted that the episode encoded both an anxiety over colonial authority and a concomitant drive in the text to 'quell[] . . . a fundamental disquiet concerning its own functions within the projects of colonial discourse' (204). Another important essay by Paul Brown related early events in Virginia (in particular, the planter Rolfe's marriage to Pocahontas, the abducted daughter of the chief Powhatan) to contemporaneous English attempts to colonise Ireland, in order to show how Shakespeare's play disclosed 'character- istic operations of the discourse of colonialism' (1985: 50). Informed by Edward Said's Orientalism, Brown argued that, through the intertwined language of 'masterlessness' and 'savagism' (50), colonialist discourse voiced 'a demand both for order and disorder' producing a disruptive other (Caliban) 'in order to assert the superiority of the colonizer' (58), who concomitantly embodied civilisation and its virtues.

Such readings eschewed the question of Shakespeare's direct knowl- edge of his putative sources to suggest that The Tempest was more broadly and conflictedly shaped by early modern colonialism than mere source study could reveal. Nixon (1987) and Loomba (2002a) have built on this framework to consider how gender and sexual politics inform the colonial contexts shaping the play's inception as well as those that influenced the history of its reception. Other readings – including Griffiths (1983) Fuchs (1997), Gillies (1986), Brotton (1998), and Baker (1997) – flesh out the play's connections to America, Spain, North Africa and Ireland, but do not develop further the basic theoretical issues.

Ultimately, the more capacious historicist sense of *The Tempest* as a colonial text is sacrificed by Kastan's attempt to reclaim for Europe primacy 'in its own historical moment', wresting it from the perceived hegemony of colonialist/postcolonialist interpretations. Asking us to consider 'how thin is the thread on which the play's relation to the new world hangs' (1999: 186), Kastan points out – rightly – that it seems to be set in some unnamed Mediterranean island rather than any of the main colonial arenas, and that its only explicit references to those sites occurs via negative comparisons – particularly Ariel's remarking to Prospero that the Italian ship is safe in a harbour 'where once / Thou call'dst me up at midnight to fetch dew / From the still-vex'd Bermoothes' (I.ii.227–9). Even Trinculo's observation that the English 'would not give a doit to relieve a lame beggar' but 'will lay out ten to see a dead Indian' (II.ii.31–2) is at best only an indirect reference to Caliban, and the play's clear debt to Michel de Montaigne's essay on the Brazilian cannibals 'has little relevance to the dreams and desires of the Italian courtiers' (Kastan 1999: 187). The absence of direct historical allusion beyond these few scraps leads him to suggest that far from identifying the play's 'articulatory principle' (Barker and Hulme 1985: 204), the 'Americanization of *The Tempest* may itself be an act of cultural imperialism'. In short, it is less the play itself that is a colonial text than the readings that proclaim it as such.

Now, one might easily reverse this charge, applying it instead to Kastan's own 'Europeanisation' of the play. But to do so would also mean acceding to the terms of his analysis, including its surprisingly restricted sense of what constitutes historical context. His approach not only evades Barker and Hulme's contention that the erasure of its traces is a strategy constitutive of colonial discourse, but papers over the extent to which European politics and colonial politics were far from being mutually exclusive in the play's own historical moment. To understand colonial interpretations as accruing to the text primarily as a result of our contemporary concerns is to posit too sharp a distinction between past and present, then and now. Desirable though it may be, such clarity is untenable, if only because we can only 'know' (or, at any rate, surmise) what the play meant in its time through the lens of our present, a lens itself shaped by intervening colonial histories (not least those per-taining to how Shakespeare's text has been received, revised, interpreted and transmitted). Indeed, as Barker and Hulme show, the question of what kind of a text *The Tempest* is rapidly expands to engage the interpretive complexities that attend textuality as such. Like colonialism itself, a play-text is a mobile object, its contours shaped and reshaped by the para-texts constellated around it. Thus, even if Kastan is right in claiming that colonial readings are products of 'our uneasy conscience in the postcolonial world we inhabit', it does not follow that they *neces-sarily* attribute to *The Tempest* something not present at or alien to its inception (though they might). The near-invisibility until the twentieth century of the play's colonial investments expresses an important aspect of the necessary entanglement of the colonial with the postcolonial: unveiling colonial imperatives depends upon a postcolonial perspective able to unravel more fully how it is that colonial discourses veil their own operations. Re-inserting the play into its own historical moment is also a retrospective act: it makes visible dependencies and relationships not easily seen before, attachments that the play's immediate context may have led it to conceal.

Postcolonial Reactivations of *The Tempest*

There is no doubt that for a number of writers and critics outside the Anglo-American world, Shakespeare's play offered – and continues to offer – a powerful template through which to explore their own colonial and postcolonial situatedness. These appropriations emphasise the other sense in which a text may legitimately be construed as colonial, along-side the complex relationships to its own era: even if it was not (then) a colonial text, *The Tempest* has surely become one (now). According to Hulme and Sherman, the play 'has been re-read and re-written more radically, perhaps, than any other play' (2000: xi), a consequence many of its editors attribute to its imprecision both in geographical loca-tion and delineation of characters (see, for example, Orgel 1987: 11; Vaughan and Vaughan 1999: 73–5). This studied vagueness, along with the breadth of its thematic engagement with 'the dynamics of freedom and restraint, obedience and rebellion, authority and tyranny' (Vaughan and Vaughan 1999: 74), has proved especially conducive to re-imagining its import.

The conflicts between Spain and the US around 1898 triggered the first wave of *Tempest* appropriations in Latin America; the play became the basis for unabashedly allegorical interpretations directed against the

American military aggression that culminated in the takeover of Puerto Rico, the Philippines and Cuba. The most important figures in this politicisation of Shakespeare's play were the Cuban José Marti (1853–95), the Nicaraguan Rubén Darío (1867–1916), and the Uruguayan José Enrique Rodo (1871–1917). Interestingly enough, their inaugural interventions did not adopt the solidarity with Caliban that would dominate subsequent appropriations. Quite the reverse: in Rodo's *Ariel* (1900) and *El mirador de Próspero* (1913), it was Shakespeare's 'airy spirit' who came to symbolise the affirmation of

> an idealist sense of life against the limitations of utilitarian Positivism; the spirit of quality and selection, as opposed to the equality of false democracy; and the feeling of *raza*, Latin ancestry, as a source of the energy we need to save and sustain the personality of our nations before the triumphal expansion of others. (Rodo 1914, cited in Hulme and Sherman 2000: 217)

By contrast, Caliban remained a monster, much as he had been for the nineteenth century, only this time the monstrosity at issue was the brutality, greed and crude materialism that these Spanish-American modernists saw epitomised in the US, and in Anglo-American civilisation more generally.

While 'a certain contradictory admiration' for the 'vigorous, sensual and bacchic' Caliban was not entirely absent in such writers as Darío (Brotherson, in Hulme and Sherman 2000: 214), Caliban's rehabilitation would have to await the radical re-working of Shakespeare's play by Caribbean writers of the 1960s, when numerous African and Caribbean colonies were undergoing the arduous experience of decolonisation. In essays by the Barbadian writer George Lamming and the Cuban Roberto Fernández Retamar – 'A Monster, A Child, A Slave' (1960) and 'Calibán' (1969), respectively – as well as in the Martiniquean Aimé Césaire's play *Une Tempête* (1969), the earlier allegorical affiliation with Ariel was cast off in order to unearth a more problematic identification with Prospero's monster. If earlier Latin American allegorisations had embraced the desire to locate the play in their own historical moment – for Kastan, the impetus driving *all* colonial/postcolonial readings of *The Tempest* – these Caribbean responses were simultaneously appropriations and readings: they tuned the text to resonate with contemporary decolonisation but also identified this resonance as coming from the text itself, a consequence of its own engagement with its colonial context. As Hulme puts it, Lamming 'engages at both levels – appropriation and reading – without obvious changes of gear', moving smoothly between 'the allegorical level where the address is outwards, either historically or politically, and the textual, addressed back, both to the text Lamming actually studied and to the institution of Shakespeare criticism and performance' (in Hulme and Sherman: 2000: 223–4).

A similar understanding of the inseparability of colonial from postcolonial imbues Retamar's turn to Caliban as the hybrid figure expressing the historical essence of Caribbean identity:

> Our symbol . . . is not Ariel, as Ródo thought, but Caliban. This is something that we, *mestizo* inhabitants of these same isles where Caliban lived, see with particular clarity: Prospero invaded the islands, killed our ancestors, enslaved Caliban, and taught him his language to make him understood . . . I know no other metaphor more expressive of our cultural situation, of our reality . . . [W]hat is our history, what is our culture, if not the history and culture of Caliban? (quoted in Vaughan and Vaughan 1999: 106)

Even as Retamar offers Caliban as a symbol for the *mestizo* American, he anchors his allegorisation in the actual history of the Caribbean, which he leads back to Shakespeare and his antecedents. Symbolic appropriation of *The Tempest* to represent an ongoing condition thus merges with a historical reading of the play as the original colonial allegory to which the postcolonial present can be traced. Like Lamming, then, Retamar refuses the tidy separation that Kastan and others would later assert, revealing instead the necessary entanglement of history and allegory.

In Lamming and Retamar, we see the lineaments of a further sense in which a text may be construed as colonial. Borrowing a term from biblical hermeneutics, we might call this the typological. Arguably, the particular typological antecedent which inspired these Caribbean writers – even as they rejected its implications – appeared in yet another, slightly earlier, reading of Shakespeare's play: Octave Mannoni's *Psychologie de la Colonisation* (1948), translated into English in 1956 under the title *Prospero and Caliban: The Psychology of Colonisation*. Mannoni was a French social scientist and psychologist, who administered for a number of years France's largest colony, the southeast African island nation of Madagascar. The theory of colonisation Mannoni developed in his important re-reading of *The Tempest* 'only fell into place', Rob Nixon writes, 'through his exposure to one of the twilight moments of French colonialism – the Madagascan uprising of 1947–49 in which sixty thousand Madagascans, one thousand colonial soldiers, and several hundred settlers were killed' (1987: 562). The horrors of this colonial crisis led him to advance an account in which Prospero and Caliban became psychological types pitted against one another.

The 'typical colonial', exemplified by Prospero, becomes so, Mannoni argued, not because of experience acquired in the colonies, but because 'of traits, very often in the nature of a complex, already in existence in a latent and repressed form in the European's psyche, traits which the colonial experience has simply brought to the surface and made manifest' (1956: 97). Central to this psychological formation is anti-sociality, 'the lure of a world without men' (101), coupled with a 'pathological urge to dominate' (102):

> What the colonial in common with Prospero lacks, is awareness of the world of Others, a world in which Others have to be respected. This is the world from which the colonial has fled because he cannot accept men as they are. Rejection of that world is combined with an urge to dominate, an urge which is infantile in origin and which social adaptation has failed to discipline. (108)

The colonial context provides, then, the necessary conditions for this 'Prospero complex' to emerge, and in Madagascar these involved the confrontation of the colonial with a non-European culture marked by a different complex, that of the Caliban-type. What characterises Mannoni's Caliban is a dependence complex that has developed from being 'forced out of a secure "tribal" society and into the less stable, competitive edged hierarchies of a semi-Westernized existence' (Nixon 1987: 563). Thus it is that Caliban seeks not self-determination but, paradoxically, what Brönte's Jane Eyre would later also voice, a longing for: 'a new servitude' (Brönte 1947: 87).

> Caliban . . . begins plotting against Prospero – not to win his freedom, for he could not support freedom, but to have a new master whose 'foot-licker' he can become. He is delighted at the prospect. It would be hard to find a better example of the dependence complex in its pure state. In the play the complex must be a projection, where else could it have come from? The dependence of colonial natives is a matter of plain fact. (Mannoni 1956: 106–7)

As Freud memorably put it, the unconscious has no history; for this very reason its structures and formations enable us to collapse the temporal separation between two historical moments, the early modern and the contemporary, the colonial and the postcolonial. Mapping the colonial situations in Madagascar and in *Tempest* onto one another discloses for Mannoni the enduring typology which underlies the cultural conflicts of colonialism.

The generation of anti-colonial writers who followed Mannoni would take affront at the 'insinuation that Caliban was incapable of surviving

on his own and did not even aspire to . . . independence in the first place'
(Nixon 1987: 564). Lamming, Césaire, Fanon and others emphatically
rejected the Frenchman's identification of Caliban as the psychological type of native colonial dependency – an assessment that in any case
curiously echoed fifteenth- and sixteenth-century Spanish descriptions
of the Amerindian natives as 'natural slaves'. Nonetheless, a differently
directed sense of Shakespeare's Caliban as a prototype for the native
intellectual in an era of decolonisation emerges out of their reflections.
Inflected by Lamming through the history of the slave trade, Prospero's
admission that he 'cannot miss' – that is, do without – Caliban, for he
'does make our fire / Fetch in our wood, and serves in offices / That
profit us' (I.ii.312–14), opens up a point of identification: 'I am a direct
descendant', Lamming writes, 'of slaves, too near to the actual enterprise to believe that its echoes are over with the reign of emancipation'
(1991: 15). In contrast to Mannoni, it is the openness and undecidability of the future that Lamming emphasises: Caliban's abandonment
at the play's end, so 'near the actual enterprise' of his enslavement by
Prospero, produces an uncertain freedom, not least because Lamming,
like his Shakespearean ancestor, has been altered by the colonial
passage, Europeanised and schooled in the coloniser's language:

> Moreover, I am a direct descendant of Prospero worshipping in the same
> temple of endeavour, using his legacy of language – not to curse our
> meeting – but to push it further, reminding the descendants of both sides
> that what's done is done, and can only be seen as a soil from which other
> gifts, or the same gift endowed with different meaning, may grow towards
> a future which is colonised by our acts in this moment, but which must
> always remain open. (1991: 15)

As with Retamar's description of Caliban as prototype for the *mestizo*,
Lamming ambivalently embraces the hybridity of Shakespeare's original, seeing in him and the play 'a certain state of feeling which is the
heritage of the exiled and colonial writer from the British Caribbean'
(1991: 9). The dynamic of decolonisation is expressed here through
'the desire to mount an indigenous countertradition, with a reinterpreted Caliban from 1611 and the contemporary, about-to-be-liberated
Antillean of 1959 flanking that tradition' (Nixon 1987: 569). The
remarkable assertion that past colonial conditions themselves constitute
the grounds for a different kind of colonisation (that of the future 'by
our acts in this moment') makes sharply visible a corresponding possibility in *The Tempest*. A projection onto the Shakespearean text it
may be, but it discloses something essential to the text's own moment,

occluded for centuries by the very colonial dynamic the play so deeply engages.

'You taught me language; and my profit on't / Is, I know how to curse' (I.ii.366–7): Stephen Greenblatt observes of these lines that 'what we experience . . . is a sense of their devastating justness' (1992: 25). This insight, Peter Hulme argues, does not imply that our experience of Caliban's famous response to Prospero grows out of our project-ing our own postcolonial concerns onto the play. If the lines 'refuse to be taken as the self-indictment that Prospero would read them as', it is not because of a 'decision to find postcolonial themes present, to land a seventeenth-century play with a late-twentieth-century agenda'. Rather, in locating their postcolonial readings in the very language of Shakespeare's text, such writers as Mannoni or Lamming

> claim to discover something of significance about the play that was obscured or ignored for many years. That discovery may have been enabled in some sense by the whole process of decolonisation, but the readings invent nothing, whatever the supposed political motivation for them doing so. (in Hulme and Sherman 2000: 234)

A further implication of this line of argument is that a text is a colonial text not just by virtue of a historical relationship to its past but through a historical relationship to its future. And it is by producing that con-nection anew that the most powerful postcolonial readings operate. Colonial texts and the postcolonial readings that reveal them to be colonial might thus be said to constitute acts of temporal insertion; they create gaps in time through which pasts and futures emerge, to act upon one another – and upon us.

Theory after Shakespeare

Colonial processes break in the middle the very continua of European thought upon which they feed, thereby producing the beginnings of new beginnings. They make new worlds and new experiences of those worlds. I would like to close this section by suggesting that *The Tempest* is also a colonial text because it makes this dynamic visible.

In his *Shipwreck with Spectator* (1996), Hans Blumenberg identifies the contraposition of dry land and deep sea as a fundamental metaphor through which human beings have sought over centuries to grasp the nature of their existence. This metaphorical frame is far from static, being regularly transformed to accommodate the changing conditions of life. The archetypal – and perhaps most influential – version is owed to the poet-philosopher Lucretius, whose *De Rerum Natura* [*On the Nature of Things*] develops an emphatic contrast between a shipwreck at sea and the secure spectator on dry land:

> When on the great sea the winds are tossing the waters, it is sweet to watch from the land the great struggles of some other – not because it gives you pleasure and delight that anyone is distressed, but because it is a joy to discover from what misfortunes you yourself are free . . . (Lucretius 1965: 40)

A related juxtaposition is central to *The Tempest*'s opening scene of a shipwreck. The opposition between imperilment at sea and the 'great comfort' of land underwrites Gonzalo's 'warrant[ing]' the bos'n against drowning as he seeks to make the 'rope of [the boatswain's] destiny our cable': 'If he not be born to be hanged, our case is miserable' (I.i.30–1). The Shakespearean twist on Lucretius is that survival depends upon exchanging deaths – theirs at sea for the boatswain's on land. Death is the ultimate certainty; the questions that remain concern who and how. And so Gonzalo hangs his hope of life on the boatswain's hanging. How thin that cable is becomes clear with Gonzalo's lines concluding scene one: 'Now would I give a thousand furlongs of sea for an acre of barren ground – long heath, brown furze, anything. The wills above be done, but I would fain die a dry death' (I.i.65–8). This admixture of desire and resignation lays bare the underlying opposition: any land, however little or sterile, rather than this death by water.

To borrow a line from T. S. Eliot, 'I had not thought death had undone so many'. 'Poor souls, they perished' (I.ii.9): with Miranda's entrance, the play explicitly introduces the Lucretian motif of the secure spectator looking upon a nautical disaster. But the emphasis on Miranda's compassionate specular identification with the shipwreck's victims – 'O, I have suffered / With those I saw suffer' (I.ii.5–6) – contradicts Lucretius on a decisive point. Unlike Lucretius, she does not insist on a mode of self-reflection that constitutes a properly philosophical relation to reality. For him, the paradigm has nothing to do with feelings engendered by the sufferings of others. Rather, the spectator's physical distance becomes an epistemological attitude, allowing him to blunt the consequences of living in an unstable, ever-dissolving universe. '[N]othing is sweeter', as Lucretius says, 'than to occupy the high and quiet places fortified by the teachings of the wise, from which you can look down on other men and watch them as they wander to and fro, seeking in their wanderings a way of life . . . ' (1965: 40). For Lucretius and his Greek predecessors the spectator was the existential figure for theory itself. It represented in purest form a distanced, objectifying relationship to the world, one which led to the contemplation of order and the sublimity of objects revealed. The existence of order is not guaranteed as such by *De Rerum Natura*, which reassures one only that *at most* a firm ground may exist beyond the sea's hostile reach. But without theoretical distance even this possibility cannot be achieved. The indifference of theory thus makes 'itself into the equivalent . . . of reality's indifference to man, its constituent part' (Blumenberg 1996: 27). Far from indifferent, Miranda rejects the Lucretian coordination of knowing one is untouched by events and thus being untouched by them. 'I pray you, sir, / For still, 'tis beating in my mind', she asks her father, 'your reason / For raising this sea-storm?' (I.ii.175–7). For her, the tempest without is the tempest within.

'The direful spectacle of the wreck' has, Prospero in turn acknowledges, 'touched the very virtue of compassion in thee' (I.ii.26–7). Not the wreck itself, as Miranda assumes, but the *spectacle* of the wreck. Prospero's art has, he insists, 'so safely ordered' the spectacle that there is 'not so much perdition as an hair, / Betid to any creature in the vessel / Which thou heard'st cry, which thou sawst sink' (I.ii.29ff.). Not the creature's lament, but Miranda's hearing its cry; not the vessel's sinking, but Miranda's seeing it sink. This gap between the putative event and its sensory and emotive repetition in the compassionate spectator reintroduces the question of theory – recall, the Greek word *theoría* derives from *theoros*, or 'spectator'. 'Be collected; / No more amazement. Tell your piteous heart / There's no harm done' (I.ii.13–15). By virtue of his artful transformation of reality into spectacle, Prospero creates a distance from the wreck and from those who seem to suffer its consequences. This theoretical remove occasions a temporal distance as well: it makes room for memory, for stories that might otherwise have been blocked by the self's fixation on the event.

This complex engagement with an inherited classical tradition and its theories of knowledge may seem far removed from exigencies of early modern colonialism, much as Prospero remains distant from the wreck. But such distance also bespeaks the transformation of theory from a looking-on – at best defensive in its Lucretian sense – into an assertion of the self upon the world. Prospero's mastery allies theory with an active technological control over nature, to which Francis Bacon famously subscribes. Insisting that 'knowledge and human power are synonymous, since ignorance of the cause frustrates the effect' (1854: 3.345), Bacon concludes that 'the sovereignty of man lieth hid in knowledge . . . [N]ow we govern nature in opinions, but are thrall unto her in necessity: but if we would be led by her in invention, we should command her by action' (1854: 1.254). The links between this attitude and early modern colonialism run deep. As Bacon proclaims, in a sentence resonating with Prospero's status as magus: 'Those who become practically versed in nature, are the mechanic, the mathematician, the physician, the alchymist, and the magician' (1854: 3.345). In how it revivifies the metaphor of shipwreck and spectator, then, *The Tempest* echoes the new configuration of knowing and being made available by the intertwined discourses, both scientific and colonial, surrounding the 'discovery' (or, better, the production) of worlds new and old.

However, the play also immediately complicates our understanding of theory as an action exerted from a distance, a power wrested from and turned upon nature. For Prospero does not quite address the 'cry' that 'did knock against' Miranda's 'very heart' (I.ii.8–9). Whether the wreck be real or not, the fact of a positive outcome – the saving of ship and crew – does not address the suffering of those who endure the event *as if* it were real. And indeed how could he? As the scene repeatedly makes clear, for Prospero suffering is paramount. From the tortured syntax of his description of Antonio's treachery and his own experience of a potential shipwreck; to his threatening account of Ariel's imprisonment in a 'cloven pine'; to his obvious relish in detailing the torments to which Caliban will be subject: Prospero repeatedly reveals his investment in pain, his own and others'. He justifies his pleasure in what others suffer on the grounds of his own suffering: his is the power of the survivor, who, in mastering suffering, successfully brings nature under his own service. Beyond Ariel's delight in the spectacle he 'performs' lies Prospero's 'strong bidding': 'Hast thou, spirit, / Performed to point the tempest that I bade thee? (I.ii.193–4). Rather than merely ratifying the distance that separates the subject from what he sees and controls, remembering the past reveals a projective involvement; it thereby reinvests the fantasy of a control both technological and colonial with the pleasure that arises from exerting it.

To be sure, minimising involvement has never truly been an option for Prospero. His studied refusal to engage 'worldly ends' and to 'dedicate' himself instead 'to closeness and the bettering of my mind' (I.ii.89–90) – an attitude closer to the antique ideal of theoretical distance – has already been exposed as an unsustainable luxury: it leads only to 'sea-sorrow' (I.ii.170). 'Vous êtes embarqué', as Pascal would later say. Prospero has always already been at sea, the existential situation revealed most clearly when he finds himself clinging to a 'bark' that is not much more than a floating plank: 'a rotten carcass of a butt, not rigged, / Nor tackle, sail, nor mast' (I.ii.146–7). Under such circumstances preserving the self means not only taking pleasure in survival, but in one's very ability to do so – an ability that underscores one's difference from those who cannot, and whose suffering sustains the fantasy of control.

Such pleasure is writ large in proto-colonial narratives of discovery, above all in the spectatorial relationship to the land, once the ship enters a foreign and distant harbour. Knowing that one has survived allows one to project the distance travelled into an epistemological distance between the re-found self and what is thereby laid open to its gaze; further, it enables the re-encoding of that distance as an experience of power, and in fact the power of theory – figured here as the books that first distanced the distracted ruler from reality (only later to enable him to assert his control over reality).

While such control is deeply entwined with the domain of colonial discovery, it is not restricted to that domain. Here, Montaigne's 'Of Physiognomy' is instructive in juxtaposing the sea of history to theatre:

> Thus do we eagerly seek to recognise, even in shadow and in the fiction of theatres, the representation of the tragic play of human fortune. Not that we lack compassion for what we hear; but the exceptional nature of these pathetic events arouses a pain that gives us pleasure. Nothing tickles that does not pain. And good historians avoid peaceful narratives as if they were stagnant water and dead sea, in order to get back to the seditions and wars to which they know we summon them. (1958: 800)

And this Prospero knows. The would-be magus' fantasy of control is equally that of the dramaturge and playwright who avoids dead seas to give us instead seditions and tempests, the very events that we desire. Indeed, to relinquish the fantasy would seem to imply relinquishing the self that has come into being through the fantasy: to retire to Milan, 'where every third thought shall be my grave' (V.i.312).

But to see it only thus would be to make *The Tempest* Propero's play alone. As Miranda reminds us, suffering is convertible not only into a kind of power born of epistemological distance but also into a kind of fellow feeling born of contemplating parallels between one's own and others' suffering. Like las Casas' *History of the Destruction of the Indies* (1552), *The Tempest* engages the very question of what it means to 'be' a new world text. And engages it in part as the question of theory itself: of the relationship to the world that our looking-on produces.

Others and Selves

Thus far I have intentionally sidestepped another fundamental question brought to the fore by colonial/postcolonial studies: What is an other?

Edward Said's *Orientalism*, moreover, ensured that this question would be coupled with another: What is the self? Their conjunction reflects Said's understanding that such apparently neutral designations as the East in fact express interpenetrations of material and imaginary geographies: the Orient referred not simply to a place but to a discursive construct (sited upon a set of places) through which another discursive construct, Europe, constituted and maintained its identity. To put it another way: European texts and practices produced the East as an object of knowledge and as a site upon which colonial power was exercised; simultaneously, this process projected abiding differences between Europe and the East, between self and other.

In early modern studies, the doubled questions of self and other convey rich possibilities as well as limitations. But for the relative abstract issues of identity and difference to be made palpable, they need to studied through their concrete manifestations in specific contexts. In what follows, I primarily address England's proto-colonial efforts, seeking to illuminate how literary criticism has dealt with its complex, differential relationships to Ireland, Spain and Turkey. As we shall see, although Said's original argument has been extensively criticised (see the overview in Loomba 1998: 47–51), supporters and detractors alike have not fully shaken off its logic, even as they have extended, complicated, or proffered themselves as yet more fodder for the broad dynamic he identifies.

A territory that was already a sort of internal colony, Ireland curiously preceded and postdated the historical trajectory of England's emergence as a colonial power. As Tudor policy transformed England's relationship to that 'other' island during the sixteenth century, the Irish experience in turn deeply affected expansion westward to the Americas. Ireland thus offers an opportunity to examine fractures and fissures resulting from the overlay of colonial – and, indeed, postcolonial – policies and identities.

By contrast, Spain and Turkey were throughout this era imperial forces in their own right, aggressively seeking to expand into neighbouring territories, Christian and non-Christian alike. There could be no question of bringing them under English sway: still, these were both empires with which England had to engage. One of the enduring ironies is that England exerted no little effort in trying to build monopolistic mercantile alliances with Turkey, in spite of the threat this Islamic state posed to the wider Christian diaspora, thereby alienating European neighbours such as Spain, with whom England might otherwise seem to have a closer affinity. It was no simple matter to tell one's friends from one's enemies – and as hard to decide when to call them friends, and when enemies.

Ireland: Civilised Selves and Barbarous Others

For early modern Ireland, we are fortunate to have as our guide a canonical poet who complexly negotiates the demands of nation and empire: Edmund Spenser. Arriving in Ireland in 1580 as private secretary to the new Lord Deputy, Arthur, Lord Grey of Wilton, Spenser administered English interests there almost until his death. Grey was a militant Protestant bent upon realising the policy of Irish 'pacification' set into motion by Henry Sidney (father of Philip Sidney), and the twenty-eight-year-old Spenser probably accompanied Grey on his most notorious military expedition to Fort d'Oro, Smerwick, where the Deputy 'ordered the slaughter of some 600 Spanish and Italian troops who had surrendered' to him (Matthew and Harrison 2004: v. 51, 921). This action ignited an uproar not only in Ireland but in the English court as well, leading to Grey's recall in 1582. Nevertheless, Spenser vigorously defended the Deputy in print – directly in *A View of the Present State of Ireland* (written c. 1596) and more elliptically in book V of his magnum opus, *The Faerie Queene*. Spenser gradually elevated both his social and economic status in Ireland, ultimately acquiring a 3000 acre estate, Kilcoman (a tiny portion of the roughly half a million acres confiscated for English settlement). In 1598, when the Munster plantation was under threat from the forces of the Gaelic lord Hugh O'Neill, he was appointed sheriff of Cork (see Judson 1945: 200). But the settlement was soon overrun and the poet's estate sacked and burnt, forcing him to take refuge in Cork before fleeing to Westminster. He died in England shortly thereafter.

Even so brief a biographical sketch suggests how large Ireland looms in Spenser's life. And yet its avoidance was for centuries the norm in studies of his writings. This nigh automatic foreclosure was noted in Said's *Culture and Imperialism*, his remarks anticipating – and perhaps even spurring – the postcolonial turn in Spenser criticism: 'it is generally true that literary historians who study the great sixteenth-century poet Edmund Spenser . . . do not connect his bloodthirsty plans for Ireland, where he imagined a British army virtually exterminating the native inhabitants, with his poetic achievement or with the history of British rule over Ireland, which continues today' (1993: 5). The last two decades have produced a welcome correction, with numerous critics seeking to relate Spenser's involvement in Ireland to his poetic *oeuvre* in systematic and sophisticated ways (see Hadfield 1997; Maley 1997; Highley 1997; Carroll 2001; Palmer 2001; and McCabe 2002).

For Said, an imperial and a nationalist Spenser are two sides of the same coin, the representation of Irish barbarity a necessary correlative to the projection of British civility and superiority. This binary opposition between other and self is certainly visible throughout Spenser's *View*. Written in the form of a dialogue between Irenius and Eudoxus, the work seeks to make 'known thoroughly and discovered' Ireland's 'malady', so that it may be 'cure[d]' through 'a diet, with straight rule and order to be daily observed, for fear of relapse into the former disease' (1970: 3). Spenser's elaborate genealogies (based on such chronicles as William Camden's *Britannia* and Richard Stanyhurst's description of Ireland) develop the foundational opposition most clearly, by asserting that the native Irish (the 'meere Irish', Spenser and others often call them) were descended from savage Scythians and Gauls. The ineradicable signs of these origins are revealed, for example, in their 'cries . . . which savour greatly of Scythian barbarism, as [do] their lamentations at their burial[s], with desperate outcries and immoderate wailings'. Compounding their 'uncivil and Scythian like' howling are bad habits stemming from the Gauls, such as drinking their enemies' blood and 'painting themselves therewith' (55–6). In fact, Spenser's Irenius claims to have seen these 'heathenish' (56) folk drinking even the blood of their own friends and families: at 'the execution of a notable traitor', his 'foster mother took up his head whilst he was quartered and sucked all the blood running out there, saying that the earth was not worthy to drink it, and therewith also steeped her face and breast . . . crying and shrieking out most terribly' (62).

Ireland appears, too, as thinly disguised allegory in Spenser's epic *The Faerie Queene*, where Artegall, 'the Champion of true Justice' (Bk V, I.3.2), is chosen by the Faery Queen herself (one of the poem's many figures for Elizabeth I) to 'restore' Irena (the figure for Ireland) 'to right' (Bk V, I.4.8). Accompanying Artegall is the 'yron man' Talus:

Immoveable, resistlesse, without end.
Who in his hand an yron flale did hould,
With which he thresht out falshood, and did truth unfould.

(Bk V, I.12.7–9)

He now went with him [Artegall] in this new inquest,
Him for to aide, if aide he chaunst to neede,
Against the cruell Tyrant, which opprest

The faire Irena with his foule misdeede,
And kept the crowne in which she should succeed.

(Bk V, I.13.1–4)

The figuration of Ireland as Irena cleaves the land from its people, and particularly its oppressive ruler, the Tyrant Grantorto, whose name translates to 'great wrong'. (Grantorto has also been read as an allegory for the Pope, indicating the Protestant polemics of Spenser's epic, to which I shall return.) This separation allows Artegall and Talus's interventions to be represented as returning the island to its natural, free state of quietude – Irena also means peace – and justice. Irenius's glowing praise of Ireland's natural beauties introduces a corresponding moment in the *View*: this 'most beautiful and sweet country' has been 'utterly wasted and left desolate' by the rebellious Irish. And so the land itself calls for restoration, being 'full of very good ports and havens opening upon England and Scotland, as inviting us to come unto them, to see what excellent commodities that country can afford' (18–19).

The connection between Book V and the *View* goes deep. A central claim bruited throughout Spenser's political tract is that, given Ireland's present state, true reformation cannot be achieved through the normal enforcement of law – meaning, English common law. The impossibility results not from the law's limitations but from the inaptitude of the Irish themselves, 'being a people altogether stubborn and untamed' (4) upon whom no instruction can stick. Consequently, true Justice demands a cleansing violence 'by the sword, for all those evils must first be cut away with a strong hand before any good can be planted, like as the corrupt branches and unwholesome boughs are first to be pruned, and the foul moss cleansed or scraped away, before the tree can bring forth good fruit' (95). (This image recurs in the Bower of Bliss episode in Book II of *The Faerie Queene*.) Spenser thus defends Lord Grey's violent Irish tenure, representing his actions as necessary to ground anew constitutional authority, which has been eroded by Irish intransigence. The implacable Irish hatred of 'all reformation and subjection to the English', argues Irenius, demands the violence of equity, 'new framing as it were in the forge all that is worn out of fashion; for all other means will be but lost labour by patching up one hole to make many' (93).

Book V of the *Faerie Queene* is equally concerned with the paradoxes of Justice in this colonial context. At its very outset it takes Bacchus as a normative model, who 'with furious might / All th'East before untam'd did overrone, / And wrong repressed, and establisht right, / Which lawlesse men had formerly fordonne' (I.2.1–4). Book V departs from the main Aristotelian tradition, which saw equity as a form of mercy that tempered the rigorous application of law (as in Portia's famous paean to the 'quality of mercy' in Shakespeare's *Merchant of Venice*). Instead, as 'true Justice', equity embodies a higher legality, a supra-legal and remorseless power able to re-establish the very foundations of law by purging and punishing. (I return below to the one apparent exception – the invocation of mercy at Canto X's beginning.) Artegall's adventures therefore have as their necessary counterpart Talus's unstoppable violence. For Grantorto's defeat in single combat turns out to be only the beginning; reforming Irena's kingdom relies even more heavily upon the 'iron groom's' unpitying stance towards the indigenes:

> During that time, that he [Artegall] did there remaine,
> His study was true Iustice how to deale,
> And day and night employ'd his busie paine
> How to reforme that ragged common-weale:
> And that same yron man which could reveale
> All hidden crimes, through all that realme he sent,
> To search out those, that usd to rob and steale,
> Or did rebell against lawfull government;
> On whom he did inflict most grievous punishment.
>
> (Bk V, XII.26)

In the regular rhythm of Talus's nigh-unstoppable 'yron flale', we hear the *View*'s insistence that the 'necessity of the present state of things enforced [Lord Grey] to that violence' with which he would be identified. And such 'necessity' is laid at the barbarians' door: 'Ius Politicum, though it be of itself not just, yet by application, or rather necessity, is made just, and this only respect maketh all laws just . . .' (1970: 22), 'for when a people are inclined to any vice or have no touch of conscience, nor sense of their evil doing, it is bootless to restrain them by any penalties or fear of punishment' (24).

Yet, if the opposition between civility and barbarity seems cleanly to distinguish coloniser from colonised, self from other, recent studies have emphasised (*pace* Said) that the actual case was never quite so simple. For, even as the *View* rails against Irish barbarity, it reserves its harshest words for the representatives of English authority there: 'the chiefest abuses in that realm are now grown from the English, and the English that were are now much more lawless and licentious than the wild Irish, so that as much care as was then by them had to reform the Irish, much and more must now be used to reform them' (63). On another level, then, Said's picture of a monolithic Britain subjugating an equally mon-

olithic Ireland obscures as much as it reveals. Not only is Britain not synonymous with England, but the opposition fails to address adequately
the fragile, even precarious, construction of individual and national
identities. The ambivalence of Spenser's status as poet of nation and
empire forces us to recognise how fluid the resulting identities could be.

To see what is at stake in Spenser's attack on 'the English that were'
for degenerating into barbarians worse even than the 'wild Irish', we
need to dip briefly into the shifting currents of history. England traced its
territorial claims to twelfth- and thirteenth-century Norman conquests
of Ireland. Spenser often recalls these colonial origins, as in the declaration that Henry II had given his laws to 'those new [English] inhabitants'
responsible for driving the native Irish 'into deserts and mountains'
(1970: 13). In this sense, re-making Ireland as England's first modern
colony was already a postcolonial endeavour: the renewed push towards
effective domination took its impetus from the contention – buttressed
by mythic histories – that Ireland's contemporary situation was the
aftermath of an anterior colonisation.

Nevertheless, the gap between the assertion and the actual exercise of
dominion remained vast in the sixteenth century. In intervening years,
the displaced natives had recovered much territory, effectively reducing
English control to the so-called Pale, a small eastern sector. However, in
English eyes, the Irish had not established legal title despite this success,
since that standing allegedly belonged by right of conquest to the crown
and to descendants of the original invaders. At any rate, the island's hab-
itable area was divided *de facto* between Anglo-Irish overlords descended
from the Normans, who professed loyalty to the English crown, and
Gaelic chieftains who refused to recognise the crown's authority. Even
among the former, though, allegiance was largely 'theoretical': the long
separation from England had made them 'jealous of their independence,
and their subjection to the government was a polite fiction. In reality,
therefore, they were little different from the Gaelic lords . . . who were
independent kings in their own localities' (Canny 1976: 27–8).

Intractable disputes among (and rebellions by) these ostensible representatives of England's right along with regular attacks by the Gaelic
Irish made it difficult to maintain a hold even over the small, though
rich, demesnes of the Pale. To defend that territory, Henry VIII had
to provide a standing force of 1000 men, making Ireland even in later
years the only place where 'a sizeable English army was maintained in
the queen's pay' (Canny 2001: 5). The crown's growing concern about
costs spurred a drastic change, one initially triggered by the Palesmen's
offer to eliminate the need for an army by persuading the Gaelic lords

to accept English standards of civility and law. The Anglo-Irish decision to elevate Henry VIII from Lord of Ireland to King of Ireland in 1541–3 brought matters to a head, since it encouraged the king to assert his authority and common law over the entire island, the Palesmen expecting that they would be the executors (and beneficiaries) of the crown's expanded commitment. This offer was politically motivated, of course. These 'Old English' settlers too denigrated the Gaelic Irish, but their aim was less to insist (as Spenser would) upon the latter's ineradicable barbarity than to convince 'the English that they [that is, the Anglo-Irish], being the only civilized people in the country, should be supported militarily and financially in their struggle for survival' (Canny 1976: 127). While the king took on this additional burden somewhat reluctantly, the policy was nonetheless energetically pursued in the 1540s, but led only to more turmoil (which ironically meant that the army had to be further beefed up to protect the primary bastion of English influence).

The very desire to reduce the English government's financial burdens resulted in an increasingly draconian – if often haphazard – policy during Elizabeth's reign, gradually transforming what had largely been a colony primarily in name into a colony in reality. If the expense of extending effective control over the entire island was seen as prohibitive, leaving Ireland alone was not thought an option either, for fear that a foreign European power might use it as a base to invade England. Thus in 1560, the Earl of Sussex, Lord Lieutenant of Ireland, complained that he was 'forced by duty to give advice . . . not so much for the care I have of Ireland, which I have often wished to be sunk in the sea', but because of his worry 'that if the French should set foot therein, they should not only have such entry into Scotland as her majesty could not resist . . . but . . . they should take utterly from England all kind of peaceable traffic by sea, whereby would ensure such a ruin to England as I am feared to think on' (quoted in Canny 1976: 30). England's colonial policy was driven less by a coherent vision than by just such conflicted impulses.

Against this background, the ends to which Spenser's fractured rhetoric is directed become more comprehensible. Beyond the 'meere' Irish, Spenser's other primary target in the *View* is the Anglo-Irish or Old English, the descendants of the original Anglo-Norman settlers. (Though nothing is straightforward where Spenser is concerned: he married an Anglo-Irish woman, Elizabeth Boyle, and wrote the 'Epithalamium' as well as many of the sonnets of his *Amoretti* for her.) Seeking to allay discontent with the standing army, Sir Henry Sidney described the Anglo-Irish as 'a nation derived from our ancestors, engraffed [i.e. engrafted] and incorporate into one body with us, disturbed by a sort of barbarous people, odious to God and man, that lap our blood as greedily as yours' (Campion 1633: 136). John Derricke's *Image of Ireland* echoes this complex evocation of hybridity, of identity and difference, further fragmenting Irish and English identities by regional geography (1581: b2v). Nevertheless, the Old English would be increasingly assimilated to the Gaelic Irish, while an emerging English colonial class, militantly Protestant, sought firmer hold of policy.

Repeatedly calling Ireland a colony, Spenser's *View* advocates thoroughgoing colonisation, inspired, like others, by Roman antecedents (and by ongoing developments in the New World). Sir Henry Smith, Queen Elizabeth's secretary of state from 1572, was motivated by his study of the classics to propose a privately financed English venture to settle Ulster based 'almost entirely upon Roman methods of colonization' (Canny 1976: 88). He approaches Lord Fitzwilliam with this precedent in mind:

> This I write unto you as I do understand by histories of things past, how this country of England, once as uncivil as Ireland now is, was by colonies of the Romans brought to understand the laws and orders of the ancient orders [sic] whereof there hath no nation more straightly and truly kept the moulds even to this day than we, yea more than the Italians and Romans themselves. (quoted in Canny 1976: 129)

In effect, Smith wanted to drive out the ruling elite and retain the majority of the population as docile cultivators, pointing – as Spenser does – to Roman example. If the analogy seemed pertinent, it was because England was now 'the new Rome, the centre of civilisation' (Canny 1976: 130).

During Elizabeth's reign, England's army in Ireland steadily grew. Garrisons were established in key areas; land was confiscated from Anglo-Irish lords and Gaelic chieftains for settlement; buffer zones were created to protect the Pale. Opposition was suppressed with Talus-like harshness. Facing resistance to the 1569 colonisation of Munster, Sir Humphrey Gilbert's brutal retaliation made no distinction between combatants and non-combatants, as Thomas Churchyard's approving description makes evident:

> His manner was that the heads of all those . . . which were killed in the day, should be cut off from their bodies [and brought to his encampment] . . . so that none could come unto his Tent for any cause, but commonly he must pass through a lane of heads, which he used *ad terrorem*, the dead feeling nothing the more pains thereby: and yet did it bring great terror to the people, when they saw the heads of their dead fathers, brothers, children,

kinsfolk, and friends, lie on the ground before their faces . . . (Churchyard 1579: q3v)

An outburst in a 1572 letter from Ireland's Lord Deputy Fitzwilliam to Lord Burleigh captures the prevalent attitude towards Irish inhabitants, whether Old English or Gaelic Irish:

> this people . . . hath been long misled in beastly liberty and sensual immunity so as they cannot abide to hear of correction, no, not for the horriblest sins that they can commit. Till the sword have thoroughly and universally tamed . . . in vain is law brought amongst them: nay dangerously is the bridle thereof shaked towards them . . . this makes them all tooth and nail . . . to spurn, kick and practice against it. (quoted in Canny 1976: 128)

The acts perpetrated by the so-called New English to pacify the whole island are supported unequivocally in the *View*, which criticises them only for not being adequately sustained. Throughout, Spenser echoes the viewpoint of an influential cadre of young men, so steeped in Renaissance humanist discourses of civility that they had become blind to its darker implications: the often violent rejection of all that seemed alien to its definitions of civilisation. Redeploying the opposition of civility and barbarity to re-fashion both English and Irish identities, Spenser speaks, then, less for the English as a whole than for the growing subset of new English settlers who had come to view all earlier inhabitants of Ireland as 'beyond the pale'.

Moreover, it is the outlook of this emergent group which Spenser seeks to project as representative of Britain as such. This ideological gambit becomes evident in the close association Book V of *The Faerie Queene* posits between its protagonist Artegall and the 'Briton Prince' Arthur (Bk V, 8.29.31). Together, they echo the narrator's praise of Mercilla's power and mercy as she metes out justice to the treacherously rebellious Duessa (a transparent allegory for Elizabeth's treatment of Mary, Queen of Scots):

> Who then can thee, *Mercilla*, throughly prayse,
> That herein doest all earthly Princes pas?
> What heavenly Muse shall thy great honour rayse
> Up to the skies, whence first deriv'd it was,
> And now on earth it selfe enlarged has,
> From th'utmost brinke of *Americke* shore,
> Unto the margent of the *Molucas*?
> Those Nations farre thy iustice doe adore:
> But thine owne people do thy mercy prayse much more.

> (Bk V, 10.3)

Since Duessa is executed in the space between Cantos IX and X, Mercilla's mercy seems less than effectual, bowing readily to the 'strong constraint' seconded by both Arthur and Artegall. English justice by the sword, re-written as mercy, expands here to engulf the globe, reaching from the 'utmost brink' of American shores to the famed Spice Islands of the east, the Moluccas. And Arthur provides the connection between Britain's imperial desires and England's regime in Ireland. For the historical – or quasi-historical – claim to Ireland was supported in English histories and chronicles by a mythical one: even before Henry II's invasion in the 1170s, the Arthur of legend, it was asserted, had conquered all of Ireland, before absorbing Iceland, Norway, Denmark and Gaul into his empire (Hadfield 1997: 90). The standard source for these accounts was Geoffrey of Monmouth, whose influential *Historia Regum Britanniae* described how Arthur, 'determined to subject [Ireland] to his authority' (1966: 221), defeated the King Gilmaurius, leading all other Irish princes to surrender. This legendary precedent would repeatedly be cited – as, for instance, in Richard Hakluyt's *The Principall Navigations* (1589: 243) – by those Elizabethans most concerned with setting their nation's expansion on a firm footing.

In short, to justify a struggle that defied a clear separation between Irish and English, Spenser ultimately redirects the opposition between barbarity and civility in a manner that fractures the very notion of Englishness. Civilisation is arrogated to the new settler class, which is now posited as representing Britain as such. The category of the barbarian is concomitantly extended to include the Old English, who have degenerated through their long association with the native Irish. In particular, the 'dangerous infection' of fostering their children with Irish nurses has led, says Irenius, to English babies drawing 'into themselves together with their suck, even the nature and disposition of their nurses, for the mind followeth much the temperature of the body, so as they proceeding from the mind, the mind must be needs effected with the words; so that the speech being Irish, the heart must needs be Irish, for out of the abundance of the heart the tongue speaketh' (1970: 65). Given such contamination, true reformation could only take place once English civilisation – whose epitome was English common law – had been effectively implanted. And to do so, the iron had to be thrust deep into the Irish/English body.

Spain and Turkey: Protestantism and its Others

At the very least, the distinction between selves and others in Ireland's case had to negotiate tripartite differences among the Gaelic Irish, the

Old English, and the New English. However, even this triangulation remains insufficient: England's arduous occupation transpired within yet wider transnational contexts that reveal the fluctuating interdependence of religious and nationalist polemic in constructing the colonial self. Examining how the rhetoric of religious difference was used to represent complex and shifting relationships to Spain and Turkey, I hope hereby to chart as well an important movement in postcolonial studies towards recognising multiplicity and hybridity. While Ireland's colonisation reveals the limits of binary oppositions, further enlarging our view to include different kinds of colonial 'others' emphasises the mobility of colonial and postcolonial identities, their perpetually being in formation:

> where nations start and stop will never be a settled question. It will never be possible to determine exactly what forms of difference a nation will be prepared to include and what will have to be castigated as the alien 'other' against which such a body will seek to define itself. (Hadfield 1997: 2–3)

Again, Spenser offers a toehold, revealing amidst Book V's overarching, Ireland-directed allegory the inseparability of England's Irish interventions from its conflicted relations to at least two other empires already in ascendancy: the Spanish and the Turkish/Ottoman. One episode in particular speaks simultaneously to both these imperial threats. In Canto VIII, immediately after Artegall has been freed to pursue again Irena's rescue, that primary quest is temporarily sidelined once more by the Souldan [Sultan], who 'with most fell despight and deadly hate / Seekes to subvert' the 'Crowne and dignity' of Mercilla, the 'mayden Queene of high renowne' (see Book V.8.17 and 18). The Souldan's presence suggests the relevance of English–Ottoman relationships for Spenser's epic, but Artegall's encounter with this pagan king has also regularly been interpreted as an allegory for England's increasingly fractious relationship with Spain's Philip II and the Roman papacy (see Upton's commentary to his 1758 edition: 2.623–6; also Aptekar 1969: 82–3). Thus, for example, the climactic battle between the knight and the 'proud Souldan with presumptuous cheare, / and countenance sublime and insolent' (Book V, 8.30.3–4) echoes England's victory over the Spanish Armada in 1588, not least in how the battle concludes. Rather than being able directly to overcome the Souldan's attacks by force of arms, Artegall achieves this end indirectly. He finally unveils his shield, whose powerful light burns and maddens his opponent's flesh-eating steeds, and it is they who bring about the monarch's end.

At last they have all overthrowne to ground
Quite topside turvey, and the pagan hound
Amongst the yron hookes and graples keen,
Torne all to rags, and rent with many a wound,
That no whole peece of him was to be seene,
But scattred all about, and strow'd upon the greene.

(Bk V, 8.42.4–9)

The manner of the demise recalls the defeat of the Spanish fleet, ultimately destroyed less by its battering at English hands than by irresistible natural forces – the gales which crippled its ships, dispersing them across the sea much as the Souldan's corpse is scattered and strewn over the field of combat. It is perhaps no accident that Artegall and Arthur meet here to pledge their joint support for Queen Elizabeth's stand-in, Mercilla. English colonial policy towards Ireland (embodied in Artegall's quest) and the character of Britain (embodied by Arthur) are aligned in the mutual admiration of these allegorical figures, 'swearing faith to either on his blade, / Never thenceforth to nourish enmity, / But either others cause to maintaine naturally' (Bk V, 8.14.7–9).

Set against the historical record, however, there appears more than a little irony in Spenser's aligning English/British interests in Ireland *against* the putative tyranny of Spain and Roman Catholicism. After all, a scant thirtysome years prior Spanish colonialism in America had provided a model not just for England's ventures in the New World but for its Irish programme as well. Sir Thomas Smith was only too aware of the parallels between Ireland and the New World, fearing that his proposal regarding Ulster (described above) might be tarnished by association with Thomas Stukely's earlier, fraudulent subscription for funds. In 1563, Stukely had raised money from private investors ostensibly to support an Anglo/French-Huguenot colonisation venture in America, only to use the resources to pursue Atlantic piracy. Smith worried that he and his son would be taken as 'deceivers of men and enterprisers of Stukely's voyage of *Terra Florida*, or a lottery as some evil tongues did term it' (cited in Canny 1988: 1). Stukely's name would have been especially fresh in English minds because he, too, had been engaged in military service in Ireland, but had recently turned Catholic and provided support to Irish rebels against the crown.

Smith's thoughts were undoubtedly also shaped by the text of one of his Cambridge students, Richard Eden, who in 1555 published his *Decades of the New World*, an English rendition of extracts from Peter Martyr d'Anghiera's influential descriptions of early Spanish colonialism. Eden's preface lauds Spain's ongoing conquests as a model for

England. His extravagant commendation of a nation soon to become an inveterate enemy is revealing, especially when juxtaposed with later English insistence on the gulf between their own colonial civility and Spanish barbarity.

Not surprisingly, Eden begins with the Romans, citing Cicero to remind the reader how far 'the dignity of man's nature' exceeds 'the condition of brute beasts', who are driven only by their senses and 'beastly appetites'. By contrast, man's mind is 'nourished with knowledge' and seeks thereby to leave behind 'a memory of his immortal nature'. Such immortality is epitomised by Alexander and the Roman empire. And yet, Eden insists, the Spanish have gone beyond even those illustrious precedents because their burgeoning empire confers its true benefits not upon the colonisers but the colonised:

> And surely if great Alexander and the Romans, which have rather obtained their deserved immortal fame among men for their bloody victories only for their own glory and amplifying their empire obtained by slaughter of innocents and kept by violence, have been magnified for their doing, how much more then shall we think these men worthy just commendations which in their merciful wars against these naked people have used themselves toward them in exchanging of benefits for victory, that greater commodity hath thereof ensued to the vanquished than the victors. They have taken nothing from them but such as they themselves were willing to depart with, and accounted as superfluities, as gold, pearls, precious stones and such other: for the which they recompensed them with such things as they much more esteemed. (1555: ai-r)

Trade, gift-giving and military action become inseparable: commodity exchange turns, via the unasked-for 'mercy' of war, into a generosity that relieves the unclothed, uncivilised natives of their unwanted 'superfluities' in order bestow upon them what they truly desire.

It is not that Eden is unaware of an opposing viewpoint, which would draw attention to the loss of land and liberty that is the precondition of such colonial beneficence. But to this possible objection he has a ready rejoinder:

> But some will say, they [the Spanish] possess and inhabit their regions and use them as bondmen and tributaries, where before they were free. They inhabit their regions indeed: yet so, that by their diligence and better manuring the same, they may now better sustain both, then one before. Their bondage is such as is much rather to be desired than their former liberty which was to the cruel Cannibals rather a horrible licentiousness than a liberty, and to the innocent so terrible a bondage, that in the middle of their full idleness, they were ever in danger to be a prey to those manhunting wolves.

Eden's rhetorical strategy is familiar. The earlier freedom of the natives is qualified by an alleged failure to manage their own lands. Spanish right of conquest thus derives from a superior ability to exploit fully territories that have suffered from the 'full idleness' of their occupants. Further, Eden insists that even their ostensible liberty prior to the conquistadors' arrival was anything but. He divides the indigenes into two groups: the 'cruel Cannibals' (for whom liberty is merely a cover for unnatural lusts), and their victims, the other native 'innocents' (whose original condition was one of bondage and terror). Consequently, brutality is simply the necessary means to impart the true liberty of Christian civility:

> But now thanked be God, by the manhood and policy of the Spaniards, this devilish generation is so consumed, partly by the slaughter of such as could by no means be brought to civility, and partly by reserving such as were overcome in the wars, and converting them to a better mind, that the prophecy may herein be fulfilled that the wolf and lamb shall feed together ... [T]he Spaniards as ministers of grace and liberty brought unto these new gentiles the victory of Christ's death, whereby they being subdued with the worldly sword are now made free from the bondage of Satan's tyranny, by the mighty power of this triumphant victor, whom ... god hath ordained ... to deliver the bound out of prison and captivity. (aii-r,v)

Such is the bounty of colonialism.

The parallels between Eden's legitimation of Spanish New World depredations and Spenser's support for colonial cleansing in Ireland are striking. The citing of classical precedent as colonial model; the distinction between native barbarity and colonial civility to justify violence as necessary and ultimately munificent; the separation of land from its inhabitants; the representation of colonial intervention as a liberation from the tyranny of the few; the legitimacy of Christian law over the pagan law of the jungle; these are all features that sixteenth-century English colonial writings borrow from the Spanish. They persist through Spenser and beyond, even as England's relationship to Spain underwent a sea-change.

Nonetheless, by Spenser's time, such parallels are increasingly underplayed, to insist instead upon the English difference from its colonial competitor. Spenser's *View*, for instance, often links the Irish with the Spanish, suggesting that the Gauls who contributed to the Irish stock had originally been inhabitants of Spain. This lineage is made to seem yet more disreputable by casting aspersions on the Spanish: as a result of the waves of conquests on the Iberian peninsula, the Spaniard himself is 'the most mingled, most uncertain and most bastardly' of Europeans, so the Irish do 'most foolishly . . . think to ennoble themselves, by wresting their ancestry from the Spaniard, who is unable to derive himself from any nation certain' (1970: 44). The putative dubiety of Spanish ancestry underwrites *The Faerie Queene*'s curious superimposition of Catholic Spain onto the Islamic Ottoman. Such an identification was, Benedict Robinson notes, far from unusual in the English context, where contemporary Spain was often polemically associated with its Islamic past. As Edward Daunce laconically remarks, 'The *Mores* ruled Spain for 800 years, during which time, we must not think that the *Negroes* sent for women out of *Aphrick*' (1590: E3r; see also Robinson 2007: 41–2).

Indeed, the conflation of Spain and Turkey rests upon an even deeper impulse recognisable in *The Faerie Queene*: the desire for a Protestant imperium (see Gregerson 1995). As is well known, Spenser's epic responds to two important European antecedents: Torquato Tasso's *Gerusalemme Liberata* and Ludovico Ariosto's *Orlando Furioso*. Both these texts evoke – directly in Tasso's case, more mediatedly in Ariosto's – a fundamental divide between Christendom and Islam. Shaped by the medieval crusades, which had driven the Moorish Islamic powers from the Iberian peninsula but had failed to recover Jerusalem, Tasso's epic in particular envisions a unified (Catholic) Christendom able finally to win back Christianity's birthplace from its Islamic occupiers: 'Tasso's text encodes a Counter-Reformation polemic that blames Protestantism for the continued power of the Turks, and sees in crusades the solution to Christian schism' (Robinson 2007: 39). An oft-cited early Italian history of the Ottoman empire, Paulo Giovio's *Short Treatise upon the Turkes Chronicles* (1532), suggests the currency of the idea of a shared Christian crusade in the sixteenth century. Recalling 'the great slaughter and bloodshed of the christians' and 'the extreme tyranny and cruelty of the Turks towards us' (Dedicatory epistle, nn), Giovio concludes by lamenting the absence of such unity in the face of Ottoman puissance:

> But certain men there be which think that the Turk may be more easily vanquished and put to flight, if he be suffered to invade either Austria or Italy, then if the Christians, marching forth in his provinces, should there set upon him . . . This opinion peradventure were not far from the truth, if the Christian princes were so wholly of one mind and consent, that at the first rumour of the Turks coming they would assemble and gather together power and strength of men able to resist and withstand him. But certes we can scant trust that this shall happen . . . (1546: cxxxviii, r-v)

Because defence remains uncertain, Giovio concludes with the hope that the Spanish Emperor Charles V, 'being now of sufficient age', will take 'this occasion' to unify all Christian powers 'to vanquish and bring under the Turks', thus advancing himself to 'the highest step of sincere praise and glory' (cxl, r-v).

The Faerie Queene's numerous encounters with the Saracens and Paynims, as well as the Souldan, echo the crusading drive of these epic and historical antecedents. However, Spenser re-directs the religious rhetoric to express instead the desire for a specifically Protestant crusade (see Lim 1998: 144–60; Robinson 2007: 40–56). The conflict with the Souldan in particular 'recalls and reverses Tasso, using the romance narrative of crusade to reassert the singleness of Christian faith while reserving that singleness not for a reunited Christendom but for the Protestant nation' (Robinson 2007: 43). From this perspective, both Catholicism and Islam, Spain and Turkey are inimical to England, as instantiations of false religion. Hence Spenser's epic conflates opposed religious persuasions, one internal to Christendom and the other external, in order to project a militant Protestant identity, with England as its standard bearer.

Spenser's logic finds an important precedent in John Foxe's *Actes and Monuments*, among the most influential publications in sixteenth-century England. Foxe's monumental compendium of the lives of martyrs who sacrificed themselves for the Reformed cause deviates significantly in one place from its pattern of recounting individual lives: an extended 'discourse . . . of the Turkes story' outlines 'their cruell tyranny, and bloody victories, the ruin & subversion of so many Christian Churches, with the horrible murders and captivity of infinite Christians' (1610: 675). In content, this redaction of existing histories may not immediately seem to offer anything new. However, what is striking about the *Actes* is its deeply ambivalent tone.

On the one hand, 'the fierce and barbarous hostility of the cruell turks' (689) towards Christians is never in doubt, allowing Foxe to identify the Ottomans with the Antichrist: 'the whole power of Satan, the prince of this world', he says, 'goeth with the Turks' (676). On the other hand, Foxe repeatedly represents their actions as the 'scourge of God for our sins, and corrupt doctrine', a punishment for 'such great defection and decay of Christian faith' (575). In other words, the Turk's relentless expansion is primarily enabled by the schism within Christendom, which has led the Pope to attack Protestantism rather the true enemy. And this Catholic failure leads to the burning issue that brings Foxe's discussion of Europe's future to a close:

> Now in comparing the Turke with the Pope, if a question be asked, whether of them is the truer or greater Antichrist, it were easie to see and judge, that the Turke is the more open and manifest enemy against Christ and his Church. But if it be asked whether of them two hath been the more bloody and pernicious adversary to Christ and his members: or whether of them hath consumed or spilt more Christian blood . . . neither is it a light matter to discern . . . (710)

Just such a superimposition of Islam and Catholicism as belief systems diametrically (and violently) opposed to the true faith of the Reformed Church underwrites Spenser's double allegory in Book V, where the Souldan combines the Islamic and Catholic threats to Protestant England.

This blurring of doctrinal opposition echoes as well in Spenser's sense of the difference between the new English (including himself) and the other inhabitants of Ireland. The fault, as Irenius puts it, 'is but one, but the same universal throughout all that country, that is that they are all Papists [that is, Catholics] by their profession, but in the same so blindly and brutishly informed . . . as that you would rather think them atheists or infidels' (1970: 84). Here, too, an internal doctrinal difference (Protestant versus Catholic) merges with an external one (in that Irish 'Papists' are assimilated to atheists and infidels), reinforcing the interrelationship between England's production of its colonial identity vis-à-vis Ireland, on the one hand, and against the competing empires of Spain and Turkey, on the other.

But what neither *View* nor *The Faerie Queene* quite disclose is how England's relationship to its European rivals did in fact differ from its relationship to the Ottoman, and thus the extent to which England's belated incursions into the New and Old worlds were not fully consonant with the kind of muscular Protestantism Spenser advocates. A sense of the change in the years following Eden's rousing call for the English to emulation of the Spanish may be glimpsed in an early colonial manifesto, circulated when tensions between Spain and England were running high: Richard Hakluyt the Elder's 'Reasons for Colonisation' (c. 1585), written to support English expansion into Virginia. On the surface, colonial motives seem not have changed greatly in the intervening period:

> The ends of this voyage [to Virginia] are these:
> 1. To plant Christian religion.
> 2. To traffic.   Or, to do all three.
> 3. To conquer.

Hakluyt recognises both the interdependence and the challenge of these objectives: '[t]o plant Christian religion without conquest will be hard. Traffic easily followeth conquest; conquest is not easy'. Nevertheless, he posits trade rather than warfare as likelier to constitute the optimal solution: '[t]raffic without conquest seemeth possible and not uneasy'. At the same time, even trade presumes that each party engaged in exchanging goods desires something the other possesses, and if perchance the Virginian natives 'be content to live naked and to content themselves with few things of mere necessity, then traffic is not. So then in vain seemeth our voyage ...'. Consequently, it is necessary that the natives be transformed by being taught what they ought to desire, that is, their 'nature [must] be altered, as by conquest and other means it may be ...' (1965: 31).

It is these 'other means' that will ostensibly distinguish the English from the Spanish. Hakluyt proposes that the natives be

> drawn by all courtesy into love with our nation, that we become not hateful unto them as the Spaniard is ... for a gentle course ... best answereth the profession of a Christian, best planteth Christian religion, maketh our seating most void of blood, most profitable in trade of merchandise, most firm and stable, and least subject to remove by practice of enemies. (32)

Given the impending conflicts with Spain and the recent publication in England of las Casas' *Brevisima Relacion* (translated in 1583 as *The Spanish Colonie*), Hakluyt's remarks dovetail with the broader attempt to assert English colonial benevolence over and against Spanish malevolence (see Greer et al. 2008; Maltby 1971), turning a blind eye to the similarities between their actions in Ireland and the Americas respectively. Despite Hakluyt's emphasis on Christianity, there is little evidence that English colonists were actually accompanied by a minister, and documents dealing with the practicalities of colonial settlement suggest that little provision was made for transmitting religion to indigenous peoples (Fuller, personal communication).

No surprise, then, that Hakluyt's vision of peaceable mercantilism continues to rely on methods reminiscent of Spanish practice. He stresses the need for strong fortifications both 'to preserve our bodies, ships, and goods in more safety', and to carry out reprisals by 'scourg[ing] the people there, civil and savage', whenever necessary. That fortification aims as much at colonial domination as at maintaining a trading foothold soon becomes clear, for by such means

> we may be lords of the gates and entries to go out and come in at pleasure, and to lie in safety and be able to command and to control all within, and

to force all foreign navigation to lie out in open road subject to all weath-
ers, to be dispersed by tempests and flaws, if the force within be not able to
give them the encounter abroad. (32–3)

Tearing a page from Portugal's attempts to control Indian Ocean trade,
Hakluyt insists on the strategic use of force to control who and what
can move. To 'command and control all within' has as its corollary the
power to exclude competitors by refusing them access to domains under
English control.

Regarding the Ottoman empire and the North African regencies,
however, such control was recognised as being impossible. Notably,
Foxe's *Actes* does not not hold out hope that European lands overrun
by the Turks can ever be regained (see 1610: 709). And so he calls on
Christ's mercy to 'stand up for his church and stir up zealous princes
and prelates' not so much to 'recover that that is lost' as 'yet at least to
retain that little that is left' (686). Encountering the Ottoman in particular could not be seen by any European nation, let alone England, as
an exercise to be settled by military might: 'at this stage in its history,
Islam could neither be ignored nor "dominated"' (Matar 1998: 184).
Therefore, engagement had to emphasise 'traffic', the development of
peaceable trade relations that could benefit England, while holding at
bay the threat posed by that formidable sultanate.

England's eastern policy prompted different self-definitions than its
Irish, shaped by economic possibilities and hazards. To export English
commodities (wool, tin, lead etc.) and circumvent Iberian control over
the movement of goods, new trade routes were needed. The Ottoman-
Venetian war and Antwerp's conquest by the Spanish in 1572 made
the situation especially urgent: the two main ports for England's inter-
national trade were no longer readily usable. Consequently, Elizabeth
I opened official relations with the Turks in 1579, jostling with other
European nation states to obtain preferential trading privileges (see
Brummett 1994 and Bisaha 2004). These negotiations led to the
founding of the Levant or Turkey Company in 1581.

But a precondition for a Turkish alliance was finding (or constructing) a shared ideological space. Surprisingly, religion provided a means.
Even Foxe's account of Constantinople's fall to the Ottoman in 1453
hints at the possibility of a different configuration of religious affinities. After excoriating the victorious Turkish soldiers for spitting on
images of Christ, he unexpectedly veers into chastising the Catholics
for having afforded this 'occasion of slander and offence . . . unto the
barbarous infidels by this our ungodly superstition, in having images

in our temples, contrary to the express commandment of God in his word' (1610: 682). Iconoclasm would in fact furnish the grounds for an English-Ottoman compact against Catholic powers, to the extent that 'support for Protestants and Calvinists [became] one of the fundamental principles of Ottoman policy in Europe' during the period (Inalcik 1995: 117). Soon after his accession in 1574, Sultan Murad III wrote to Protestants in Flanders and Spain, stressing the similarity between Islam and the reformed cause:

> As you, for your part, do not worship idols, you have banished the idols and portraits and 'bells' from churches, and declared your faith by stating that God Almighty is One and Holy Jesus is His prophet and Servant ... but the faithless one they call Papa [the Pope] does not recognize his Creator as One, ascribing divinity to Holy Jesus (upon him be peace!), and worshipping idols and pictures which he has made with his own hand ... (in Skilliter 1977: 37)

Queen Elizabeth echoed the sentiment. A letter to the Sultan emphasised her status as 'the most invincible and most mightie defender of the Christian faith against all kinde of idolatries, of all that live among Christians, and falselie professe the name of Christ' (Hakluyt 1589: 165). The increasing importance of England's mercantilist aspirations contributed to bifurcations in how the Ottomans were represented, and consequently altered English self-representations as well (see Matar 1998, Burton 2005, and Brummett 1994).

Texts such as *The Faerie Queene* and Foxe's *Actes* aspired towards a Protestant imperium able to assert itself against Catholics and Muslim alike, even as they modelled such an imperium on Spanish and Ottoman achievements (as well as classical antecedents). In contrast, travel narratives and drama tended to engage more directly with the mercantilist impulses evident in the elder Hakluyt's manifesto, articulating religious affiliations along different, and often more fluid, lines. Drama's aptitude in this regard has been shown by a number of critics (for example, Vitkus 2003; Bartels 1993 and 2009; Barbour 2003). Reliance on 'Islamic themes, characters, or settings' became rife in the theatre during the last decades of the sixteenth and early years of the seventeenth century, yielding 'complex and nuanced' representations of Islam 'moved by a variable nexus of economic, political, and cultural forces' (Burton 2005: 11). These included famous plays – for instance, Christopher Marlowe's *Tamburlaine the Great* (1587–8) – but also lesser known works (at least, for us), such as Thomas Kyd's *Soliman and Perseda* (1592), the anonymous *Captain Thomas Stukely* of 1596, and Philip Massinger's

1624 *The Renegado*. Moreover, as itself a mobile and commercial space, the London stage seemed particularly suited to present 'the spectacle of variety and alterity' whereby its audience could come 'to know and recognize what it meant to be properly English, Protestant, lawful, virtuous . . . '. Engaging otherness both as the 'pleasure of staged exoticism' (Vitkus 2003: 27–8) and as a threat to be overcome, the early modern theatre helped negotiate the multiple, unstable differences between England and its others.

Thinking Differently about Others: Olearius's Travels

Through English perceptions of Ireland, Spain and Turkey, I have delineated the shifting status of the relationship between self and other in colonial/postcolonial studies of the early modern period. The initiating binary oppositions between 'the West and the rest' soon came under pressure, leading to consideration of triangulated and hybrid identities. We have seen that there can be no single 'other' against which colonial 'selves' are defined; rather, identities take shape in fluid, fluctuating fields of differences and multiplicities. This does not mean that an opposition between, say, civility and barbarism entirely loses its force or analytical value. As the cases of Spain and Turkey show, ideological contrasts persist, but their deployment becomes unstable, for the era in which recognisably modern modes of colonialism developed was equally one during which political and physical geographies were in flux, identities constantly re-negotiated and re-formed. Engaging different actors and interactions in an increasingly global world, postcolonial perspectives have expanded our sense of the Renaissance and its legacies.

At the same time, such perspectives are not immune to the histories of their own origins. Impelled by the (still urgent) ethical mission of confronting colonialism and its consequences, postcolonial studies as an academic endeavour began by deconstructing Eurocentric structures of thought, seeking to 'recover historical voices that were overlooked because of an entrenched ethnocentrism'. Recognising the limits of binary forms of analysis led in turn to the call for reconfiguring '"identity" . . . in the midst of a multiplicity of cultural influences that more closely resembles what Homi Bhabha has called the "lived perplexity" of people's lives' (Powell 1999: 1). Yet even this formulation suggests the tendency in postcolonial studies to reduce the question of difference to that of identity, addressing multiplicities predominantly in terms of how these constitute the 'self' (or 'selves') – even if closer examination ultimately reveals this 'self' to be fractured, internally divided, and so on.

This may be especially true for the early modern period, where we have fruitfully multiplied the colonial 'others', but have not always been able to move beyond how we see these 'others' in relation to 'selves'. Daniel Vitkus's observation thus seems apt: '[i]n early modern studies, English identity is compared and contrasted to the Irish Other, the Spanish Other, the Islamic Other, the Amerindian Other, and so on'. Despite attention to multiple sites of identity formation, the persistent 'use of the singular noun "other" to signify the status of a foreign entity beyond the pale of the homeland relies' on a questionable analogy between 'individual consciousness and collective identity' (2003: 1). Indeed, the often strident demands for a truly multicultural or transnational understanding of early modern colonialism sit uncomfortably beside the actual analyses of literary texts, which overwhelmingly rehearse the different ways in which colonial identities were consolidated out of projections – be they dual or triangular – onto different cultures and nations. Scholars of a comparativist bent, such as Barbara Fuchs (1997 and 2001) and Roland Greene (1999), have pushed beyond the Anglocentric bias of Renaissance studies, but even their useful work does not ultimately relinquish a dynamic whose implicit or explicit telos is the constitution of colonial identities.

In part, we owe this dynamic to the texts we analyse. In his *Actes*, Foxe evinces some pride in laying out clearly distinctions which 'otherwise in other authors and writers be so confused, that it is hard to know . . . what difference is between Saracens, Turks, Tartarians, the Sultans or Soldans, Mamelukes or Janizarites' (1610: 709). Yet, he unfolds this diversity only to collapse it again into the image of the Islamic Antichrist, against which Christendom – English Christendom in particular – finds its own shape. A similar logic may be glimpsed in a recent study of Islam and early modern Europe: Benedict Robinson's treatment of the Saracen in Spenser's *The Faerie Queene*. After acknowledging real differences among Turkish, Persian, and north African Muslims, the interpretation quickly treats the Saracen as *the* 'mobile and resonant term of difference' (2007: 33), seeing in that figure a paradigmatic 'encounter with Islam . . . vital to the self-constitution of Protestant England in the late-sixteenth century' (55–6). Recognising multiplicity dissolves into a specification of identity, thereby echoing the very dynamic from which postcolonial criticism elsewhere distances itself.

This attention to identity formation derives in some measure from our seeking to establish the continued relevance of early modern colonialism to present concerns. Following and going beyond Said, much important work has shown how the ways we think about national, racial, and gendered identities persistently reveal patterns of misrepresentation and inequity traceable to early modern colonial pasts. It is worth pondering, however, whether such studies retain the critical force they once had. In a recent, provocatively titled collection, *Postcolonial Studies and Beyond*, David Scott wonders whether postcolonial studies may have begun 'to slide from criticism toward method . . . from a revolutionary paradigm toward a normal one', its critical energies vitiated by 'the conditions of its normative institutionalization [as well as] the conditions of its scholarly regularization and canonization' (in Loomba et al. 2005: 386). Consequently, he recommends a renewed self-consciousness, that 'we persistently ask what the point is of our investigations of colonialism for the postcolonial present, what the question is to which we are fashioning an answer' (399).

In early modern studies, the deconstruction of binary logics has certainly led us to rethink the connection between past and present, most evidently in attempts to relate contemporary globalisation to the redrawing of boundaries among nations and continents during the period. As the editors of *Postcolonial Studies and Beyond* suggest, an important need today is 'to recapture a history of transoceanic and transcontinental trade, travel, and conquest so as to avoid a shallow embrace of the contemporary notion of the global' (4; see also Mignolo 2000). But how we recapture such histories, our 'style of reasoning' (in Scott's phrase) about them, matters. Consider, for example, the rather unconvincing links proposed by Robinson (as by Burton) between Renaissance understandings of Islam and the so-called war on terror. Robinson's monograph closes by asserting the parallel between 'Milton's moment' and 'our own moment, when images of Islamic fanaticism are again being circulated in order to provide cover for the most radical transformations of state power, citizenship and the rule of law' (2007: 179). The likeness is never more than loose, but it nonetheless expresses an urge characteristic of his book: his use of the category of the transnational plays out a contemporary politics of globalisation on early modern terrain. Differences thus tend to be subsumed by identities.

My aim is not to single out Robinson's otherwise engaging historicist account of why the romance genre remains central to 'explor[ing] a new world of conflicting and uncertain identities' (2005: 8). Similar reservations could voiced about my own earlier work (Raman 2002) or that of other critics cited here. The relationships obtaining between a (wouldbe) colonial power and its multiple others (both within and beyond its domain) remain important. But I do want to suggest that reconstructions of these relationships have often been as constraining as productive.

Speaking of the English response to the Irish, for example, one critic rightly notes that '[t]he recognition of one's own past in another by no means implies an acceptance of that other; it instead establishes a temporal dynamic in which that other must be made the same' (Fuchs 1997: 52). So far, so good. However, what dominates her critical response is another kind of sameness, born out of the very critique of colonialism: the exposure, over and over again, of how colonial discourses establish such a 'temporal dynamic', using the other to stabilise the self. The logic of such critique does not accept the other *as* other any more than do the discourses of colonialism; the 'other' remains a slot or a function upon which the self depends for its making. Does the proliferation of others in the service of making early modern European identities adequately capture emerging fields of difference? And further, following Scott's line of thought: how does attending to difference change – how does it make a difference to – our ways of thinking about the postcolonial present and its specific exigencies?

I do not pretend to have answers to these questions. But I would like to open possible avenues by considering briefly a popular seventeenth-century travel narrative largely ignored by the English-speaking world: Adam Olearius's *The Voyages and Travells of the Ambassadors sent by Frederick Duke of Holstein to the Great Duke of Muscovey and the King of Persia* (1647 and – as an expanded second edition – 1656). Olearius's book not only went through numerous German editions, but was published several times in French, English, and Dutch, and once in Italian (see Baron 1967: vii). Even today, it remains a significant source for information about early modern Russia and Persia, and has occasioned substantial scholarly activity outside the Anglo-American context. Olearius's reception usefully reminds us of the wide, multivalent contexts of travel and travel writing. Accounts such as his are important not only because they reveal the limits of the usual tendency to focus on the 'big' powers (particularly, England, France and Spain); they also provide a sense of what postcolonial studies misses by leaning heavily on identity formation as a paradigm. Olearius's journey from Holstein to Persia and back again offers at least a glimpse of alternatives.

But where is Holstein and who was Olearius? The northernmost remnant of the Holy Roman Empire, Holstein was a small duchy bordering the North and Baltic seas, in effect independently ruled by Duke Frederick III (1616–59), who was descended from Danish royalty. In the early 1630s, Otto Brugman [Brüggemann], a Hamburg merchant proposed to take advantage of Holstein's geographical position to catapult the tiny state into the ranks of major commercial powers.

His idea was simple if grandiose: to reach Persia using Swedish and Russian waterways in order to turn Holstein into an entrepôt for Asian trade, win for it a monopoly on European silk commerce, and possibly make it a centre for manufacturing silk cloth (see Baron 1967: 6). However, to achieve all this, the relatively powerless principality of Holstein needed the cooperation of the other more powerful states: Sweden, Russia and Persia. Sweden was favourably inclined, though it demanded a hefty price for the privilege of using its rivers. The Persians, too, were likely to agree: the proposal earmarked a large annual gift for the Shah, and shifting the trade route northwards would greatly benefit his political interests. The current route through Aleppo advantaged the Shah's 'neighbour and foe, the Turkish Sultan, who levied a 100 per cent duty on Persian silk passing through his domains' (Baron 1967: 7).

In negotiations with Muscovy, Holstein's insignificance was its greatest advantage, since (unlike Denmark or Sweden) it posed no threat. Duke Frederick offered Tsar Mikhail Feodorovich assistance for munitions, soldiers, and skilled technicians – much as England had done in the 1550s to gain trading privileges from Ivan IV – along with a substantial financial sweetener. These varied agreements required two embassies: the first from 1633–5 to secure Russian permission, and the second (1635–9) to finalise negotiations with Persia's Shah. It was to these two voyages that Olearius was attached as secretary. Born Adam Oelschläger, the son of a tailor, Olearius had pursued astronomy and mathematics in Leipzig until the advent of the Thirty Years' War. Duke Frederick's opportune invitation offered a route out that would lead to his settling permanently in Holstein, ending up as court mathematician, librarian and counsellor.

The actual embassy turned out to be a failure. High costs of obtaining trade clearances; the difficulty of navigating the Volga; attacks by Cossacks and Tartars en route; a violent storm on the Caspian sea that wrecked the ship purpose-built for the voyage; the Shah's unexpected coolness; and the disastrous behaviour of Brugman himself: all these combined to douse the Duke's initial enthusiasm, so that by 1640 he was striving 'as zealously to disengage himself from the contract with Russia as he had earlier been to obtain it' (Baron 1967: 9). We should not forget (as literary scholars too often do) that such failures were in fact endemic to early modern colonialism. No matter where one looks, be it in the New World or the Old, they were the norm rather than the exception (see Fuller 2008). And it is precisely by experiencing failure that European colonial empires gradually, often haltingly, grew (see Bauer

2003: 30–76) – no matter what their rhetoric of success and superiority or our sense of their retrospective inevitability might suggest.

Olearius's engaging description of the embassy's arduous journey through Muscovy and Persia is certainly not free from prejudice. '[A] German by nationality, a Protestant by faith, a scholar by training, and a high functionary by social rank' (Baron 1967: 18), Olearius was prone to scathing judgements about the Russians in particular (on topics ranging from their alleged superstitiousness and xenophobia to their lack of moral character). However, his devotion to faithful description acts as a counterweight to such interpretative excesses. This fidelity appears regularly in his willingness to question and revise classical sources (such as Herodotus or Pliny) as well as important contemporary ones (for example, Johannes de Laet's *De imperio magni mogolis sive India* or John Cartwright's *The Preacher's Travels*) in light of empirical experience.

More remarkably, the descriptions of Persia do not usually lead to the kind of invective evident in the Muscovy sections. Even Olearius's relations with the Persian religiosi lack the edge one might expect. Thus, for instance, he speaks glowingly of a mullah, Maheb Aaly, 'who was a very young, but mighty good natured man, and of an excellent humour, and one who did all that lay in his power to serve me, doing me the greatest kindnesses he could on all occasions, especially in my study of the Arabian tongue'. Aaly and his friend Imanculi visit Olearius on alternate days

> to teach me their Language as to learn mine . . . Which they did with great improvement daily, especially Imanculi, who no doubt had in short time arrived to the perfection of it, had it not been for the envy or jealousy of some of our own, which proved so great, as to make it suspected that those people had some design to change their religion: so that they were forced to keep out of the way, and for the most part make their visits in the night. (1669: 160)

The episode is a complicated one, for the objections to the meetings are communicated by the embassy's interpreter, who purports to convey the Persian Governor's concern. The fear of changing religion, then, appears to be the reverse of what has become a standard trope in current scholarship on European relationships with Islam and the East, that is, of the Christian turning Turk. The anxiety seems rather on the side of the Persians themselves. However, it transpires that there was no such fear at all. Not only does the mullah decide that this must be 'some trick', because 'Persians are never forbidden the company or conversation of Christians' (160–1) but the interpreter himself later admits that he had not been sent by the Governor at all; his intervention was arranged by Brugman, who wanted to prevent Olearius from learning Persian – for reasons entirely unrelated to religion. If the episode seems primed to exploit the kinds of faultlines visible in Foxe's *Actes* or *The Faerie Queene*, it reveals instead internal divisions within the embassage, attempts by one member to use the (potential) cleavage of religion for his own ends.

Certainly, there was no love lost between Olearius and the ambassador, and if the account is true, blame for the mission's failure largely rested upon the Hamburg merchant's head. Among the goods carried by the embassage were pieces of artillery, which Brugman insisted on taking everywhere. However, in order to transport these from Niasabath, he commits one of his many gaffes:

> The Ambassador Brugman would need cut some certain beams, which the Sophy had, with vast charge, brought to the sea-side, to be employed in the building of his ships, and cause carriages to be made thereof for our artillery, not regarding the remonstrance of the Persian, who told him, that if he made use of these beams, the Sophy could not build his ships that year. (151)

The last laugh would belong to the Persian officer, who had tried to dissuade the ambassador, telling the travellers that 'he could not imagine what pleasure we took in carrying with us Sails, brass Guns and Carriages, which could only put us to trouble and retard our journey' (152). He supplied them with so few horses that 'not being able to draw our artillery, we were forced to leave our carriages behind, and to load our guns upon camels' (151).

I do not describe Brugman's misadventures with cannons, wooden beams and horses as evidence for the assertion of will and arrogant dismissal of native 'others' all too familiar to scholars of colonialism. Ideological presumptions are certainly present in the merchant-turned-ambassador's insistence that 'it was the humour of that Nation, not to do anything until they are forced to, and the only way was to domineer over them' (151), an attitude that seems to characterise his actions throughout the journey (to the embassy's detriment). Instead, I want to draw attention to the sails, brass guns, beams, camels and horses themselves. Their presence reminds us that Olearius's narrative is not only about human beings, and what they believe or do. The embassy is part of a world filled with non-humans who are not simply tools to be directed by human interests, but instead form – conjoined with humans – hybrid agents and assemblages. Nor should hybridity be understood here in the manner that postcolonial studies (drawing on Bhabha) has usually stressed: as an interstitial trace, a 'third term' emerging between two identities, a difference that undermines their opposition. It indicates rather the interrelation of 'the technological, the economic, the political, the social, and the natural' in early modern European encounters with foreign worlds. Animals and material artefacts do not stand apart 'as means or tools to be directed by social interests'; they constitute 'integral parts ... whose form' is a function of how 'they absorb within themselves aspects of their seemingly non-technological environments' (Law 2001: 1–2).

Brugman's domineering defined his vision: he could not see that a man is not the same when encumbered with cannons and sail. His mobility is reduced, dependent upon successfully incorporating horses, camels, and gun carriages if he is to achieve the desired control over (and distance from) his environment – and these make him other than he was; they each have their costs (and, potentially, benefits). What seems an irrational desire to take guns and sails wherever the embassy goes is in fact perfectly rational: the objects bespeak the necessary capacity to exert force and the ability to return, two indispensable requirements for colonial mastery. But he sacrifices other requirements, among them mobility and durability (both social and physical). To acquire one's own mobility in the short term by robbing the Sophy of his for 'that year' does not seem the best way of ensuring the long-term durability of an as-yet uncertain trade. Olearius offers many such instances of what he calls Brugman's 'untowardness' and 'incivility', and the merchant would ultimately pay a heavy price. Upon returning to Holstein, he was held to account, a number of his fellow travellers testifying against him. Found guilty, he was executed.

Given its ethical investments, postcolonial studies tends to valorise opposition, allying itself with resistance to colonial and neo-colonial representations and practices. This is a principled, attractive stance. The example of Brugman suggests, however, the need to think differently about what resistance entails, who its agents are, and how it is articulated. Developments in science studies, for instance, offer new avenues for reconceptualising postcolonial agency, opening it up to the clamour of what Bruno Latour felicitously calls 'the parliament of things': 'we don't assemble because we agree, look alike, feel good, are socially compatible or wish to fuse together but because we are brought by divisive matters of concern into some neutral, isolated place in order to come to some provisional makeshift (dis)agreement' (in Latour and Weibel 2005: 23). Brugman lacked, it would seem, a sense of that 'neutral place' that his diplomatic endeavour demanded, and the things he carried with him resisted, undermining the possibilities he was seeking to create. Overcoming such resistances was central to early modern colonialism. The 'durability and fidelity' of its structures owed not just to people acting in requisite ways but to new assemblages that could overcome the counter-forces of wind and sea, animals and germs – and, of course, other peoples.

Let us juxtapose Brugman's travails with Olearius's brief but eloquent description of the Persian region of Mesanderan. Its chief city Ferabath had been renamed by Shah Abbas, whose pleasure with its location had led him to give it

> the name it now hath, from the word Ferah, which signifies pleasant or delightful. Indeed, the whole country is such ... [T]he plains are very populous, and very fertile, and so pleasant, that the Persians say it is the Garden of the Kingdom, as Touraine is of France. Whence the Hakim, or poet, Firdausi had reason to say,
> Tschu Mesanderan, Tschu Kulkende Sar?
> Nikerm we nesert, henis che besar?
> That is, What is Mesanderan? Is it not a place set with Roses? Neither too hot, nor too cold, but a perpetual spring? (147)

Olearius's eagerness to enter the place and the language is infectious, reminding us that early modern encounters with foreignness were not always predictable. They were replete with possibilities – pleasant and unpleasant – not immediately reducible to logics of self and other. In this episode, the differences between Europeans and Persians do not disappear. Quite the contrary: the transliterated verse maintains the alterity of the experience, even as the traveller reaches for the familiarity of French geography to convey to his European readers a sense of place. But the parallel does not assimilate the Persian other to the European self, nor does it evince anxiety about the self. Differences simply remain differences. They certainly *make* a difference, for the new language and its rhythms mark the eruption of something new into the traveller's consciousness. The journey would indeed remake Olearius. Despite failing to achieve its intended purpose, it would lead to Olearius's reputation as the best Persian linguist in Europe: pursuing his linguistic studies back in Holstein, he translated the poet Saadi's *Gulistan* and constructed the first Persian-Arabic-Turkish dictionary (see Baron 1967: 11–13). His experience abroad did transform the self, but not in a way that echoes the paradigms of identity-construction central to postcolonial critiques.

The instance cited is small, just as Holstein itself would remain relatively inconsequential. But such moments point to another avenue for postcolonial studies, following a line of thought espoused by such thinkers as Gilles Deleuze. In his reading of Michel Tourneur's *Friday* – a rewriting of Defoe's classic text – Deleuze locates the novel's contribution in its emphasis upon interactions with strangers bringing into visibility the very act of seeing. What comes into view is an Other not as 'an object in my field of perception nor a subject who perceives me', but as 'a structure of the perceptual field, without which the entire field could not function as it does'. But, asks Deleuze, 'what is this structure?' His answer:

> It is the structure of the possible. A frightened countenance is the expression of a frightening possible world, or of something frightening in the world – something I do not yet see . . . [T]he possible is not here an abstract category designating something which does not exist: the expressed possible world certainly exists, but it does not (actually) exist outside of that which expresses it. (1990: 307)

Responding to unexpected worlds, even 'colonial' texts often hew to this imperative, grasping the Other not – or at least, not only and immediately – as judgement, but by unfolding the possibility expressed in and as what is. Doubtless, the unfolding of new worlds cannot escape inherited ideological frames. Nevertheless, to varying degrees, even these anamorphisms open on to potentialities that strangers and their even stranger worlds express.

One promise of postcolonial studies has always been that it makes us see our present, our own worlds, anew. But the question remains: how? Let me close by returning to the Shakespearean text with which this chapter began. It seems to me increasingly unclear what yet another colonial reading of, say, *The Tempest* will yield, *unless* conjoined with different styles of reading able to draw into the picture different kinds of sources – that is, those beyond what are now the usual suspects, namely, travel writings, geographical descriptions, chronicle histories, and so on. We might learn more – or, at any rate, differently – by juxtaposing Caliban's indigenous knowledge of 'the qualities o'th'isle: / The fresh springs, brine pits, barren places and fertile' (I.ii.329–30) with, for instance, Garcia da Orta's *Coloquios dos simples e drogas he cousas medicinais da India*, first published in Goa in 1563. This massively influential medicinal work, 'organised on non-European precepts of Middle Eastern and South Asian ethnobotany' (Grove 1995: 78), lay at the intersection of European colonial expansion and the diffusion of indigenous botanical knowledge across Europe, knowledge gleaned by Orta from Malayali and Persian doctors in south-west India.

Rather than simply empathising with Caliban's sense of the dispossession he has suffered – 'This island's mine by Sycorax, my mother' (I.ii.332) – we might then also read in his description the traces of what could be called an anti-colonial flow of knowledge, whose impact is no less significant for being ignored or denied. Prospero may respond by calling Caliban a 'most lying slave' (I.ii.345), but the history of Orta's botanical text reveals what Shakespeare's play set on an unnamed island does not quite say: how indigenous sciences of plant life in fact shaped European knowledge. '[A]lmost all . . . substantial "European" texts' subsequent to the *Coloquios* and the comparable *Hortus indicus malabaricus* by the Dutchman Hendrik van Reede (compiled in response to the medical needs of the Dutch East India Company after they had displaced the Portuguese in Malabar) retained essentially indigenous structures of Arabic and South Asian classifications of affinities, rather than adopting available European models (see Grove 1995: 80–90). 'Dr. Orta often knows better than all of us', the Portuguese physician boasts of himself to his interlocutor, 'for we only know the Gentoos [that is, the Indian Brahmins], but he knows Christians, Moors and Gentoos better than all of us' (1913: 86). Orta's authority comes from combining these different strands of knowledge, but 'given the choice between Christian and Arab authorities' he nonetheless 'unhesitatingly chooses the latter' (Grove 1995: 82).

By contrast, what Shakespeare's play reveals, if read a certain way, is a disjunction: between Caliban's claim to have freely offered Prospero local knowledge essential for his survival and the latter's refusal to even acknowledge that gift, deflecting the native's reproach instead onto the issue of attempted rape. And it is in that gap between conflictual assertions which do not quite meet one another that resonant histories lie, producing colonised selves and colonial others.

Chapter 3

Case Studies

The early modern period made a truly global history possible. Indeed, the Oxford English Dictionary credits the mid-sixteenth century with first using the world 'globe' in connection with the terrestrial world, citing Richard Eden's 1553 *A Treatise of new India*: 'the [w]hole globe of the world ... hath been sayled aboute' (*OED* 3a). No set of case studies can do justice to the sheer variety of nation states, polities, and social groups invested in the 'age of discovery' that Eden celebrates. Nonetheless, the readings developed below do at least take the reader beyond the Anglo-American sphere, signalling the importance of a broader, more capacious understanding of how we began to become global.

Britain's dominance in later centuries has led to our over-emphasising England's importance, and neglecting the Iberian beginnings of early modern colonialism. Asymmetries persist within the Iberian domain as well, with Spain garnering most attention – not only because of Columbus's famous (if fortuitous) landfall but also because its South American conquests brought control over the vast silver mines of Potosí. Nevertheless, the treaties of Tordesillas (1494) and Saragossa (1529) divided the newly discovered lands beyond Europe between *two* kingdoms: Spain and Portugal (see Brotton 1997). Only later would other European nation-states successfully jostle for their shares, gradually eroding the empires claimed by their Iberian forerunners.

To help balance subsequent trends, I begin these case studies with Portugal. Readings of playwright Gil Vicente's *Auto da Índia* (c. 1509) and Luis Vaz de Camões' epic poem *Os Lusíadas* (1572) [*The Lusiads*] suggest two different ways early modern Portuguese texts imagined history to remake the 'original' events of colonialism. A second set of paired case studies then takes us to the New World and China through the eyes of the engraver-cum-publisher Theodore de Bry and his sons.

Their massive travel-writing compilations circulated striking visual representations of foreign worlds and peoples across Europe. The complex interplay between image and text in de Bry's rendition of narratives by the English polymath Thomas Hariot and the Dutch voyager Jan Huygen van Linschoten illustrates how the idea of writing functioned in such works to address otherness, producing both differences and similarities between civilised and savage, European and native.

Traversing these different geographical areas enables a return to England with a richer context for how its forays westward and eastward unfolded. Mercantile competition fundamentally shaped the actions of later entrants, such as England and the Netherlands, into the colonial sphere (see Brenner 1993).

> [W]hen in the late sixteenth century, a London-based venture attempted to enter Euro-Asian trade, it was a Company, a quasi-private entity with some state sanction and some diplomatic privileges, that did so – and not the state itself. Similarly, Dutch trade to Asia – although sanctioned by the States General – was conducted after 1602 by an ostensibly autonomous body, The Verenigde Oost-Indische Compagnie. (Subrahmanyam 1993: 45)

If in retrospect a global mercantile – rather than monarchical – empire was the legacy of English (and Dutch) colonial belatedness, its beginnings can be glimpsed in sixteenth- and seventeenth-century literary texts (on Dutch colonial literature, see Beekman 1996).

Richard Brome's *The Antipodes* (1636) shows how rapidly travel was becoming routinised in the seventeenth century. It is in relation to changes wrought by a new mercantilism that the play ultimately negotiates between a medieval past and an early modern present, re-imagining the promises and perils of going beyond one's home. I close with two case studies that emphasise less the material contexts of colonial voyaging than the literary responses to its conceptual implications: a study of elegies by John Donne reveals the reconceptualisation of economic value spurred by Renaissance colonialism; and a brief reading of Christopher Marlowe's *Tamburlaine* emphasises the emotive force of colonial change itself, visible in the ambiguous coupling of desire and horror it engendered.

Amidst the diversity of texts, genres, and worlds examined, certain themes recur. The repeated use of the female body as a metonym for the territories to be possessed discloses the work of gender in colonial representation. The market provides another prominent trope, dramatising a world in flux, where people, commodities, and ideas are constantly on the move. The much older comparison of life to a voyage achieves new life, too, in this era, continually re-adapted to changing contexts of discovery. Such threads bind together the multifarious encounters that would coalesce into what we now call early modern colonialism.

Two Ways of Looking at Colonial Beginnings

Spanish and Portuguese exploitation of colonial territories was subject from the outset to royal control. According to Fernão Lopes' *Crónica de el-rei Dom Fernando* [Chronicle of King Fernando], the Portuguese ruler (r. 1367–83) included a number of his own vessels in a commercial company in the last year of his reign. His successors continued this practice, leading the French King François I (r. 1515–47) to refer insultingly to Portugal's Dom Manuel (r. 1495–1521) as *le roi épicier* or 'the grocer king' (see Boxer 1969: 70). The derogatory phrase carried more than a touch of envy, since the reigns of Dom Manuel and his son Dom João III (r. 1521–57) marked the zenith of the Portuguese Renaissance as well as of Portuguese colonialism. Their rule culminated in the colonisation of Brazil; trade monopolies in Asia; and the first sustained European contact with China and Japan. Overshadowed by Britain's rise in the eighteenth and nineteenth centuries, these accomplishments often pass unacknowledged, with consequences both historical and literary: relegated to the shadows are writers whose work emanated from other European centres of power. For Portugal, the rapid decline of its empire in the late-sixteenth century has only exacerbated our neglect.

Unfinished Histories: Gil Vicente's *Auto da Índia*

Among the under-recognised is one of Portugal's greatest dramatists, Gil Vicente. The sixteenth-century playwright nonetheless shines brightly, along with Camões and the modernist poet Fernando Pessoa, in the nation's literary canon (see Bell 1922: 108). And one of Vicente's plays, *Auto da Índia* (c. 1509), offers a fascinating glimpse into tensions and struggles in the royal court that was the crucible of Portuguese imperialism.

Surprisingly, given his exalted place in Portuguese literary history, we are not entirely certain who Vicente was. Scholarly consensus nevertheless identifies an eponymous goldsmith, whose most famous work is the beautiful Belem monstrance (wrought, Audrey Bell tells us, of the first tribute of gold from the East). Born around 1465, Vicente came to prominence during João II's reign, but produced his major dramatic works between 1505 and 1531 for the courts of Manuel and João III. He died in 1536 or 1537, leaving an *oeuvre* of short plays ranging from the twelve major *Farsas* (farces or comedies) – of which *Auto da Índia* is an early example – to religious works and tragicomedies.

Vicente's life and work were closely bound to the court and its vicissitudes. Precisely this dependence makes *Auto da Índia* a rich source for understanding the specific exigencies of Portugal's attempts to establish an Eastern colonial empire. We should not assume, though, that the courtly arena was a unified one. Between 1300 and 1500 'Portugal witnessed a complex struggle between centralising tendencies inherent in the monarchy, and the resistance of other privileged groups: the Church, the Military Orders, and the nobility' (Subrahmanyam 1993: 33). Portuguese colonial endeavours reflected a force-field of competing interests rather than a monolithic nationalist outlook. Even as the voyages of discovery received their primary direction from the Portuguese court, the court itself expressed an often precarious balance among different upper class factions, of which the king and his immediate retinue were just one.

Portugal's relationships with its Mediterranean neighbours complicated these internal divisions. Not only was the memory of Spanish interference in Portuguese succession fresh, but a conflict with North African Moorish powers – ousted from the Iberian peninsula through the long *Reconquista* – was ongoing. Bitter struggles continued between adherents of the so-called Castilian party (the territorial nobility and clergy that had sought to proclaim the Spanish Juan I of Castile king of Portugal upon Pedro I's death in 1367) and the future Dom João I (Pedro's bastard son, who had garnered the support of the urban aristocracy and artisanal classes), influencing court politics. In addition, Portugal's obsession with neighbouring Muslim powers remained uneasily conjoined with its push towards India and the East. Indeed, the rapid collapse of Portuguese imperial ambitions would be tied to an event not far in the future, which realised several fears simultaneously: the disastrous defeat (and demise) of King Sebastian at El-Ksar-El-Kaber in battle against the Moors (1580) resulted in Portugal's North African campaigns coming to a halt, as well as in the nation's very sovereignty being ceded to the Spanish crown.

To these conflicting pressures Gil Vicente's *Auto da Índia* bears witness. At first glance, this slender farce (not much more than 500 lines long), seems an unlikely text to bear the burdens of so involved a history. Vicente's deceptively simple courtly entertainment concerns the domestic goings-on that ensue after a Portuguese merchant's departure to India in 1506, as part of a fleet commanded by Tristão da Cunha. Eager for her husband's departure, his wife – ironically named Constança, that is, Constance – immediately begins to dally with two lovers, an impoverished 'escudeiro' or squire named Lemos and a bombastic Spanish soldier, Juan de Zamora, playing off one against the other. The mouse-play abruptly ends when the cat returns in 1509, the year of both the performance and the fleet's homecoming after an apparently successful and profitable voyage. Vicente's farce ends with the cuckolded husband and his irrepressible wife going down to the port together to see the sweetly decked-out ship, 'a nao . . . bem carregada' (Vicente 1997: line 513).

The festive, playful exterior of Vicente's farce nevertheless raises the spectre of a threatened domestic space and its potential violation. The merchant's wife, identified at one point as 'luz de todo Portogal' [light of all Portugal, l. 124], functions as the site upon which a class-based, proto-national competition is enacted. The 'threadbare squire' [escudeyro . . . çafado, ll. 211–12] Lemos, for instance, recalls the declined, perhaps once landed, Portuguese nobility whose position has been partly usurped by a rising mercantile class, of whom the husband is representative. The return of her 'namorado perdido' [lost lover, l. 209], as the wife calls Lemos, thus marks a comic *ressentiment*, whereby the displaced squirearchy gains a measure of revenge by invading the bed of the departed merchant Master. The reversal echoes the traditional nobility's resurgence after its rough treatment at the hands of João II. Upon accession, his successor Dom Manuel pardoned nobles who had been exiled earlier for conspiracy, and restored properties to the new duke of Bragança, the most powerful of these territorial nobles. He further 'made the nobility into a court circle, recognising seventy-two families . . . Many of these were established in Lisbon or the neighbourhood, receiving grants or pensions from the royal household or the military Orders' (Livermore 1976: 132).

The presence in *Auto da Índia* of a Spanish lover, Juan de Zamora, further encodes an intra-Iberian tussle for control over Portugal itself (and, consequently, over the newly discovered lands east and west). This struggle marked every succession crisis in Portugal from the fifteenth through the seventeenth centuries. But it was less a national struggle in the modern sense than a complicated series of responses by different noble houses to a monarchy bent on asserting its authority. It was, after all, the collusion between the Portuguese Braganças, and the Spanish royal couple, Ferdinand and Isabella, that had led to the former's downfall in João II's reign. The need to deal carefully with a dangerous, rich neighbour left its mark on tricky negotiations such as those that led to the treaty of Tordesillas, as well as, finally, to Portugal's provisional absorption into the Spanish realm following the El-Ksar-El-Kaber disaster.

In *Auto da Índia*, the debased courtly hero, de Zamora, represents both the Spanish threat and its limits. In fact, the threat is even more specific: the printed text attributes his lines to the 'Castelhano', thereby emphasising the particular importance of Castile to Portuguese politics. If Vicente's Castilian does not quite succeed in entering the desired space of the wife's bedroom, he does nonetheless, in mock-epic and mock-biblical terms, threaten entry from the street below her window, barely stopping himself (or so he claims) from 'pulling down the house' and 'raging war' like Samson. He bombastically swears to 'burn down the house' [quemar la casa, l. 331] and 'destroy the world' [destruyr el mundo, l. 332] even if his defeat means being 'drawn through all the town' [arrastado . . . por la cuidad, ll. 323–34] like Hector by Achilles. On at least two dimensions, then, the domestic spaces of the play – the house and the bedroom – invoke tensions constitutive of the public spaces surrounding the play-world: the shifting balance of power among class-fractions within the Portuguese court; and the complex game of thrones Portugal was engaged in with its more powerful Iberian competitor.

It is the voyage to India that brings these tensions to the surface. The journey triggers a potential threat to the domestic world in that it creates an absence of authority – and provokes in turn the desire to fill that absence. And yet, the anxiety about national identity and integrity that often characterises later colonial texts (see, for example, the discussion of Camões below) seems missing from this play. Its comedic treatment of the Indian venture contrasts with Vicente's celebration of Portugal's North African campaigns in such theatrical pieces as *A Exortação da Guerra* and *Auto da Barca do Inferno*. The eloquent *A Exortação*, for instance, was composed in 1513, when the current duke of Bragança was embarking on a military expedition against the North African town of Azamor. In it, a necromancer priest delivers a rousing call to war: 'Arise, Arise, Lords / because with its grand favours / all of heaven graces you, / the King of Fez loses heart / and the Moroccans clamour'. The contrast in attitudes could not be more striking: 'the expansion in North Africa is exalted and arises as an entirely justifiable crusade, whereas India does not provide anything more than the primary material for a farce, the pretext for risible situations' (Castelo-Branco 1966: 133, my translation; see also Roig 1990: 15ff.). The tonal difference alerts us to the fact that Portuguese colonisation of India was still very much a work-in-progress at the time of the play's writing. The *Estado da Índia* had only been established in 1505, and da Cunha's 1506 voyage was only the third assay east in the decade following Vasco da Gama's historic journey. Indeed, the consolidation of Portuguese power in the East would later be traced to the achievements of da Cunha's fleet: the convoy included ships under the command of the so-called Caesar of the East, Afonso de Albuquerque, whose conquest of key seaports in the Indian Ocean littoral would lay the basis for Portuguese dominion over eastern trading routes.

The contrast between *Auto da Índia* and Vicente's other North Africa directed plays can be explained by the difference between two forms of Portuguese expansion: broadly speaking, the North Africa campaigns were supported by the nobility, while the Atlantic expansion (leading eventually to India and Brazil) reflected the impulses of merchants and the urban bourgeoisie. While this distinction simplifies a more complex distribution of interests, it usefully locates a standing tension and antagonism between two class fractions, both of whom were represented at court (even as their relative strength shifted from reign to reign). Vicente's farcical denigration of the India enterprise reflects the charged situation of the later Manueline court. For Dom Manuel, the notion of becoming Emperor of the East remained largely couched in terms of suzerainty rather than sovereignty, the push towards India being driven as much by a messianic dream of finding potential allies in a crusade against the Moorish powers, as by a commercial interest in Indian Ocean trade (see Thomaz 1991: 98–109). The military actions undertaken in the Indian Ocean, leading to the Portuguese commercial control of Goa, Hormuz and Melaka, were not responses to direct royal initiatives. Rather, the very possibility of a seaborne trading empire became conceivable for Dom Manuel because of Albuquerque's decisions, particularly his understanding of the spatial structure of Indian Ocean trading routes.

In light of this overdetermined context, Vicente's attitude to the India voyage in his earlier *Auto da Índia* indicates the playwright's alliance with those very groups once threatened by João II. In so far as the squire Lemos successfully (if temporarily) takes possession of the merchant's bedroom, we might see the voyage to India as fulfilling a class-inflected desire, whereby the nobility regains land/woman at the expense of the upwardly mobile mercantile bourgeoisie. The play's mockery of the India venture, then, subtly enunciates the political positions of one faction at the Portuguese court, echoing in inverted form, as farce, its ambivalence about the consequences of investment eastward.

However, Vicente's apparent denigration of the India voyage in the context of domestic politics is complicated by a second layer of identification: for Constança, the figure of Portugal and the domestic space, also stands for the extra-domestic, colonial space of India. Thus the 'Castelhano' attempts to seduce her by underscoring her husband's mistaken priorities: 'what more India could there be than you', he apostrophises, 'what more precious stones, / what more things of beauty / than both of you to be together?' (ll. 131–4). Further, insisting on his own colonial rights, he exclaims that 'God has made India / only so that we two / could go through this together; / and, solely for my happiness / to partake of this joy / God had India discovered' (ll. 145–50).

The entanglement of the drama of domestic desire with the drama of Eastern conquest becomes even clearer as de Zamora's rhetoric of seduction pre-figures the husband's description of travails endured on the India voyage. In expressing superiority to the absent merchant, the Spaniard's self-interested, debased courtly language employs, for instance, images of storms and contrary winds: 'Juan de Zamora he was not; / drawn through the streets be my lot / if . . . I'd leave you even half an hour. / And, even if the sea be humbled / and the sea storm cease, / and the wind obey me . . . / I'd not leave you for a moment' (l. 135ff.). In turn, the returning husband evokes the memory of a three-day storm, thereby suggesting the manner in which he and de Zamora function as mimetic doubles competing for the riches of India/woman: 'I went through many dangers', he tells his wife, 'a hundred leagues from here, / there rose up such southwesterlies / southwest and west-southerlies / such that I'd never seen such storms [tormenta]' (l.430ff.). As with the Spaniard's journey to Constança, the husband's journey to India is beset with difficulties. He may have successfully 'fought and robbed' [pelejamos & roubamos, l. 465] his share of India's riches, as he freely admits, but his journey was by no means a smooth one: 'We went out into the ocean / almost, almost changing direction, / Our Garça flew along, / and the sea split asunder' (ll. 460–3). And Constança, too, merges Zamora's fruitless voyage to conquer her affections with her husband's search for eastern riches: 'May yours be a bad voyage', she intones dismissively, 'on the way to Calicut' [Ma viagem faças tu, / caminho de Calecu, ll. 433–4].

But identifying Constança with India also significantly shifts the play's evaluation of the voyage eastward. While Vicente mocks the journey to India in the context of courtly politics, that voyage nonetheless becomes the mainspring of the play's actions, the organising metaphor for all dramatic interactions: as a figure for India, Constança stands for the return anticipated by all the anxious investors competing for her charms (see Ferreira 1994: 106). The Portuguese squire Lemos invests his pittance in a loaf of bread and pitchers of wine in the hope of her favours, whereas the Castelhano repeatedly insists from the street that she 'open up to him' [¡ Abrame . . . ¡, ll. 251 and 314] and 'fulfil' what she has promised, anticipating a corporeal return on the courtly discourse he has expended. (The wife's response makes clear her disdain: she refers to de Zamora as the 'vinegary Castilian', wanting 'to be paid for the vinegar he gave me' (l. 261 ff.).) Even the lower classes seem caught up by the mercantile ethos of investing now in hope of magnified – if deferred – profit: the maid, Constança's feisty accomplice, turns down the immediate gain of a silk cap, opting instead for a future share in eastern wealth. 'Or, when [your husband] gets back', she tells the wife, 'give me something he's brought you' (ll. 50–1).

The theatrical mechanisms of *Auto da Índia* likewise rely on the logic of departure and return characterising mercantile voyages to India. Not only does the play begin with the incipient departure of the master (and the threat of his not leaving), but the ensuing action is itself structured around the arrivals and departures of competing lovers; the return of the husband from India at the play's conclusion also signals the departure of the married couple to see the boat bearing Eastern riches. As *both* pretext for the play *and* its central metaphor, the India voyage thus functions as an empty cause present everywhere in its effects. India appears always as an absence: the missing ship we never get to see, the wife standing in for the space of the East, the repeatedly invoked riches the play never reveals. The play thereby draws attention to itself as theatre and as a figure for the historical event – da Cunha's voyage – which it simultaneously references and brackets.

Notably, the *Auto* chooses as its occasion not Vasco da Gama's momentous inaugural voyage, but one of its far less flashy successors. The latter would indirectly have far-reaching implications for the actual demarcation of Portugal's colonial dominions. But the playwright could not know these effects at the time of writing: the history of Albuquerque's achievements was yet to be composed. True to the uncertainties of its time, *Auto da Índia* thus conveys an understanding of history as living event, as a series of actions whose status as events depends upon their theatrical recreation. The play transforms the colonial language of investment and return into a theatrical principle, into its very motor – and yet the voyage remains outside the play, resisting the theatrical appropriation it enables. In this sense, 'India' stands as the uncertain promise of a history to be fulfilled, not yet endowed with the shape it will eventually acquire. While the play skilfully engages different forms of temporal closure – ritual, secular and theological – it nonetheless holds open the space of possibility, of that which has not been and cannot yet be written. Just as the wife's inconstancy is evoked but never quite affirmed, suspended via the ironic disjunction between the theatrical events and her name, so too are the riches of the East always projected but never fully attained, even when the well-laden ship returns.

And it is here that generic form and historical location become doubly significant. For the *Auto* is tied as theatre to the singularity of the performative event. The singularity emphasised is not just the initial court performance but the historical event upon which the play's ending depends: the homecoming of Tristão da Cunha's fleet. According to the play's last stage direction, husband and wife 'go to see the ship' and 'so ends this first farce'. Anthony Lappin speculates that this conclusion might have been the signal for the entire courtly audience to walk down to the docks to greet the returned ship, thereby participating in a social ritual, a public theatre of colonial homecoming. If so, the ending captures the moment when text, subtext, and context fold into one another. Though we do not see the ship, *Auto da Índia* nonetheless projects the walking-down as fulfilling the desire it represents – but that action only completes the play offstage, for only there does theatre merge with the domestic and colonial performances making it possible.

History as Myth: Luis Vaz de Camões' *Os Lusíadas*

If *Auto da Índia* is enmeshed in the uncertain beginnings of Portuguese colonialism, Camões' *Os Lusíadas* undertakes the task of retrospectively rewriting those origins, re-telling in heroic vein the story of Vasco da Gama's 'discovery' of India in 1497–8, the eastern counterpart to Columbus's famous voyage. History ensures, however, that the epic's celebration of Portuguese imperialism would soon acquire an ironic edge. Dedicated in 1572 to the young King Sebastian, the poem looks forward to future heroic deeds in keeping with Portugal's past, but cannot see that a scant six years later the king would be dead (as would Camões himself) – and with him any hope of expanding Portugal's colonial imperium. A future unknown to Camões – but known to us – thus casts a shadow over the epic's primary aim: to transform the openness of historical events into the fixity of memory, history into myth.

Some of this history Camões knew firsthand, having played a role in its making. Born into Galician nobility in 1524, circumstances eventually led him to sea and to India, as they had earlier led his father, a sea captain. After being banished from Lisbon in 1546 for an unknown transgression, he became a soldier at Ceuta in Morocco, where he lost an eye in battle, learnt tactics of war, and developed a lifelong hatred of his Moorish enemies. Upon return to Lisbon, he joined the king's service for about three years, before sailing to India in 1553 with Fernão Alvares Cabral's armada. He did not see his native land for seventeen eventful years, which included near shipwreck en route to Goa and numerous military campaigns in Malabar, Ormus, the Moluccas, and Macao. Legend (and his own boast) has him swimming to safety, clutching the manuscript of *Os Lusíadas*, after a shipwreck off the Mekong river in Thailand. His monumental work was published in 1572, earning him a small pension from the appreciative King Sebastian. Camões died of the plague in 1580, the very year that Philip II of Spain absorbed Portugal into the Spanish empire.

The epic reveals a double allegiance: on the one hand, to the demands of its classical models (above all, Virgil's *Aeneid*), and, on the other, to the burden of recounting a contemporaneous history. This two-fold loyalty bespeaks the mutual dependence of these generic forms during the period. 'Through [the epic's] song of remembrance heroes are transformed into the men of old and thus represent a collective "past"' (Hartog 1992: 84). Like the epic, historiography, too, seeks to dispense *kleos*, an everlasting glory that overcomes death and oblivion. Remembering heroic exploits brings into being an enduring collective identity, constituted through but transcending individual action.

The affinity with epic imbues contemporary chronicles with a sense of the magnitude of Portugal's colonial achievements. Dedicating in 1551 a history of the '*descobrimento & conquista da India*' to King João III, Fernão Lopes de Castanheda emphasises the need to preserve and perpetuate 'the notable and grand actions' performed by discoverers 'which have never been surpassed in valour, or even equalled, in any age or country' (1551: 1; my translation). Alexander the Great's victories cannot be compared to the 'noble deeds' performed by the Portuguese, the Lichefield translation dismissively adds, any more than 'a dead lion can be likened to one alive'. Nonetheless, the 'memory' of these glorious recent actions remains confined to four persons, 'so that if they had died' all remembrance 'would have ended with them, the which would have been imputed to their great shame and rebuke' (1551: 4). Fighting against the death of memory, Castanheda's *História* represents one way in which sixteenth-century Portugal shaped itself by rehearsing its colonial accomplishments.

Camões' *Os Lusíadas* aims even higher than its historical and literary progenitors:

> Of the wise Greek, no more the tale unfold,
> Or the Trojan, and great voyages they made.
> Of Philip's son and Trajan, leave untold
> Triumphant fame in wars which they essayed.
> I sing the Lusian spirit bright and bold,
> That Mars and Neptune equally obeyed.
> Forget all the Muse sang in ancient days,
> For valor nobler yet is now to praise.
>
> (1950: 1.3.1–8, 3)

Camões holds before us the very epic and historical precedents we are urged to forget. Not content with memory, he calls instead for oblivion, advocating the erasure of mythic pasts by a living history that has taken their place. These opening lines evoke the *Aeneid*, the *Odyssey* and the Macedonians as limits of the thinkable and the achievable. By rejecting them he challenges the possibility of worldly limits as such for the Portuguese, who have tracked 'the oceans none had sailed before' [mares nunca dantes navegados], who have sailed 'even beyond Taprobane's far limit' [ainda além da Taprobana] (1.1.3–4, 3).

Yet, this self-conscious engagement with a classical inheritance also reveals a tension between its demands and those of history. For Camões '[t]he subject of heroic poetry is necessarily historical. The epic is not simply narrative, but historical narrative' (Livermore 1976: 12). Rather than relay the inspiration of the Muses, Camões claims that *his* voice replaces theirs. *His* song shall 'sow' [espalharei] the Portuguese's glorious deeds far and wide, *his* 'genius and art' [engenho e arte] (1.2.7–8, 3) will make us 'forget all the Muse sang in ancient days' (1.3.7, 3) Camões' epic is no less fantastic and hardly less fictional than those written by his precursors; but this strategic reduction of classical myth allows him 'to assert a historicity and human truth for his fabulous classicizing invention' (Quint 1993: 117). Historical memory is eternalised in order to unveil the existing nation as a living embodiment of the 'Lusian spirit bright and bold, / that Mars and Neptune equally obeyed' (1.3.5–6, 3).

However, the forced conjugation of history and epic remains fraught. In contrast to those 'foreign muses' [estranhas musas], who extol 'empty deeds / Fantastical and feigned and full of lies' [vãs façanhas, / Fántasticas, fingidas, mentirosas], Camões insists that his work celebrates a historical truth that 'exceeds' [excedem] such 'dreams' [sonhadas] and 'fictions' [fabulosas]: 'the great and true' acts of the Portuguese adventurers [verdadeiras vossas são tamanhas] (1.11.1–8, 5). But the insistence on his own voice's mythical status betrays an uncertainty, for lost with the Muses' authority is their guarantee of his narrative's truth. Embracing history in order to make the Portuguese its privileged agent, *Os Lusíadas* itself falls into history's grasp; its legitimacy is rendered suspect, dogged by the fear of being taken as 'fantastical and feigned'.

The difficulty of coordinating epic and history in *Os Lusíadas* illustrates a deeper tension within Renaissance historiography regarding origins and meaning. Discussing humanist methodology, David Quint sees in early modern textual practices a distinctive coupling of history and allegory. Seeking to recover 'original' texts from classical antiquity, Renaissance philology implicitly evoked an understanding of culture as a human creation, its meaning determined by historical circumstances and the individual dispositions of authors. However, humanism shied away from the fullest consequences of this insight: the impossibility of an absolutely fixed and authorised meaning in the face of historical change. Hence, the turn to allegory: when the 'counterfeit' productions of human endeavour threaten to engulf the 'original' text, an allegorical reading became necessary to recover the divine meaning that had once authorised the cultural sign (see Quint 1983, Chapter 1 *passim*).

An important episode from *The Lusiads* sheds light on how allegory was adapted to legitimate colonial history. The situation is as follows: after a perilous passage, Vasco da Gama has at last reached safe harbour in the East African town of Melinde. Its ruler asks him to describe the West, Portugal and its history, and his own voyage to this point. Obligingly, the explorer begins 'first [his] giant continent to explore, / And after tell the tale of bloody war' (3.5.7–8, 82). The annals of Portuguese history finally reach the reign of the present King Manuel, who had entrusted to the narrator Vasco da Gama this expedition east. Camões attributes Manuel's imperial impulse to a dream in which two ancient men urge him to embark on India's 'discovery', prophesying his success:

It seemed to him [Dom Manuel] that he had climbed so high
He must have touched on the first sphere at last,
Whence many various worlds he could descry
And, of strange folk and savage, nations vast,
And near the place of Dawn's nativity, . . .
He saw spring forth two clear and noble fountains (4.69.1ff, 152) . . .
From the waters issued (or so fancy told)

Two beings, who, far-striding, near him drew (4.71.1–2, 152) . . .
And one of them approached with weary air,
As who had had the longer way to go. (4.72.3–4, 153)
He, as the person of chief dignity,
Thus to the King from far his thought made plain:
'Know a great cantle of this world shall be
Awarded to your crown and to your reign.
And we, whose fame so far abroad doth flee,
Whose necks to bow none ever could constrain,
Warn you 'tis time for you to make demand
For the great tribute given by our hand. (4.73, 153)
'I am illustrious Ganges. In the earth
Of Paradise I have my cradle true.
And this, O King, is Indus, he whose birth
Befell among the heights you have in view.
Fierce warfare is the price that we are worth.
But if your ends you constantly pursue,
Unfearing, after victories untold,
You'll bridle all the nations you behold.' (4.74, 153)

Manuel's dream is poised between the culmination of an aggressive expansion that has reclaimed all Portugal from the Moors and a new phase in the nation's history that will make it a dynamic *imperium* in its own right. Joining past to present, the dream signals the origin of a new age posited as a break, even as this origin is re-inscribed within the encompassing history of the 'Lusian' (1.1.5) – that is, Portuguese – spirit the epic celebrates.

Camões' invocation of the prophetic source whence the two rivers spring also introduces, though, a different way of addressing the tension between divine truth and its debased human imitation. If the Renaissance figure of the original seeks allegorically to connect the products of human history to a transcendent source of meaning, then the epic achieves that linkage in the colonial context by re-writing history as prophecy. After all, from Camões' vantage point, the events that Ganges and Indus prophesy as da Gama's future are already past: they have come true. Prophecy thus ties time-bound human actions to the timeless, anchoring the instability of human meaning in the stability of a truth outside history. But it does so only at the proper time, when an accomplished history is itself in the position to legitimate vatic utterance. Colonial events can thus be marked as original – that is, as a break from what has come before and therefore intrinsically inimitable – while the uncertainty of those beginnings is overcome by referring them to an absolute and transcendent source.

But King Manuel's dream does even more. For the prophecy is uttered by Ganges, namely, the very figure personifying the Orient. Willingly acceding to its own subjugation, Asia legitimates the Portuguese imperial project by predicting its own future. Thus is the dominance that the Portuguese are to win by force underwritten by precisely those upon whom force is to be exercised. And conversely, the present fact of dominance legitimates Camões' representation of the East as a place inviting its own colonisation.

Revealed herein is an important strategy of European colonial representation. The narrative stages a moment in which the colonising power assumes the ability to represent and speak for the 'Orient'. In turn, the 'Orient' is re-constituted as an entity that *needs* to be spoken for. In this, *Os Lusíadas* prefigures a colonial logic that extends well beyond the sixteenth century. As Michael Harbsmeier argues, only European civilisation came to make its own ability properly to describe and understand the other into the very definition of its own identity (in Barker et al. 1985: 1.72–88). Increasingly, the possibility of adequately representing newly discovered lands is assumed by European 'civilisers', replacing (multiple) indigenous histories. What thereby occurs is a 'worlding' (see Spivak in Barker et al. 1985: 1.128–51) of the East in accordance with the economic and territorial project of western colonialism.

Spivak's notion of 'worlding' does not only conceptualise how European representations remake the worlds that come under colonial sway. As importantly, it indicates how native inhabitants are 'worlded', that is, induced into acceding voluntarily to those representations and their place within them. Underwriting this latter process is a prior assumption that domains to be colonised are 'uninscribed earth', blank and homogeneous spaces unmarked by an indigenous history. Thus, Manuel's dream depicts the terrain into which the King enters as an undiscovered country that no traveller has ever reached, where no humans reside: 'wild fowl' and 'savage beasts' abound, and the very shrubs and trees conspire to 'block all passage where no man can go' (4.70.1ff, 152). And yet, at the same time, this monstrous and untamed space is associated with the Christian paradise, the garden of Eden ('For not since Adam sinned until our day / Has human foot across them broke the way', 4.70.78, 152). The imagined space is *both* associated with the privileged origin of the Christian world *and* pictured as an unwritten-upon space awaiting civilisation's hand. And, if Ganges is to be believed, Manuel's is the hand into which these lands will fall.

The texts accompanying Portugal's discovery of a sea-route to India reveal how early modern colonialism was shaped through stories that reinterpreted as well as set the coordinates for the actual practices of discovery. Thus, justified by the East's prophecy of its own subjugation are also the violent means through which Portugal would in reality achieve its dominion. The sixteenth-century Portuguese chronicler Manuel de Faria y Sousa's description of Vasco da Gama's reception upon returning to Portugal hints in passing at the violent underlying realities:

> There were Public Thanksgivings through the Kingdom for the good success of this Voyage ... And all men's expectation being raised with the glory of the Action and hope of ensuing Profit, it was now consulted how to prosecute what was begun, and resolved, that according to the disposition they had found in the People of those Countries there was more need of Force than Intreaty, in order whereunto thirteen Vessels of several sizes were fitted, and Peter Alvarez Cabral was named Admiral. (1695: 53)

'[T]here was more need of Force than Intreaty': a phrase tucked in a subordinate clause, as if its truth were self-evident. In many ways, far from being a 'good success', Vasco da Gama's first voyage was a fiasco: of the initial crew of 160 men, he lost 105 to sickness or disease, and failed – largely because of his own misinterpretations – to establish friendly trade with Calicut's Zamorin. But the need for force was in fact independent of success, being an implicit assumption from the very beginning. Wresting control over trade from the Arab and Gujerati ships plying the Indian Ocean littoral required the continual exercise of violence: first actually to break into existing trading networks, and then to maintain them in a way that yielded acceptable results.

On his second voyage a few years later, da Gama eschewed even the pretence of friendly negotiation:

> The Admiral arrived the 12th of July at Quiloa, having lost two Ships in bad Weather. He entered furiously, firing all his Cannon, and battering the Town in revenge of the ill usage others had received from that King. But he to prevent his total ruin, came in a Boat to appease the Admiral, offering to be a subject, and pay a Tribute to King Emanuel. Thus the Storm was converted into Joy. (Faria y Sousa 1695: 64)

This description of Quiloa's capture skilfully merges the town's brutal conquest with a rhetorical statement of Portuguese mastery over nature. The ships arrive in 'bad weather', but with the Quiloan king's conversion into a Portuguese vassal, the storm is itself 'converted' into joy. Neatly slipping from the storm's natural power to the storming of Quiloa, the historian asserts the equivalence between the Portuguese forces and the forces of Nature, while also establishing the Portuguese as a force over nature, capable of 'converting' – note, too, the monetary resonance – nature's power to their own ends.

In this movement, colonial history, having displaced myth, itself becomes mythical. As we have seen, just such a logic pervades Camões' *Os Lusíadas* too. To recall King Manuel's dream, it was the East itself that had, in the shape of the Ganges and Indus, underscored the necessity of colonial violence: 'Fierce warfare is the price we are worth. / But if your ends you constantly pursue, / Unfearing, after victories untold, / You'll bridle all the nations you behold' (4.74.4–8, 153). By 'faining' a prophecy which 'the strange folk and savage, nations vast' (4.69.4, 152) cannot themselves utter, the brutality of colonial history assumes the mantle of heroic inevitability.

Two Ways of Writing the Heathen: Theodore de Bry

From different treatments of colonial origins, I turn now to contrasting ways of representing the diverse peoples that European voyagers encountered. I also move from literary representations to the interplay between images and texts, contrasting two cases drawn from the widely circulated and influential illustrated books published by Theodore de Bry. The instances examined below – one from the thirteen-volume compilation of voyages to the New World, called *America* or *India Occidentalis*, and the other from its twelve-volume companion of voyages to the east, *India Orientalis* – focus on how the concept of writing was used to shape relationships to foreign worlds and peoples.

Writing the New World Native: de Bry's *America I*

The collection of European voyages which would come to be called *America* was set into motion by Richard Hakluyt. With his encouragement, de Bry illustrated and published Thomas Hariot's account of the 1585 English expedition to Virginia. Although based on watercolours by John White (a painter who had travelled with Hariot), de Bry's engravings were not identical to White's 'very original[s]' (Hariot 1590: nn). De Bry selects twenty-three images from those he was provided, ignoring pictures of botanical and zoological novelties, and his engravings introduce slight modifications (for example, adding local crops such as maize or tobacco; see van Groesen 2008: 144–6).

Beyond abridging and altering visual sources, though, the most significant change in de Bry's volume is the medium of illustration, substituting copper engravings for drawings and watercolours. There seems little doubt that Hakluyt's desire to publicise the English claim to Virginia throughout Europe brought him to the well-known Flemish engraver, then domiciled in England. The introduction of copper engraving around 1565 in Antwerp and its environs (where de Bry resided from 1578 to 1585) had led to a refinement of this technology for printed books aimed at a more affluent readership. As Donald Lach writes, because of 'the need for finer technique' in reproducing maps, '[b]y the last generation of the sixteenth century prints derived from [copper] plates began to replace the woodcut in a variety of scientific and techni-cal books that required sharp and accurate illustrating' (1977: II, pt. 1, 78–9). It was the prestige and reach of this new medium that Hakluyt wished to harness for England's expansionist forays, and that the de Bry images for *America* and *India Orientalis* would come to epitomise. Before this monumental undertaking gathered steam, however, only one volume was conceived, not yet called *America* but more modestly (fol-lowing Hariot): *A Briefe and True Report of the New Found Land of Virginia*.

Here, Theodore de Bry brings together in the New World context graven image and written word. How such beginnings are seen and re-seen lies at the heart of Michael Gaudio's excellent study of de Bry's *America* engravings. As his *Engraving the Savage* shows, the White watercolours used as models for Hariot's *Briefe and True Report* alert us to how, even before the images convey meaning within de Bry's published volume, they point, bearing witness. Indexing a new visible reality, they testify to the very act of seeing the savage (see also Campbell 1999). Conceptually preceding the text, the 'ethnographic image . . . is the thing against which the text *generates* itself' (Gaudio 2008: xi). The text comes after the image.

But if, as witnesses to otherness, the pictures seem prior to the 'dark forest of the text' (de Certeau 1980: 37), another kind of writing belongs to the de Bry images themselves: their material inscription. For the early modern printed image – and, consequently, its role in producing ethno-graphic knowledge – relied on technologies closely related to writing: the incisions constitutive, first, of woodcuts, and then, most importantly, of copper engraving. Attending to this material act of engraving thus 'has the effect of bringing us back to the earth, back to the workshop where the engraver, at work with his tools, crafts alterity out of lines cut with a burin onto a copper plate' (Gaudio 2008: xii). As we shall see, Gaudio's compelling reading of one particular image brings to light the rich interplay between seeing and writing in what is – retrospectively – a primal scene of Europe's encounter with alterity, suggesting the complex work of writing in establishing the relationship between Europeans and natives. Yet, even while embracing his analysis, I want to suggest that it offers only one possible paradigm for understanding the uses to which writing would be put during the course of 'discovery'. Its limits become evident when we juxtapose de Bry's visual representation of the New World encounter with other scenes, other places, and other worlds disclosed by the *Indias* series.

One of the roughly two dozen engravings devised for Hariot's text shines more luminously for Gaudio than any other, since it foregrounds scriptive techniques connecting the native's body to early modern writing: the *Report*'s final Virginian image, showing '[t]he Marckes of sundrye of the Cheif mene of Virginia' (Figure 1). Translating the tattoos on the native's body into an alphabetical writing that can be consumed by the European reader, this engraving 'decode[s]' the savage: it 'translates the otherness of a New World body . . . into the familiarity of a European sign system' (Gaudio 2008: 5). But its manner of doing so is far from simple. As a type of 'metapicture' (Mitchell 1994: 48), de Bry's engraving self-consciously sustains two contradictory readings in circulation, thereby inviting the reader to meditate upon how images produce meaning.

On the one hand, de Bry illustrates the difference between the marks of ownership or domicile 'rased on [the] backs' of the Virginian natives and the familiar alphabetical script which decodes these tattoos. The contrast suggests that the savage cannot go beyond bodily communication; lacking letters, he also lacks the fundamental constituent of civilisation. The civilised European must speak for him, translate his corporeal marks into 'proper' writing. Concomitantly, the image also projects a civilised viewer, who can read the savage page/body and thereby know the savage.

On the other hand, the image leads also in the opposite direction, hinting at the similarity between tattoos and writing as practices of inscription. And it is precisely engraving that blurs the distinction between improper and proper marks, tattoos and alphabet, because it brings into relief the material act it shares with both tattooing and alphabetic writing.

> The process of making tattoos, which among North American Indians involved the pricking of flesh with sharp instruments (fish teeth, needles, thorns, sharpened bones) dipped in charcoal or cinnabar, is itself analogous to the two European techniques . . . for constructing letters: the scratching of a sharpened goose quill dipped in ink onto paper or parchment, and the cutting into a metal plate with a sharp burin. (Gaudio 2008: 22)

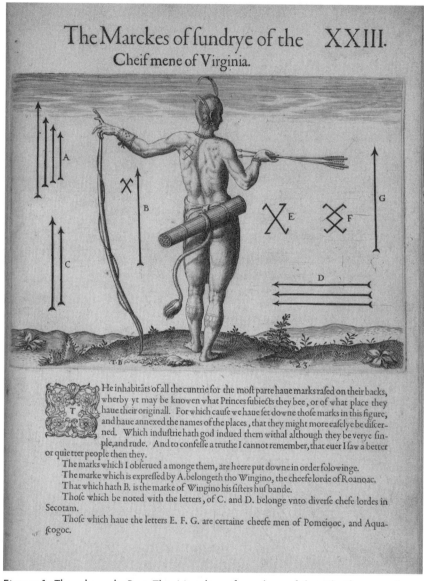

The Marckes of fundrye of the XXIII.
Cheif mene of Virginia.

He inhabitãts of all the cuntrie for the moſt parte haue marks raſed on their backs, wherby yt may be knowen what Princes ſubiects they bee, or of what place they haue their originall. For which cauſe we haue ſet downe thoſe marks in this figure, and haue annexed the names of the places, that they might more eaſely be diſcerned. Which induſtrie hath god indued them withal although they be verye ſimple, and rude. And to confeſſe a truthe I cannot remember, that euer I ſaw a better or quietter people then they.

The marks which I obſerued amonge them, are heere put downe in order folowinge.
The marke which is expreſſed by A. belongeth tho Wingino, the cheefe lorde of Roanoac.
That which hath B. is the marke of Wingino his fiſters huſbande.
Thoſe which be noted with the letters, of C. and D. belonge vnto diuerſe chefe lordes in Secotam.
Thoſe which haue the letters E. F. G. are certaine cheefe men of Pomeiooc, and Aquaſcogoc.

Figure 1 Theodore de Bry. The Marckes of sundrye of the Cheif mene of Virginia, from Thomas Hariot's *A Briefe and True Report* (1590), Ill. 23. Courtesy of the Rare Book Division of the Library of Congress.

This shared materiality is especially disconcerting because it subtly reminds a Christian viewer that even the European alphabet is a fallen, historical form, radically separated from the originary, divine Word. The difference between the savage and the civilised, New World native and European engraver, collapses in the face of their shared separation from the biblical origins of humankind. De Bry makes the complex relationship of writing to the Fall explicit in the *Nova alphati effictio* [Newly Fashioned Alphabet], an alphabet book of engravings he published in 1595 (see Figure 2). In the letter *A*, 'Adam and Eve have, so to speak,

Figure 2 Johan Theodore de Bry after Theodore de Bry. Letter A, from *Nova alphati effictio* (1595). Typ 520.95.241, Houghton Library, Harvard University.

fallen upon the extended arms of the letter itself, which is intertwined with the branches of the Tree of Knowledge and the snaky limbs of Satan, who assumes the form of a female serpent resting on top of the A' (Gaudio 2008: 13).

Thus, the de Bry engraving of the Virginian superimposes two contradictory understandings of writing's function in the New World encounter, seeing it as the site both of difference and likeness, simultaneously disavowing and acknowledging human resemblance across cultures (compare Juliet Fleming's discussion of the double logic of tattoos in 2001: 79–112). If the native's back is the page upon which a European viewer inscribes his separation from the savage, the engraving also evokes the savage as a concrete reminder of how far the viewer too has fallen. It thereby exposes the ineradicable residue of the savage within the ostensibly rational, civilised self. This, then, is the writing lesson Gaudio draws from de Bry: writing separates 'us' from 'them' – but it is also writing which undermines that separation.

Gaudio's elegant discussion of writing's ambivalent place in de Bry's engraving nonetheless prompts a further set of questions. Does writing always function the same way in colonial contexts? What if writing is unable so to constitute the boundary demarcating (and joining) self and other? What if writing produces differences that do not easily reduce to conventional oppositions between civilised and savage, literate and illiterate, rational and irrational? For it must be noted that Gaudio's discussion of the relationship between writing and seeing requires that we understand difference primarily in terms of binary opposition. And yet, even in the *Marckes of sundrye of the Cheif mene of Virginia*, the gulf separating viewing subject from viewed object grows out of a multiplicity that exceeds the simplicity of binarisms (unstable as these are shown to be).

For 'Virginia' projects as an ideologically unified place what are in fact the multiple and fractured spaces that actually constitute the New World encounter. 'Virginia' dissimulates, whereas the tattoos and their alphabetical translations, as the engraving's elaborate caption shows, also simply register differences *among* these inhabitants and their spaces:

> The marke which is expressed by A. belongeth tho Wingino, the cheefe lord of Roanoac.
> That which hath B. is the marke of Wingino his sisters husbande.
> Those which be noted with the letters, of C. and D. belonge unto diverse chefe lordes in Secotam.
> Those which have the letters E. F. G. are certaine cheefe men of Pomeiooc, and Aquascogoo.

In short, Hariot and de Bry reproduce a plurality that only subsequently becomes meaningful as a dynamic play of oppositions. Prior to the opposition between tattoos and alphabet are differences that image and caption bear witness to. Tattoos are themselves a form of social inscription, expressing a differential space divided along genealogical, geographical, and tribal lines. They make visible the fact of a sheer multiplicity. Here, differences ultimately dissolve into the overarching opposition between uncivil savage and civilised self identified by Gaudio. But extending our gaze beyond the Virginian encounter shows the extent to which such multiplicities become the norm – especially in European engagements with the Old worlds of China and India.

Let us leave, then, this scene from *India Occidentalis* to contrast it with a scene of writing from the other India. A very different understanding of writing's place and function may be found in the second volume of *India Orientalis*, which reproduces portions of Jan Huyghen van Linschoten's Dutch *Itinerario, Voyage ofte Schipvaert . . . naer Oost ofte Portugaels Indien* (1596).

> The men of China have many speeches, but in writing they understand each other in every place, for they write everything with figures and characters, whereof their alphabets are sundry and innumerable . . . which is the cause that among them such as are learned are so much esteemed. Their paper is like that of Europa, but not so white, but thinner and smoother: they make also of all colours, which is very fair, they write with pens of Reeds, wherein there sticketh a pencil, such as painters use. Painting, printing, & gun-powder . . . have been used in China many hundred years past, and very common, so that with them it is out of memory when they first began . . . Printing is likewise very ancient with them, for . . . there are books found in those countries of China, which were printed at the least five or six hundred years before printing was in use with us in Europe, so that it is not found when it first began there. And there are many books in China, for that they are very curious and desirous to write and register all things, as well that which is done in their kingdom or which belongeth thereunto, as also other memorable things, cunning and fine devices, laws and ordinances, all policies & governments in their towns, wherein they much resemble and surpass the ancient Grecians and Romans. (1598: 41–2)

Consider a few salient features here. First, Linschoten does not distinguish his overview of Chinese writing in any significant way from other information in this section. Entitled 'Of the Provinces, Towns, and other things worthy of memory in the kingdom of *China*', the chapter contains a hodgepodge of details: the names of all the provinces, a generic description of Chinese cities, rules constraining the use of weapons, marriage customs, descriptions of banquets and feasts, and so on. Their 'sundry and innumerable' alphabet is simply another of these 'things worthy of memory'. Second, while the description repeatedly compares Chinese and European writing – even to the latter's detriment, as in the willingness to see the Chinese desire to write things down as 'much resemb[ling] and surpass[ing]' the Greeks and the Romans – modes and technologies of writing do not establish a fundamental difference between Europeans and Chinese. Instead, distinctions are subsequent to similarities and parallels. We do not, as with de Bry, start from an opposition between tattoos and writing only to reflect eventually upon an underlying similarity; rather, Linschoten first assumes a shared literacy, which is then developed into second-order differences (for instance, Chinese paper is first likened to European, before it is distinguished as less white, thinner and smoother). Third, there is no hint here of the later European treatment of Chinese characters as a way-stage towards properly alphabetical writing (see, for example Condillac's remarks cited in Derrida 1985: 313). To the extent that Linschoten identifies Chinese writing with ideographs ('they write everything with figures and characters'), this feature is not denigrated. Far from it: despite the 'many speeches' of the Chinese, their figural alphabet enables a unified field of communication – 'in writing they understand each other in every place'. The implicit contrast is with Europe, where the multiplicity of written languages impedes communication (compare Bonifacio 1616: 11–12).

Finally, a notable absence: there is no accompanying de Bry engraving that explicitly renders writing visible. Whatever else its virtues, this Chinese 'scene' of writing hardly presents a scene at all – and certainly not one worth capturing as image. Nevertheless, Linschoten and his other European counterparts *were* different from the Chinese, the Indians, the Javans, the Malays, and the innumerable others they encountered. And Linschoten *did* indeed produce, articulate, and represent the differences between European selves and Eastern others – as did the accompanying de Bry engravings. How?

Writing the Chinese: de Bry's *India Orientalis II*

In its twenty-third chapter, Linschoten's *Itinerario* touches briefly upon Chinese religious practices:

> For Religion and ceremonies they are Heathens, without any spark or point of Mahomet's law . . . In many places they pray to the Devil, only because he should not hurt them. When any man lieth on his death bed, they set the picture of the Devil before him, with the Sun in his left hand, and a

poniard in the right hand, which Devil is painted with a very fierce look: and therefore they desire the patient or sick man to look well upon him, that he may be his friend in the world to come, and that year he may not hurt him. (Linschoten 1598: 39)

Given their usual taste for the outré, one might expect the de Brys to seize upon this curious scene of extreme unction. Not so, however. Instead, at this juncture, the 1628 Latin *India Orientalis II* draws our gaze to an image derived from an inserted supplementary text not written by Linschoten at all. Immediately after the Dutchman's assertion that the Chinese pray to the devil to avoid being hurt by him, the de Brys add an elaborate specification of these strange orisons, which their own engraving then realises (see Figure 3):

The Chinese use various ceremonies in their rites. They have a three-headed idol everywhere in their temples. And if they are preparing a matter of any import, or embarking upon a task ... that must be completed, they approach the idol and tie together two pieces of wood, both flat on one side and round on the other: these they throw up on high in order to explore their fortunes. And if both settle on the flat side, the omen is favourable; if however one lands on the flat and the other on the rounded side, it is unfavourable. In this case they implore the idol with many prayers that he assist them with a favourable will. But if the pieces of wood fall a second time in the unequal position, they become angry with the idol, but implore him anew, and test the wood a third time; and if a third time the pieces of wood are thrown in the unlucky position, they trample the idol underfoot and then throw it into the sea, or give it to the fire, where it burns for a bit, or indeed they beat it with whips for as long as it takes until the pieces of wood fall, with a favourable throw, on the flat side, at which point they replace the idol in his [original] position, apologising and offering it sumptuous sacrifices. (de Bry 1628: 56; my translation, assisted by A. Bahr)

This remarkable passage incorporates into the *Itinerario* scenes from an entirely different book, one Linschoten himself recommends, though warning against its inaccuracies:

yet if any man be desirous to see more [of these ceremonies and customs] ... let him read the book ... by a Spanish Friar named Fray Juan Gonsales de Mendosa [sic], of the description of China ... [A]lthough there are some faults by wrong information given unto the Author, notwithstanding it containeth many particular things worth the reading. (1596: 42)

The de Brys certainly found in de Mendoza's *Historia de las cosas más notables, ritos y costumbres del gran reino de la China* (1585) much that was 'worth the reading'. Despite Linschoten's admonition, though,

Figure 3 Johan Theodore and Johan Israel de Bry, The Chinese Worshipping Idols, from *India Orientalis II* (German ed., 1598), Ill. XXVIII. Courtesy of the Rare Book Division of the Library of Congress.

they could not resist taking yet further liberties with that source. For their depiction of Chinese men casting sticks before the 'idolum triceps' [three-headed idol] actually combines into a single action two disparate moments from the *Historia*. (The background scene in the de Bry image, which takes place before a more familiar and recognisable devil, interpolates yet another anecdote from the Spanish text, to which I shall return.) The elaborate casting of lots is extracted from a chapter on the superstitious Chinese belief 'in auguries . . . as a thing most certain and infallible' (de Mendoza 1588: 32). However, the idol does not itself appear in de Mendoza's description of these auguries, being only one of many that the Chinese ostensibly worship (albeit one they especially revere).

To learn more about this figure, we need to turn to an earlier chapter in the *Historia*, which focuses on the surprising connection between Chinese idolatry and Christian belief.

> Amongst the figures of all their idols . . . the Chinos do say that there is one of a strange and marvellous making, unto whom they do great reverence: they do paint him a body with three heads, that doth continually look the one upon the other: and they say that it doth signify, that all three be of one good will and essence, and that which pleaseth the one pleaseth the other: and to the contrary, that which is grievous and displeaseth the one, is grievous and displeaseth the other two: the which being interpreted christianly, may be understood to be the mystery of the holy trinity, that we that are christians do worship . . . the which with other things seemeth somewhat to be respondent to our holy sacred and christian religion: so that of very truth we may presume that saint Thomas the Apostle did preach in this kingdom . . . (1588: 24)

Far from indicating Chinese depravity, then, the tricephalic statue reveals quite the reverse: the success of St Thomas in disseminating the true Word across the world, even to these far reaches of the globe only now becoming visible to European eyes. Such passages – and there are many – are consistent with the *Historia*'s general thrust. It exhibits throughout a persistent tension between the author's avowed Catholicism – which *ipso facto* leads him to describe non-Christians as inferiors, blind and error-ridden – and his evident sense of confronting a civilisation that in many respects casts European achievements into the shade.

Here and elsewhere, the recourse to St Thomas's apostolic ventures partly serves to reconcile the contradiction between religious presumptions and the experiential evidence which confronted Spanish travellers to China. Recognising that 'there are found in this kingdom many moral things . . . which do touch very much our religion, which giveth us to understand that they are people of great understanding, in especial in natural things', de Mendoza is led to the 'certainty that the holy apostle of whom we have spoken, did leave amongst them by his preachings occasion for to learn many things that do show unto virtue' (39). What the Chinese do not see, then, notwithstanding their natural acuity and evident rationality, is not the present event of European arrival which has made their lives and customs visible to others, but the event in the past, when truth walked among them in the shape of the Apostle. Their blindness to the fullness of that moment conditions them in the here and now.

And yet: even in their misrepresentation, in their idolatrous image of the trinity, they reveal the 'sign and token that they had some notice of the true God, whose shadows they do represent' (26). Consequently, they resemble us even in their very unlikeness: '& we may presume that all which we have seen doth remain printed in their hearts from his doctrine, and beareth a similitude of the truth, & a conformity with the things of our [C]atholic religion' (37). If, as de Mendoza avers, print as a material institution travelled from China to Europe, this journey was conditioned, it would appear, by a reverse movement from West to East, whereby the Word was imprinted in Chinese hearts, surviving even now as an afterimage of what once was, as 'similitude of truth'. The fall was not the West's alone; in their own way the Chinese, too, have lost 'the clear light of the true Christian religion, without which the subtlest and delicatest understandings are lost and overthrown' (26).

Needless to say, none of this context is immediately visible in the de Bry engraving (Figure 3). The image operates with a simple (if unevenly executed) single-point perspective. The point where perspectival lines converge is not of visual importance: a nondescript spot on the column immediately above the right shoulder of the man who has just cast his sticks, roughly where his head might have been had he not moved to chance a throw. But its very ordinariness is telling: the point's location at the absolute centre of the picture plane reveals the choice to be purely geometrical. Its placement thus evokes the rationalism of geometry itself, subtly disclosing the engraver's projection of 'the tidy, regular, systematized . . . net of rationality' (Ivins 1969: 75) (emphasised by the neatly gridded tiles that make up the floor in the temple's foreground). Within this net, the engraving catches the Chinese reckoner just as he completes his idolatrous act. Perspective here expresses an impulse similar to what Gaudio uncovers in de Bry's depictions of Virginian natives: it operates as a rationalist model through which the savage (or heathen) is 'encompassed by the engraver's controlling intellect' (Gaudio 2008: 40).

But in the Chinese case the matter is not so simple. While the de Bry engraving aligns a European viewer's eye with geometry's rationalised gaze, the split status of the spaces depicted in the engraving counters that assimilation. So, on the one hand, the arrangement of balustrades, arches, columns, along with the buildings and steeple in the corner of the engraving rationalise space, confirming a model of vision that distinguishes us from the superstitious Chinese. On the other hand, these architectural elements, ostensibly representative of Chinese urban spaces, would not be out of place in, say, Italian paintings of the period, and this equivalence undoes the very distinction that geometry is meant to uphold. And the grotesque demon in the engraving's other scene would certainly be unremarkable if encountered, for instance, on the eaves of a medieval cathedral or in one of Hieronymus Bosch's fervid imaginings. Recognising such resemblances undermines the separation between 'us' and 'them', resulting in a curious tension seemingly akin to what appears in de Mendoza's *Historia*: the interplay between unlikeness and likeness, dissimilarity and kinship.

We can explore this tension further by turning to the only other de Bry engraving to make use of the Chinese idol: the frontispiece to *India Orientalis II*. Far from suggesting an anterior kinship between Europeans and Chinese, this idol announces its otherness; arms akimbo, it almost insolently flaunts its alterity from those for whom the book is intended (see Figure 4).

But here again the frontispiece as a whole pulls in the opposite direction as well. It shows a number of the different peoples described by Linschoten, arranged in a hierarchy moving upwards from the savage to the civilised. The de Brys' ethnography rarely veers from visual and conceptual codes that probably originated in sixteenth-century costume books; accordingly, we get basic information 'about the civility of a social group following the rough and ready formula "the more dress the more civility, the more nudity the more savagery"' (van den Boogaart 2004: 97; see also Wilson 2005: 70ff.). A virtually unclothed 'Caffre' [Kaffir] or 'Mor' [Moor] from Mozambique and a likewise scantily-clad Cochin warrior hold up the right and left of the title page respectively; a more fully dressed Malaccan and Javan gaze at one another across the middle of the page. While the Mozambiquan invites us into the image and the book by holding our gaze, his counterpart from Cochin points up with his sword toward what we should look at, his gaze directing ours. Thus, even as the engraving ultimately subordinates the multiplicity of worlds contained in the book to the false Chinese trinitarian idol, this figure nonetheless signifies the apex of (Oriental) civilisation.

Figure 4 Johan Theodore and Johan Israel de Bry, Frontispiece, *India Orientalis II* (Latin ed., 1628), showing the three-headed idol. US 2257.50, Houghton Library, Harvard University.

The coupling of these potentially contradictory characteristics – that is, the idol as simultaneously the epitome of civilisation and of otherness – leads us to the driving force behind the temple scene (Figure 3). For the de Brys' is an engraving generated *against* the text – and not just against Linschoten's *Itinerario* (which neither mentions the three-headed idol nor the casting of lots) but against the unacknowledged de Mendoza *Historia* as well. By seamlessly incorporating the foreign caption and the temple illustration into the very body of the narrative, the 1628 Latin edition in particular severely compromises the relative neutrality of the Dutchman's account of Chinese religion. Moreover, even the treatment of de Mendoza's book runs counter to its spirit. Not only do the de Brys alter the order of the source episodes – by directly linking the Chinese worship of the 'idolum triceps' to their superstitious casting of lots – but they suppress the context that de Mendoza establishes, namely, the idol as evidence for Christianity's enduring presence in Chinese history. By so doing, they radically invert the import of the image.

At issue here, to put the matter in terms derived from Gilles Deleuze, is the distinction between the copy and the simulacrum. For de Mendoza, the Chinese idol is a degraded copy of a Christian original (and, indeed, the copy of a copy of a Christian original, since it was the Apostle Thomas rather than Christ himself who had spread the Word). Time and distance work their distortions, gradually degrading the copy. But memory nonetheless materially persists in the idol: through it, 'the mystery aforesaid, of the holy trinity . . . doth indure to this day' (24). Infinitely diminished though it may be, resemblance there is, and this likeness, originating in a shared past, opens the possibility for a shared future. Whatever the differences now – and they are great – that slender yet undying affinity preserves an opening, the window to an eternal return. It suggests the hope invested by this Augustinian friar in a (shared) native rationality and civility as well as in the enduring power of a shared event in the past which preserves an essential resemblance between the Chinese and the Spanish.

In the hands of the de Brys, the de Mendozan copy becomes a simulacrum, an index not of underlying kinship but of radical perversion. As Deleuze argues, a simulacrum is not 'a copy of a copy, an infinitely degraded icon, an infinitely loose resemblance' (1990: 257). Rather, simulacra differ categorically from copies. For a copy's resemblance to an original is not merely that of an external likeness, but expresses instead the extent to which one thing is like another through its participation in the Idea – in this instance, the vision enabled by the 'clear light of the true Christian religion' (de Mendoza 1588: 26), which has been obscured (but not entirely lost) in the Chinese. In the simulacrum, this essential relationship is lacking; all that is left is a superficial likeness. 'The copy is an image endowed with resemblance, the simulacrum is an image without resemblance' (Deleuze, 1990: 257). The resemblance that had functioned in de Mendoza's text to establish a kinship *despite* the surface appearance of alterity, now serves in the de Bry engraving to establish an underlying alterity precisely *upon* the grounds that the similarity between Chinese and Spanish religious representations is purely external, emptied of any participation in the Idea. The Chinese have lost (or never had) the resemblance, even as they maintain the image. Moreover, in the de Bry text there is no mention of the Apostle, that is, there is no original event in the past to which the *idolum* can refer – and therefore no event to which one can return, upon which one can build. There is only the (en)graven image in the present, and what it says is: for them, there is only the image, and that says everything.

A brief return to the Virginian savages illuminates by contrast the visual treatment of the Chinese. *America I* does not close with the figure of the tattooed native (Figure 1). According to de Bry, along with the pictures of the Virginian he also received several images ostensibly derived from an old English chronicle. The first (and most often reproduced) is that of a male Pict grasping by its hair the freshly decapitated head of a foe (see Figure 5).

The connection between this residue of the English past and its present in Virginia appears in de Bry's caption: '[i]n times past the Picts, habitants of one part of great Britain, which is now named England, were savages, and did paint all their body after the manner following . . . ' (Hariot 1590: sig. E1v). The juxtaposition of images draws a direct connection between the Virginian savages and those from England's past. We were savages like them once, the engraving suggests, and its unspoken corollary is: we have since changed into who we now are – and therefore the Virginians might too.

Not so, however, with the de Bry rendition of the temple scene, which renders all likeness suspect. Unlike the Virginian savage or even the Pict – and equally unlike Linschoten's or de Mendoza's Chinese – the natives performing their demoniacal monkey-tricks (what the German 1598 edition calls *Ubel Affenspiele*) are utterly divorced from the possibility of participating in the Christian *logos*. And without that participation, the Chinese likeness can only be a dissimulation, evidence of an ingrained perversion that apes the very truth it seemingly represents. The appearance of a similitude *sans* re-presentation – that is, a likeness that has evolved entirely independently of Christian history – evidences

Figure 5 Theodore de Bry, Male Pict, from Thomas Hariot's *A Briefe and True Report* (1590). Courtesy of the Rare Book Division of the Library of Congress.

instead an irreducible categorical difference, the insurmountable gap between the true pretender and the false.

The need to deny resemblance between viewer and viewed is emphasised by the second pictorial axis which diagonally intersects – and visually substitutes for – the perspectival. For the dominant visual line of the Chinese engraving connects and relates events in the foreground to those in the background. And at this juncture, the paradigm of writing returns again, though in a manner quite different from its occurrence in the case of the Virginian native. Depicted in the recesses of the engraving is an almost occluded scene of writing through which cultural difference will be cemented. Here is de Mendoza's description of that strange performance:

> The order that they have in invocating or calling on the devil, is as followeth. They cause a man to lie upon the ground, his face downwards, then another beginneth to read upon a book singing . . . the rest do make a sound with little bells, and tabers: then . . . the man that lieth on the ground, beginneth to make visages and gestures: which is certain token that the devil is entered within him: then they do ask of him what they do desire to know: then he that is possessed doth answer, yet for the most part they be lies . . . he doth speak: although he [remains silent sometimes], yet . . . [he] always . . . answer[s] either by word or by letters . . . [the latter being] the remedy they have when . . . the devil will not answer by word. And when that he doth answer by letters, then they do spread a red mantle or coverlet upon the ground, and throw thereon a certain quantity of rice dispersed equally in every place upon the coverlet: then they do cause a man that cannot write to stand there with a stick in his hand, then those that are present do begin to sing and make a sound as at the first invocation: and within a little while the devil doth enter into him that hath the stick, and causeth him to write upon the rice, then they do translate the letters that are there formed with the stick, and being joined altogether, they find answer of that they do demand . . . (1588: 33–4)

In this bizarre scene – visually inserted by the de Brys into Linschoten's *Itinerario* – Chinese writing seems less a human invention than a direct transmission from beyond. It requires as medium precisely one who cannot produce the written word in and of himself, who thus cannot alter or resist what passes through him. The Chinese language, too, involves a kind of fall – a man lies face to the ground, another scrawls unknowingly in rice with a stick; the human intervention is limited to painting and connecting the visible signs to create an answer.

The de Bry scene also makes use of de Mendoza's assertion elsewhere that the Chinese invert Western writing: 'Their order of writing is clean contrary to ours, for that they do begin their lines from above downwards, but in very good order: Likewise they begin their lines at the righthand and write towards the left, contrary to us' (1588: 93). Such contrariness – purely descriptive in de Mendoza's account – is lent an ideological weighting in the engraving, where the Chinese language is seen to decline and to derive not from God but from the devil. If Western alphabetic writing itself – and, by extension, printing and engraving – expresses a falling away from the Word (see Figure 2), it nonetheless remains connected to its divine origin, a true copy. By contrast, the Chinese may not know the one God, but they certainly know the one Devil who answers them deceptively 'by word or by letters' in simulacra of divine grace. The enduring afterimage of such dissimulation is the mockery of the trinity in the engraving's geometricised foreground. The illustration reveals that this idolatrous image, which first holds our eyes, finds its true condition of possibility in the perverse writing scene hidden in the background. This, then, is yet another writing lesson (for there are many): if writing is indeed what separates (as it sometimes may) a European 'us' from a Chinese 'them', it is not because they do not have it while we do, or because theirs is a primitive form of ours, whose material traces we still carry, but because their writing is related to ours as simulacrum to copy. We truly possess our writing; their writing possesses them merely.

The crucial difference between travel narratives such as Hariot's or Linschoten's and the way the de Bry compilations use them needs to be located in *how* the belief that we are all simulacra shapes text and image, in how its implications are construed. And here the contradictory impulses driving the compilations become evident. On the one hand, the de Brys select texts that share to a degree an interest in registering plurality and difference, in exploring alterity as a site for alternative pasts, presents, and futures. The very choice of these texts marks the de Brys' own fascination with the inescapable novelty and variety brought to light by these accounts. On the other hand, however, their treatment of this diverse material reveals a persistent need to engrave against the texts. A de Bry frontispiece might be said to patrol the texts of which it is a distillation, asserting the primacy of what is seen over what is written – for example, by visually organising natives in terms of increasing or decreasing levels of civility. Their images thus impose orderliness on the potentially unruly mass of differences and distinctions revealed in the narratives they accompany.

Their resistance reveals itself most fully in the de Brys' anxious response to how the selected texts expose the possibility that we are all simulacra. With and against the implications of an idea that lies at the heart of their own theology, the de Brys repeatedly struggle, seeking to restore sharp delineations between true copies and simulacra, warding off the all-too-real possibility that the latter may rise up to engulf the originary dispensation of the Word.

The Brome-an Empire: Wonder and Theatre in *The Antipodes*

> Traffic and travel hath woven the nature of all nations into ours, and made this land like arras, full of device, which was broadcloth, full of workmanship . . . If we present a mingle-mangle, our fault is to be excused, because the whole world is become an hodgepodge.
> (John Lyly, from the Prologue to *Midas*, 1587)

From real voyages to imaginary ones: Richard Brome's 1636 satirical comedy, *The Antipodes*, may seem an odd choice for a case study. A sustained mockery of corruption in Caroline London, Brome's work does not address colonialism directly. Nevertheless, in structure and language the play engages deeply the changing status of travel in early modern Europe. In particular, it reflects on the uncanny connections between theatrical and proto-colonial voyaging, as its concluding plea to the audience intimates:

> And from our travels in th'Antipodes
> We are not yet arrived from off the seas;
> But on the waves of desp'rate fears we roam
> Until your gentler hands do waft us home.
>
> (V.ii.385–9)

Thus is the wonder at things far-fetched and distant transmuted into the audience's delight at theatre's homely pleasures, the spectator's applause enabling the joyous return.

As the preceding case study indicates, images of discovery were widespread in Europe by the sixteenth century's end. The fascination these exerted co-existed, though, with the pull of older inherited conceptions, even as contemporary attitudes to the remnants of classical and medieval pasts underwent a sea-change. Before turning to *The Antipodes*, I would like to highlight this admixture by recalling Othello's famous speech before the Venetian court:

> Wherein of antres vast and deserts idle,
> Rough quarries, rocks, and hills whose heads touch heaven,
> It was my hint to speak. Such was my process:
> And of the cannibals that each other eat,

The Anthropophagi, and men whose heads
Do grow beneath their shoulders. These things to hear
Would Desdemona seriously incline,
But still the house affairs would draw her thence,
Which ever as she could with haste dispatch,
She'd come again, and with a greedy ear
Devour up my discourse . . .

                                        (*Othello*: I.iii.139–49)

Through such stories does Othello 'beguile' Desdemona 'of herself'
(I.iii.66). I noted in Chapter 1 the association between 'cannibals that
each other eat' and Desdemona, who 'with a greedy ear / Devour[s] up'
Othello's 'discourse'. But not enough has been said about Desdemona's
wonder: 'She swore in faith 'twas strange, 'twas passing strange, / 'Twas
pitiful, 'twas wondrous pitiful' (I.iii.159–60). Her 'inclining' 'these
things to hear' suggests the persistence – even augmented, in many ways,
by the voyages of 'discovery' – of a medieval tradition in which 'mar-
vellous natural phenomena . . . emerge[d] as objects of unadulterated
pleasure and fascination' (Daston and Park 1998: 48).

    Othello's 'conjuration and . . . mighty magic' (I.iii.92) draws on Pliny's
Naturalis Historia and John Mandeville's apocryphal *Travels*, both
regularly reprinted in this period. Given the play's reliance on contemporary sources such as Knolles' *Generall Historie of the Turks* (1603)
for the Turco-Venetian conflict that frames its action, this recourse to
older texts seems curiously outdated. Yet the quotidian realities of discovery and conquest, for all their newness, often lacked the wonder (and
magic) so central to medieval and classical accounts of unseen worlds.
Consequently, descriptions drawn from Mandeville and Pliny remained,
in Brabantio's words, 'mixtures powerful o'er the blood'.

    At the same time, Shakespeare's play places these stories in a romantic
past that Iago mocks as 'fantastical lies' (II.i.219) and 'bombast circum-
stance' (I.i.13). Iago's cynicism anticipates the theatrical debunking of
Mandeville and Pliny in *The Antipodes*, a play that nonetheless shares
Othello's belief in the power of such stories – though precisely *as* stories,
for only as dramatic fictions shaping mental reality do they retain
their efficacy. In Brome's play, Desdemona's wonder becomes young
Peregrine's madness:

Joyless In tender years he [Peregrine] always loved to read
Reports of travels and of voyages.
And when young boys like him would tire themselves
With sport and pastimes, . . .
. . . he would whole days

And nights (sometimes by stealth) be on such books
As might convey his fancy around the world.

(I.i.131ff.)

Like Desdemona, Peregrine greedily consumes in words what he cannot experience in flesh. However, this imaginary conveyance only leads to his 'travelling / So far beyond himself that now, too late', Joyless wishes his son 'had gone abroad to meet his fate' (I.i.148–50). In a sense the son is merely living up to the etymology of his name: from the Latin *peregrinus*, namely, strange or foreign. And so, 'he talks much of

> the Kingdom of Cathaya,
> Of one Great Khan and goodman Prester John
> (Whate'er they be), and says the Khan's a clown
> Unto the John he speaks of; and that John
> Dwells almost up at Paradise. But sure his mind
> Is in a wilderness, for there he says
> Are geese that have two heads apiece, and hens
> That bear more wool upon their backs than sheep.

(I.i.188–95)

If Desdemona's wonder opens up for her the space of masculine agency, revealing possibilities unavailable in the 'house affairs' that occupy her, Peregrine's obsession with travel literature turns him instead into a woman, requiring the doctor Hughball to '[p]lay the man-midwife and deliver him / Of his huge tympany of news – of monsters, / Pygmies and giants, apes and elephants, / Griffins and crocodiles' (I.i.177–80).

Curing the madness induced by immoderate consumption of older travel literature constitutes the play's central plot: Peregrine's worried family seeks, with the nobleman Letoy's aid, to bring him back home to early modern reality (and specifically to make Pergerine fulfil his conjugal duties toward his child-obsessed wife Martha). For this they turn to Doctor Hughball, among the earliest practising psychoanalysts to appear on the English stage (Corax in John Ford's *The Lover's Melancholy* was probably the first). The Doctor's technique relies on theatre's power to possess – and thereby to transform – its audience. Rather than use rational persuasion, Hughball advocates sending Peregrine on a theatrical voyage into the Antipodes of his own mind, so he may produce of his own accord an aversion to its far-fetched wonders by actually 'living' them in displaced fashion: through a play in which the other characters of *The Antipodes* are both participants and spectators.

Ian Donaldson aptly describes Brome's play as a complicated Russian doll-like structure, which repeatedly blurs the distinction between those who watch and those who do, turning one into the other. The play-within-the-play has five rings of spectators: Peregrine, the 'closest and most enthralled spectator'; his wife Martha, the jealous Joyless and his young wife Diana, who increasingly get caught up in the play's action; Blaze and his wife Barbara, knowing onlookers and participants whose own marital discord has been recently 'cured' through just such means; Letoy and the Doctor, who direct the play and participate in it; and, finally, the audience in the actual theatre of Salisbury Court, where *The Antipodes* was first performed (see Donaldson 1970: 90–2).

Doctor Hughball's disparaging response to Peregrine's fervid imaginings – 'O, Mandeville', he exclaims, upon hearing the litany of strange places and actions – suggests the extent to which travel had become routine by the 1630s. Seeking to gain Peregrine's confidence, Hughball expansively dismisses 'reports of those that beggingly / Have put out on returns from Edinburgh, / Paris, or Venice, or perhaps Madrid, / Where a milliner may with half a nose / Smell out his way' (I.iii.78–82). Peregrine himself ridicules Drake as 'a didapper' in comparison to Mandeville; indeed, 'Ca[ve]ndish, and Hawkins, Furbisher [Frobisher], all our voyagers / Went short of Mandeville' (I.iii.31–3). It was not that wonders had ceased in the wake of European voyaging. Rather, they had multiplied, and the very excess meant a devaluing of 'all [that was] still too near home' (I.iii.62ff.), lending renewed life to Mandeville's far-fetched tales.

The profusion of travellers' accounts had at least two further consequences. On the one hand, it exposed the inadequacies of classical knowledge of the natural world. Indeed, the rapid decline in Mandeville's credibility – despite his continued imaginative appeal – provides further evidence of the past's slackening hold upon the present. Whereas Hakluyt's first edition of *The Principall Navigations* included a Latin text of the *Travels*, the second edition dropped Mandeville altogether (see Greenblatt 1991: 30–1). And in Brome's play, too, Peregrine's insistence on Mandeville's authority – 'Read here else. Can you read? / Is it not true' – cannot sustain itself when faced with the Doctor's claim to have been an eye-witness to the marvels of foreign worlds: 'No truer than I ha' seen't' (I.iii.41–2).

On the other hand, the explosion of travellers' accounts of Old and New worlds also helped reclaim wonder as a philosophical emotion, bringing it under the purview of a rationalist empiricism able to judge each marvel and assign it its appropriate place. Such wonder was

neither the fearful wonder of the vulgar . . . nor the Augustinian wonder of the devout . . . Still less was it Aristotle's wonder at the regular and the functional. Instead it was a philosophical version of the pleasurable wonder that informed the medieval literature of topography and travel ... the wonder of the connoisseur, so familiar with a multiplicity of extraordinary phenomena that he knew which truly deserved his amazement. (Daston and Park 1998: 167)

As Blaze reminds, our wonder ought to be directed less at Peregrine's 'extravagant' Mandevillean wanderings (I.i.147) than at the Doctor's curative achievements, accomplished not by 'bodily physic' but by a 'medicine of the mind', which he infuses

> So skilfully, yet by familiar ways
> That it begets both wonder and delight
> In his observers, while the stupid patient
> Finds health at unawares.
>
> (I.i.19ff.)

The imaginative longings of Desdemona and Peregrine for distant worlds are no more than forms of distraction and stupidity. That way madness lies. Instead, their affective responses are appropriated by the doctor who restores the 'stupid patient' to health, to the 'familiar ways' of the here and now.

But ultimately, Brome's play is concerned less to undermine the wonder evoked by travel than to appropriate it for the stage as a legitimated delight. Therefore, the Doctor's cure takes the form of repetition, leading Peregrine (and others) to undertake the very theatrical journeys that had occasioned his troubles in the first place. If Mandevillean wonder leads to madness, the theatrical repetition of that wonder effects a cure, transforming the experiencing subject by restoring him (or her) to normalcy. The nature of this repetition compulsion may be better understood by charting Brome's complex response to Mandeville. For the descriptions of the strange world beyond the Holy Land in the *Travels* are arresting not merely because they are so outlandish but also in how they *combine* difference with likeness. Thus, when Mandeville describes burial customs in Tibet (themselves borrowed from Ordoric of Pordenone's account) involving dismemberment and cannibalism, he nonetheless draws liturgical parallels with the Christian practices of transforming parts of saintly bodies into relics and of the Eucharist, thereby blurring the difference that his text produces. The effect is to establish 'a kind of metaphoric circulation so that the idolatrous city seems at once the double and ironic antithesis of the Christian city, the two views constantly oscillating' (Greenblatt 1991: 44).

A similar oscillation characterises Brome's evocation of the 'farthest distant' Antipodes that lies 'foot to foot / Against our region' (I.iii.85–7), namely, 'th' antipodes of England' (I.iii.115). On the one hand, Brome's vision of an anti-London – whose inhabitants are 'extremely contrary' in 'their manners, / Their carriage, and condition of life' (I.iii.110ff.) to those in his city – pushes to a logical extreme Mandeville's geographical vision in which every point on the terrestrial globe must be balanced by an equal and opposite one. On the other hand, Brome's satire would be robbed of much of its force were it not that his Antipodean anti-London comes to resemble the city that is its contrary (see Leslie 1997: 61–2 for a related point about Joseph Hall's 1605 satire *Mundus Alter et Idem*). The effusive celebration of the doctor's achievements in the play's opening scene, for instance, locates topsy-turvydom in the very heart of the metropolis by showing the gap between real and ideal. In speaking of those 'officers and men of place, / whose senses were so numbed that they understood not / Bribes from due fees', Blaze praises the doctor for curing them so that they 'can now distinguish / And know both of when and how to take of both'. Sanity lies not in refusing bribes, but in knowing how to 'grow most safely rich' by judicious acceptance (I.i.65ff.). Corruption is thereby 'safely' installed at the foundation of the social order.

However, while the lineaments of the Brome-an dynamic are already visible in his Mandevillean source, the demands of social satire crucially transform its mode of application. In Mandeville, the oscillation between likeness and difference fundamentally depends upon distance, both geographic and experiential. The *Travels'* attitude towards the strange worlds described therein remains generally free of anxiety, in large measure because they do not challenge European values or establish a rival norm. Mandeville's descriptions thus seem motivated primarily by a desire to know of and converse about alterity (see Greenblatt 1991: 44). By contrast, Brome relocates diversity and strangeness at home, in the London of his day, and indeed in the very heart of its theatre. Such a relocation blurs distinctions between home and away, bringing to the fore questions of normative behaviours and legitimacy (see Butler 1984: 218).

Attendant upon this divergence is a significant change in attitude. Despite presenting himself as a man of the world, Mandeville's characteristic gesture is renunciation, be it of knowledge or of material objects. 'Sir John Mandeville is the knight of non-possession' (Greenblatt 1991: 28). Entering the Vale Perilous towards the end of the narrative, and seeing treasures of all kinds heaped up around him, Mandeville's response is remarkable: 'But whether that it was as us seemed, I wot

never for I touched none, because that the devils be so subtle to make a
thing seem otherwise that it is . . . and therefore I touched none' (1968:
219). Not only does Mandeville refuse to take possession of the wealth
around him, but he gives up 'the possibility of knowledge – the ability to
distinguish between truth and illusion' (Greenblatt 1991: 27).

For Brome, however, possession becomes a – in fact, the – central
issue. Peregrine's return to 'health' crucially demands his renounc-
ing wonder in favour of the very un-Mandevillean desires of owning
and possessing. Encountering the strange stage props in Letoy's 'tiring
house', and taking a 'strict survey of . . . / Our statues and our images of
gods, / Our planets and our constellations, / Our giants, monsters, furies,
beasts, and bugbears' (III.i.289–92), Peregrine's immediate response
is – like Guyon's in Spenser's Bower of Bliss – destruction: 'with thrice
knightly force / And thrice puissant arm', he snatches down a sword and
shield, and, rushing about the set, he

> Kills monster after monster, takes the puppets
> Prisoners, knocks down the Cyclops, tumbles all
> Our jigambobs and trinkets to the wall.

> (III.i.303ff.)

Overcoming wonder, Peregrine instead takes up a crusade against all
that is alien. His aggression culminates in usurpation when he seizes 'the
imperial diadem and crowns / Himself King of the Antipodes', believing
that he 'has justly gained the kingdom by his conquest' (III.i.315–17).
Having reduced the trappings of Mandevillean romance to theatrical
properties, he begins thereafter 'to govern', as Letoy remarks, '[w]ith
purpose to reduce the manners / Of this country to his own' (III.i.320–
2). A vision of empire that reduces difference to likeness thus proves necessary for Peregrine's safe return to the domestic normalcy of Caroline
London from the strange lands in which he has travelled in thought.
To be exorcised of his 'Mandeville madness' (IV.i.466) – that is, to re-
possess himself – Peregrine must be induced to take possession of the
theatrical domain.

But possession is fraught with ambiguity since returning the self to its
proper place in The Antipodes also entails possession by something else
– and that 'something' is again the theatre. The cure for errant desire is
itself a bewitching, an appropriation of desire by the stage. If Peregrine
is to come home to himself after having travelled 'so far beyond himself'
(I.i.149), he can only do so by surrendering himself 'unawares' (I.i.28)
to the theatrical experience, ceding to theatre the power to set the coordinates of his desire and fantasy. Only then can his peregrinations cease.

This requirement also exposes, however, what seems monstrous about theatre, allying it with those Anthropophagi whom Othello associates in turn with the all-devouring Desdemona. For Peregrine's is only one of the plays being staged in *The Antipodes*. Intertwined is a second performance intended to rid his father Joyless of his jealous suspicions regarding his young spouse's fidelity. A sceptical onlooker to his son's drama, Joyless becomes an unwitting participant in an entertainment that seems designed to enable the nobleman Letoy to satisfy his carnal desire for Diana. In this theatrical frame, the cure is to be effected by showing the husband that his wife remains proof against Letoy's blandishments. And, indeed, this ploy does initially work, convincing Joyless of Diana's 'well-tried virtue' (V.ii.233). But when he accidentally stumbles upon the fact that Letoy's man Byplay had been given the order to place Joyless where he could witness his wife's steadfastness, jealousy returns in full force:

> Stay, stay, stay, stay!
> Why may not this be then a counterfeit action,
> Or a false mist to blind me with more error?
> The ill I feared may have been done before,
> And all this but deceit to daub it o'er.
>
> (V.ii.145–9)

Joyless is, of course, right in suspecting the possibility of further deceit: once the reality of the world is shown to be a theatrical illusion, there is no easy route back. If the Brome-an empire rests upon theatre's power to transform mental reality – a feature it shares with travel writing – the radical unmooring of the spectatorial position also reveals theatre's monstrous aspect. The play becomes a vortex, potentially engulfing not only the self but social reality itself. With Joyless's relapse, Brome's play raises the spectre of a theatre (and a world) gone mad.

At the last moment, the play veers away from the abyss it has opened up, through a final – and entirely unprepared for – turn: the revelation that Diana is actually Letoy's own daughter. This revelation restores Joyless's sanity, convincing him that his wife's resistance to Letoy was no performance staged for his benefit. And thus the evocation of a 'natural' horror (the monstrosity of incest) enters to bring the spiral of theatrical possession to a halt, re-drawing the line between theatre and reality. The taboo provides a mooring point outside the ever-expanding domain of the theatrical to which the possessed subject can be attached, in order to return him to self-possession. The re-anchoring of the self achieved, the kit and caboodle of the social world follow: the restoration of properly hierarchical marital, patriarchal, moral and political relationships (see, for example, Harmony's celebration of a well-ordered commonwealth in the play's concluding masque, V.ii.354–61). Theatrical pleasure is not denied, discord is not rejected, but rather receive their proper bounds within the commonwealth.

In this final swerve away from its dangerously spiralling plot, the play discloses another, crucial, dimension of early modern voyaging: the coupling of travel with an emerging global mercantilism, of wandering in strange lands with the errancies of money. For the vision of a theatre unleashed would find its fullest incarnation in the market:

> [T]he Prince with his subjects, the Master with his servants, one friend and acquaintance with another, the Captain with his soldiers, the Husband with his wife, Women with, and among them selves, and in a word, all the world choppeth and chaungeth, runneth and raveth after Marts, Markets and Merchandising, so that all things come into Commerce, and pass into Traffic (in a manner) in all times, and in all places: not only that, which Nature bringeth forth, as the fruits of the earth, the beasts and living creatures, with their spoils, skins and cases, the metals, minerals, & such like things, but further also, this man maketh merchandise of the works of his own hands, this man of another man's labour, one selleth words, another maketh traffic of the skins, and blood of other men, yea there are some fou[n]d so subtle and cunning merchants, that they persuade and induce men to suffer themselves to be bought and sold ... (Wheeler 1601: 6–7)

An older world peeps through this extended list from John Wheeler's 1601 *A Treatise of Commerce*, one whose operative distinctions are hierarchical (prince and subject, master and servant), patriarchal (husband and wife) and communal (among friends, acquaintances and women). But the qualitative distinctions among relationships are gradually being dissolved by the fluid logic of money and commodity circulation. The energy of the market resides in its omnivorous absorption of all the things in the world through which it makes its presence known and felt. Likewise, Brome's theatre expresses a fascination with – even as it shies away from – the superflux embodied by a global market: the vision of an inescapable space of exchange and possession, wherein people, things, identities, and attributes endlessly circulate, ceaselessly becoming other.

A contrast with Mandeville again proves instructive. Among the wonders of China that so impress him are the Great Khan's lavish expenditures. Mandeville seizes upon currency as an explanation:

> This emperor may dispend as much as he will without estimation, for he nought dispendeth nor maketh no money but out of leather imprinted or of

paper . . . And when that money hath run so long that it beginneth to waste, then men bear it to the emperor's treasury, and there they take new money for the old . . . And there and beyond . . . they make no money neither of gold nor silver, and therefore he may dispend enough and outrageously. (1968: 183)

For Mandeville, paper money appears to free the Emperor 'from the material limitations of coinage, that is, from the scarcity of gold and silver' (Greenblatt 1991: 37). Unlike coins, paper or leather money represents the possibility of an endless renewal of value. The fullness of value bespeaks in turn the fullness of authority, whose magnitude 'is constantly reaffirmed in the subjects' willingness to treat worthless objects as signs of wealth or tokens of exchange' (Greenblatt 1991: 37).

Mandeville's image of such expenditure without reserve finds its Brome-an correlate in Letoy's extravagant wooing of Diana, shortly before we discover she is his daughter.

Letoy Wouldst have gold?
Mammon nor Pluto's self should overbid me,
For I'd give all. First let me rain a shower
To outvie that which overwhelmed Danaë;
And after that another. A full river
Shall from my chests perpetually flow
Into thy store.

(V.ii.14–19)

Outdoing the Great Khan, Letoy commands in abundance not just the signs of wealth but the very materials embodying preciousness. Like the proverbial bounty of nature, the showers and rivers of his wealth 'perpetually flow'.

But this excess – and with it the arrogation of absolute power – Brome cannot allow, even as he fleetingly recognises that it inheres in the nature of both theatrical and monetary exchange. Indeed by the late 1630s the monetary limits on Caroline royal power would be all too visible, especially in the recurrent financial crises of the crown and its forced resort to unpopular forms of taxation and extortion for survival (see Butler 1984: 16). Brome's attacks elsewhere on sumptuous spectacles such as Sir John Suckling's privately-financed *Aglaura* (whose costumes allegedly cost £3000) reveal his own sense of a theatre and market gone mad, undermining the familiar checks and balances that gave the social world its coherence, its all too fragile harmony.

Not surprisingly, then, Diana's rejection of Letoy's rich immorality takes the form of monetary analysis:

Diana . . . [I] have not loathed the sight of it [wealth] until now
That you have soiled it, with that foul opinion
Of being the price of virtue. Though the metal
Be pure and innocent in itself, such use
Of it is odious, indeed damnable,
Both to the seller and the purchaser.
Pity it should be so abused. It bears
A stamp upon't, which but to clip is treason.
'Tis ill used there, where law the life controls;
Worse, where 'tis made a salary for souls.

                                                    (V.ii.20–9)

Diana's pejorative repetition of 'use' clearly evokes usury, and with it the spectre of a reprehensible exchange in which money illicitly begets more money. Unlike Mandeville fascinated by the Great Khan's magnificence, she expresses horror at the sheer multiplication of mere signs of value. Hence, she draws a crucial distinction between the intrinsic worth of a 'pure and innocent' metal and the supplementary worth it accrues through circulation. Money transforms into commodities what should remain outside all circulation: wealth is soiled by 'being the price of virtue', 'made a salary for souls'. To counter its threat, exchange and transformation must be held within rigid boundaries. And to this end, the King is unexpendable: his 'stamp' guarantees and underwrites the coin, ensuring that the buck stops somewhere.

As with money, so with the theatre. Its errancies and peregrinations into the strange recesses of the world and the human being prove both necessary and dangerous. Ultimately, the Antipodean theatre plants its feet back home, reaffirming through its very wanderings the stability of the world that made it possible. Of course, both theatre and King would be brought to a far more abrupt halt than Brome anticipated, Charles's stamp failing to save his head and theatre deviating too far from the vision of Cromwell's model society. But that is another story. In the wake of colonial expansion, relentlessly, the market would continue to grow, coming to control us more successfully than even a monarch might wish.

Can't Buy me Love: John Donne's 'Loves Progress'

Money and colonialism are central, too, to John Donne's bawdy elegy 'Loves Progress', which is built upon an extended analogy between colonial voyaging and traversal of the female body. Suppressed by the licenser from the 1633 edition of Donne's poetry, the poem has also largely escaped sustained critical study. Whereas the companion elegy 'To his Mistress Going to Bed' – which celebrates the woman's body as 'My America, my New-found-land' – has been much examined for how the provocative equation of physical consummation with religious ecstasy complicates its colonial metaphorics, 'Loves Progress' has seemed in comparison either too outrageous or too straightforward to warrant similar attention.

Catherine Belsey's remarks about 'To his Mistress' offer a valuable corrective to this neglect, and seem apposite for 'Loves Progress' as well. She argues for the impossibility of assigning a 'final authoritative meaning' to Donne's intertwining of love and colonial conquest. And this undecidability reveals a fundamental uncertainty regarding the object of desire itself. Is it, she asks, 'a woman, self-image, writing?'

> No wonder the worlds which were gradually opening up to the gaze of Renaissance explorers and cartographers seemed the appropriate emblem of desire. They were vast, these territories, perhaps limitless, and enticing, rich and beautiful. They were also dangerous, to the degree that they were uncharted both geographically and anthropologically. (1994: 148)

But this attractive suggestion still begs the question of what makes discovery of 'uncharted' lands the 'appropriate emblem' of desire? What, in other words, is the common space that enables the transference between gender and colonialism in many of Donne's elegies? To address these questions I focus on another set of similitudes operative in 'Loves Progress': the monetary tropes linking value to love or desire. For 'one of the ends of love assumed in this poem is the economic one. From the first, the sexual is defined in relation to commercial realities' (Marotti 1986: 50) – and specifically to nautical venturing:

> Whoever love, if hee doe not propose
> The right true end of love, hee's one which goes
> To sea for nothing but to make him sicke.
>
> (Donne 1967: ll. 1–3)

Indeed, the poem's opening section does not immediately posit an analogy between female body and discovered land, but rather likens one 'valued' object, the woman, to another, gold.

> I, when I value gold, may think upon
> The ductilness, the application,
> The wholsomness, the ingenuitie,
> From rust, from soil, from fire ever free:
> But if I love it, 'tis because 'tis made
> By our new nature (Use) the soul of trade.

All these in women we might think upon
(If women had them) and yet love but one.

(1967: ll. 11–17)

The contrast between 'value' and 'love' signals the presence of two competing modes of ascribing worth. We shall return to 'our new nature
(Use)' that Donne appears to favour. But let us first linger on the position these lines ostensibly reject: that the value of gold resides in such
properties as 'ductilness', 'application', 'wholsomness' and so forth.
This stance evokes an earlier – but still vital – theologically governed
understanding of money's function. According to this doctrine, money
could signify wealth only because as gold (or silver) it was precious in
itself; its functions rested on its intrinsic worth. Thus, for the fourteenth-
century thinker Nicole Oresme, money's utility for 'the mutual exchange
of naturall Riches' required that it be 'convenient to handle', and 'easy
to carry', properties that depended upon the metal being a concentrated
form of wealth or value that was not plentifully available, 'such that a
small portion of it might buy and exchange natural Riches in greater
quantity' (1924: 82–3).

Scholastic discussions of money nevertheless contained a crucial fault-
line: the need to coordinate the worth of the material – the metal from
which money was made – with the coin's face value. For, as we have
seen in *The Antipodes*, precious metal only became money through the
'face' stamped upon it, constituting it as coin and guaranteeing its value.
If money could measure value, this was because it stood for the prince's
authority, which was in turn underwritten by a divine dispensation. In
late medieval monetary thought, then, it was necessary that the royal
impress or sign marking the metal coincide with the referent, that is,
with the metal's intrinsic preciousness, deposited in it by God. 'Loves
Progress', too, hints at a similar theological basis for determining value:
to 'value' gold leads to 'think[ing] upon' those physical characteristics
of the metal that, taken together, establish intrinsic worth in terms of
an immutable, quasi-divine purity ('from rust, from soil, from fire ever
free').

This complex play between metallic content and visible form evokes
the need for a third term which Michel Foucault perceives in sixteenth-
century European thought. Just as knowledge of any natural object
was predicated upon some similitude between it and another object,
fixing the value of money depended upon correlating the quantity of
precious metal in the coin with its nominal value (the stamp). But for
the resemblance between two objects to be recognisable, a 'signature'

was required, which took the form of another resemblance. In a similar fashion, establishing the conformity between stamped money and the quantity of metal it contained called for a further correlation: the relationship between the coin and some commodity for which it could be exchanged. The impress which the metal bears, in other words, ought to signify transparently its intrinsic 'preciousness'. But to 'recognise' this sign – to know what value it represents – one has to relate the metal, via exchange, to a determinate quantity of some other commodity, whose value in turn depends upon a similar relationship to other commodities (see Foucault 1973: 172ff.).

This potentially infinite oscillation between metal and merchandise was arrested by laying down an absolute correlation between the total amount of gold buried in the earth and the totality of existing things through which all human needs could be satisfied. Thus, according to Bernardo Davanzati's *Le Lezione delle Monete* (1588), if we had God-like perception, we could simply establish

> each day the rule and mathematical proportions that exist between things and between things and gold . . . [A]nd we would say: there is upon earth so much gold, so many things, so many needs; and to the degree that each thing satisfies needs, its value shall be so many things, or so much gold. (quoted in Foucault 1973: 172)

'Loves Progress' mockingly invokes just such an exhaustive cosmic calculation as it elaborates upon the outrageous relationship between gold and the beloved:

> Search every sphear
> And firmament, our Cupid is not there:
> He is an infernal god and under ground,
> With Pluto dwells, where gold and fire abound;
> Men to such Gods, their sacrificing Coles
> Did not in Altars lay, but pits and holes:
> Although we see Celestial bodies move
> Above the earth, the earth we Till and love . . .
> (Donne 1967: ll. 27–33)

What is sought – that is, what satisfies male desire – lies within the female body, just as gold remains buried within the earth. Projected here is a fixed correspondence between what one prays for and what 'till[ing]' unearths. Moving from firmament to the earth's caves and mines ('pits and holes'), the speaker parodies the macrocosmic structure which for Davanzati ultimately underwrote the 'rule and mathematical proportion' between things and gold.

Rejecting as inadequate valuation based upon properties intrinsic to gold or women (wholesomeness, purity, and so on), 'Loves Progress' embraces instead a language of 'love' or desire. It thereby reveals a different understanding of value, one that focuses on gold's place within a circuit of exchange: if he 'love[s]' gold, it is, as the speaker tells us, 'because 'tis made / By our new nature (Use) the soul of trade'. 'What Donne alone among the poets seemed to sense was that within his lifetime money itself had become a commodity' (Freer 1996: 501). Rather than locating money's dual function (as measure of 'natural riches' and instrument of exchange) in the 'double nature of its intrinsic *character* (the fact that it was precious)' (Foucault 1973: 174), Donne inverts the analysis just as the seventeenth-century mercantilists would do. Money's exchanging function (what Donne calls 'Use' or the 'soul of trade') becomes foundational: 'The value of things ... no longer proceed[s] from the metal itself ... the metal merely enables value to be represented, as a name represents an image or an idea, yet does not constitute it' (Foucault 1973: 176).

If revoking the criterion of intrinsic worth means that any substance can in theory serve as money, in practice the chosen substance must nonetheless possess properties that will allow it to compare the values of different commodities. In this sense, the physical properties of gold which Donne enumerates testify less to an inner 'perfection' than to a capacity to *represent* value. Since gold is malleable, imperishable and of concentrated weight, it is ideally suited to stand for the value of other commodities in the exchange process. But these physical attributes do not in themselves make gold precious; rather they merely enable gold to discharge a representational task.

I am suggesting that this transformation in what constitutes the nature of (economic) value, partially spurred by colonial venturing, permeates Donne's erotic poetry; it provides the matrix within which 'Loves Progress' locates gender and colonialism in relationship to one another. Donne reverses the moral hierarchy, making the once-essential 'virtues' of the metallic substance merely incidental. 'True value' results from a desire that only gold's use as an instrument of exchange can provoke. Such an inversion provides the basic structure informing, first, the analogy between gold and woman, and, subsequently, the descriptions of colonial voyaging over the female body.

In the case of 'woman', too, the characteristics that ostensibly comprise her worth – virtue, wisdom, beauty, goodness, and even wealth – are dismissed as incidental properties.

Makes virtue woman? Must I cool my blood
Till I both be, and find one wise and good?
May barren Angels love so. But if we
Make love to a woman; virtue is not she:
As beauty's not nor wealth: He that strayes thus
From her to hers, is more adulterous,
Then if he took her maid . . .
Although we see Celestial bodies move
Above the earth, the earth we Till and love:
So we her ayres contemplate, words and heart,
And virtues; but we love the Centrique part.

(Donne 1967: l. 21ff.)

Unlike gold, the woman may not in fact possess these qualities, but even if she did, they would simply be contingent attributes; they do not 'make' her. Just as money's value accrues from 'our new nature (Use) the soul of trade', woman's value is conferred upon her by her sexual use: her desirability depends upon the sexual availability that is embodied as the 'centrique part'.

'Loves Progress' further extends this analysis directly to the colonial frame. For the reversal enacted in the poem's treatment of gold and woman subsequently envelops the analogy between the woman's body and the to-be-colonised spaces sought by European explorers. In describing how to 'attain[] this desired place', the 'centrique part', Donne contrasts two modes of traversing the female body: the physical act of voyaging and the charting of a map route. The difference between these approaches corresponds to changes in how space was conceptualised during the early modern period. In describing the (mistaken) attempt of 'set[ting] out at the face' to work one's way from the known to the unknown and unseen, the speaker draws upon the practical navigational methods available in late-medieval Europe, and specifically the spatial practices of the so-called portolan charts. These were essentially plots of routes drawn by sailors in order to journey over relatively short distances, generally confined to the Mediterranean basin and small stretches of the Atlantic coastlines. Used in conjunction with a compass rose and plumblines, and normally drawn on durable material such as sheepskin, these pictorial aids preserved sailors' local knowledge and represented space as if one were travelling through it. They thus subordinated geometrical relationships to an experiential movement through space: like the practice of voyaging itself, the portolans followed the actual routes taken, sketching coastlines and landmarks. The navigator oriented himself by recognising a particular monument, place, or curve of land; he relied on visible signs confirming experiential knowledge (such as the direction of winds and waves, or the nature of the seabed as revealed by the plumb-line).

For Donne's speaker, journeys of this kind are always in danger of an illusory fixation on a particular place. One who voyages by beginning at the woman's face to travel towards 'her India' will be distracted and ultimately blocked by the various anatomical places encountered en route. The risk inherent in such explorations is that of error, of straying or being forced to stray from the fixed orientation toward its goal. Thus, the hair 'ambushes' the traveller, the brow alternately 'shipwrecks' and 'becalms' the sailor: the woman's body as voyaged space is a space of detours, deterrents, deflections.

Access to 'India' requires an additional representational aid: a picture that transparently renders the entirety visible at a single glance, allowing the voyager to evade the body's resistance. This attitude towards space derives from the emergent cartography, which related places geographically, against a background of homogeneous, geometricised space. Within 'Loves Progress', too, the early modern map plays a critical role. For, given the 'Symetry' it 'hath with that part / Which thou dost seek', the foot functions as 'thy Map for that' 'desired place'. To follow the shape of the foot – that is, to chart one's route upon a map as one initiates the journey – is to take advantage of the essential emptiness of space: 'for as Free Spheres move faster far then can / Birds, whom the air resists, so may that man / Which goes this empty and Aetherial way, / Then if at beauties elements he stay' (87–90). The rather unexpected symmetry between the foot and the sexualised place sought by the voyager derives from bilingual punning, which Shakespeare's *Henry V* would make explicit in the famous scene where Katherine learns the English conqueror's language. Her shock at the 'mauvais, corruptible, gros et impudique' English language comes from associating the word 'foot' with its lewder French homophone which is the speaker's ostensible concern in 'Love's Progress' (see Corthell 1997: 69).

We can encapsulate in tabular form the contrast operative between the conditions for mere 'valuing' and those for 'loving' (to use Donne's terms) in each of the domains discussed above:

	Money (gold)	Woman ('centrique part')	Colonial Space ('India')
'Value'	physical properties	moral and physical virtues	practice of voyaging
'Love'	exchangeability	sexual usability	mapping of space

As the table indicates, gold or money provides the metaphoric structure that the poem reiterates in its treatment of gender and colonial discovery.

However, Donne's analysis goes beyond the structural homology captured in this table. That the female body and the colonial voyages become the fields upon which to renegotiate the problem of value is consequent upon a more complex diagnosis: the poem treats them not only as figures for a shared problematic, but also integrally associates them with a crisis in valuation. For all his characteristic playfulness, Donne does not simply wittily reject an earlier, theologically governed conception of monetary value for an emerging 'modern' one. Beyond the arch figural analogies derived from the problem of monetary value, 'Loves Progress' sees 'woman' and 'colonial discovery' as themselves participating in, and indeed even triggering, a wider uncertainty regarding authority. It thus seems no accident that a concern with coinage repeatedly reappears in Donne's more orthodox, religiously-oriented writings that present spiritual conflicts in comprehensible, material terms. In the 1622 sermon to the Virginia Company, for example, Donne draws upon metaphors akin to those in 'Loves Progress' to warn the would-be adventurers not to expect a speedy return on their investments, despite God's promise that the 'kingdom' beyond the seas will be theirs. Representing the temporal kingdom of the colony as the potential instantiation of the promised, divine kingdom, Donne uses coinage both as the perfect sign of value and to indicate the arduous material process by which value is created (see Donne 1987: 197).

In the case of colonial voyaging, a relatively direct causation prevails between money and the perception of a crisis in valuation. The initial impetus for viewing money as a commodity like any other derived from the growth of the market in late-medieval Europe and, especially, the importance of debasement of coinage as an expedient means of generating royal revenue. But for this nascent understanding of money's commodity character to take hold, another historical event would be necessary: the sudden influx of precious metals from Spain's colonial expansion. This development impelled contemporary observers to posit an economic link between the perceived dearness of commodities in parts of Europe and the massive dissemination of New World gold and silver. The French political theorist Jean Bodin was among the earliest explicitly to articulate the connection. 'I find', he writes in 1568, 'that . . . the principal & almost only' cause for 'the high prices we see today . . . is the abundance of gold & silver' (1924: 127). The reason for this abundance is colonialism:

[The] Portuguese . . . made himself master of the Gulf of Persia . . . & by this means filled his vessels with the wealth of the Indies & of fruitful

Arabia . . . At the same time the Castilian, having gained control of the new lands full of gold & silver, filled Spain with them . . . It is incredible, and yet true, that there have come from Peru since the year 1533, when it was conquered by the Spaniards, more than a hundred millions of gold, & twice as much silver. (1924: 129)

By the time the earliest English mercantilist tracts appeared around 1600, Bodin's explanation had become widely accepted. Thus Gerrard Malynes's treatise – aimed at remedying the 'diseased' state of England's balance of trade – eschews discussion of 'fineness, weight and proportion' to consider instead the 'property of the money, or the effects thereof'. The emphasis on money's commodity character leads him without further ado to the colonial sphere: 'whereunto the great store or abundance of monie and bullion, which of late years is come from the west Indies into Christendom, hath made every thing dearer according to the increase of monie, which . . . hath caused a great alteration and inhauncing of the price of every thing . . .' (Malynes in Tawney and Power 1962: 3.387).

English mercantilist texts further rework a traditional physiological trope: the metaphor that money was to a society what blood was to the body. Patricia Fumerton's rich reading of seventeenth-century English economic tracts shows how mercantilist texts regularly conceived of trade and commodities in terms of corporeality (1991: 174–95; see also Gil Harris 2004). For example, during a downturn in colonial trade, London merchant Lewes Roberts accuses absentee farmers of failing to produce goods for market, allowing tenants to 'suck and draw . . . the present profit and daily benefit' of their estates, 'eating up the heart and marrow of the same, with greedy art' (in McCulloch 1970: 62). Through such metaphors, the movement of commodities becomes linked to consumption and venous circulation: the buying and selling of goods drives money – the blood – all across the social body. And in proposing solutions to the nation's financial crises, too, the metaphor of the diseased body remains central, as does the monetary cure: the reformation of currency transactions to ensure that 'the Canker of this exchange shall not consume [the merchants], as it hath done many of them and others, and that unawares' (Malynes in Tawney and Power 1962: 3.400).

Donne's poetry demonstrates an acute, prescient grasp of such material transformations; it insists that, by changing the nature of value, commodification and circulation of precious metals ends up undermining existing social arrangements. In 'The Bracelet', for example, Donne expertly links money to religion and politics, attacking those 'Spanish Stamps' which, 'still travelling',

> are become as Catholique as their King,
> Those unlickt bear-whelps, unfil'd pistolets
> . . .
> Which, as the soul quickens head, feet, and heart,
> As streams, like veins, run through th'earth's every part,
> Visit all countries, and have slyly made
> Gorgeous France, ruin'd, ragged and decay'd,
> Scotland, which knew no state, proud in one day,
> And mangled seventeen-headed Belgia.
>
> (Donne 1967: l. 29ff.)

Implicit here is the sense that Spanish colonial gains do not remain confined to Spain's domains; rather, through trade this illegitimate bullion venously circulates 'through th' earth's every part', drastically altering the political and religious body of Europe. At the same time, money's circulation remains inevitable, since the flow of money 'quickens' these lands even as it 'mangle[s]' their character. This double sense marks, perhaps, the continuation of a late-medieval anxiety that saw money both as necessary for society and as a corrosive that ate into social bonds (see Kaye 1998: 52–3). The terms of Donne's response are, however, very different: the poem's indignation is spurred not just by a theory of social (or divine) justice, but by the material circumstances of a changing world.

'Go[ing] to sea' in pursuit of the 'right true end of love', the speaker of 'Loves Progress' draws upon the connection between the effects of colonial voyaging and 'our new nature (Use) the soul of trade'. Journeying to 'both the Indias of spice and Myne' – to borrow a famous phrase from Donne's 'The Good-morrow' – has led, the elegy implies, to a transformation of both the desiring subject and the object of his desire. If 'sailing towards her India' retraces the trade routes opened up by European colonial powers, this is because the desired object has become valuable through its exchangeability or commodification ('Use'), just as the speaker's own desire has been re-animated by the 'soul of trade'. Colonialism transforms the 'nature' of money, which in turn redefines the 'nature' of value. To acquire what is valuable, then, demands that one imitate the process by which value accrues to things, that is, adopt the colonial voyage as the model for attaining the desired end. And thus the speaker voyages over the commodified female body that (for him) most perfectly embodies trade.

Revolutions that Have no Model: Christopher Marlowe's *Tamburlaine* plays

The rise of early modern colonial/postcolonial studies has spurred a renewed interest in Christopher Marlowe's *Tamburlaine the Great* plays. This is not surprising. The sheer geographical range of these two plays – which traverse a wide array of territories in Europe, North Africa and the East – offers a variegated picture of early modern Islamic and Christian worlds. But they also speak to a theme central to this study: an imaginative, global desire best captured in the dying conqueror's own words, when he describes on a map what he has achieved – as well what remains yet undone:

> Here I began to march towards Persia,
> Along Armenia and the Caspian Sea,
> And thence unto Bithynia, where I took
> The Turk and his great empress prisoners.
> Then march'd I into Egypt and Arabia;
> And here, not from Alexandria,
> Whereas the Terrene and the Red Sea meet,
> Being distant less than full a hundred leagues,
> I meant to cut a channel to them both,
> That men might quickly sail to India.
> . . .
> Look here, my boys; see, what a world of ground
> Lies westward from the midst of Cancer's line
> Unto the rising of this earthly globe,
> Whereas the sun, declining from our sight,
> Begins the day with our Antipodes!
> And shall I die, and this unconquered?
>
> (*Tamburlaine II*, V.iii.127ff.)

Roughly a century after the Portuguese discovery of a sea route to India, Tamburlaine imagines a Renaissance Suez Canal linking the Mediterranean to the Red Sea. Only in the nineteenth century would this vision be rendered real (along with a new set of colonial politics). Despite his own failure, however, the imperialist ethos Tamburlaine expresses is undeniably grand in scope and ambition.

And to this ethos critics have responded, tracing with increasing specificity its colonial underpinnings as well as the strange ambivalence with which the *Tamburlaine* plays seem to regard their eponymous hero. Emily Bartels, for instance, sees them as self-consciously contradictory works. Their imperialistic drive consumes itself in its unfolding, as the characters 'unfix the critical differences that they attempt to fix' (Bartels 1993: 81). Likewise, Marjorie Garber asserts that the imperialist Tamburlaine who re-writes geography with his sword is 'unwritten' by another act of writing: the one undertaken by Marlowe's pen, which 'throws Tamburlaine's ... struggles into an increasingly ironic light' (Garber 1984: 303). Complaining that such readings ignore 'the material investment of Londoners in the eastern ventures of their own exotic agents' (1995: 54), Richard Wilson instead perceives a prospectus for an emergent mercantile capitalism, expressing the current concerns of the English Muscovy Company. He argues that the titular character conforms to contemporary descriptions of Tsar Ivan IV, a despot upon whose support English commercial expansion into Persia and the Levant depended (1995: 47–68; see also Cartelli 1991: 80ff and Levin 1952: 55). The kind of historicism espoused by Wilson has become almost normative, as is evidenced by the plethora of interpretations stressing the plays' dependence upon the nuances of England's relationship to the Ottoman empire and early modern Near East (see, for example, Riggs 2004; Burton 2005; Robinson 2007; Vitkus 2003; and Hopkins 2008).

In choosing *Tamburlaine the Great* as my final case study, I do not seek either to overturn these interpretations or to propose yet another historicist alternative. Rather, I wish to advance a speculative reading that attends to the explosive, transformational force Tamburlaine embodies, to the energy which is finally transmuted into the frustrated, plaintive desire voiced in the lines above: 'And shall I die, and this unconquered?' That energy expresses, I suggest, a utopian drive at the heart of early modern colonialism. In it we glimpse, if only fleetingly, a very different (and ultimately unsustainable) comportment to the social world, one that always threatens to escape or to break open the rationalist, strategic side of the imperial mission. If the institutions and practices established by European nation states constitute an enduring aspect of early modern colonialisms, the horizon opened particularly by Part I of *Tamburlaine the Great* may be characterised by its radical exteriority to such forms. To develop this counter-principle at the core of the colonial, I draw on the grand opposition proffered by Gilles Deleuze and Feliz Guattari in *A Thousand Plateaus*: the dualism of the Nomad and the State (1987: 351–423).

In Marlowe's play, the State is embodied by diverse Kings, Emperors, Governors and Sultans. What these various figures express is the plane of Law. The State establishes the codes of conduct intended to regulate behaviour. It is an apparatus of control built upon what George Dumézil posits as the two opposed, intertwined poles of sovereignty:

the mythic founding of power, and the legislative and juridical organisation constituted by the bonds connecting individual subjects (1988:
95ff.). *Tamburlaine*'s opening scene echoes Dumézil's distinction
when Mycetes, the ineffectual King of Persia, asks whether he 'might
command' his brother to be slain for mocking him (Part I, I.i.23). The
magical dimension of sovereignty grounds a notion of absolute power;
as Mycetes then re-iterates, 'I mean it not, yet I know I might' (I.i.26).
The language of absolute potency reverberates through the play. Recall,
for example, Bajazeth's grandiose self-conception as a power before
whose magnificence 'all flesh quakes' and 'tremble[s]', before whose
breath 'all the trees are blasted', and before whose 'smothering host'
'spring is hindered . . . / For neither rain can fall upon the earth, / Nor
the sun reflex his virtuous beams thereon' (Part I, III.i.50ff.). By contrast, the Persian Lord Meander's response to Mycetes – 'Not for so
small a fault, my sovereign lord' (I.i.25) – hints at the opposing pole: a
juridical organisation that constrains the actual exercise of sovereignty.
The tension between these conjoint impulses is suggested by the barely
audible pun in Mycetes' query whether he 'might command' Cosroe's
death: 'might' as the absolute power to impose sovereign will collides
here with 'might' as an index of the need for permission (emphasising
limits on the exercise of power).

From these leaders' perspective, the nomadic Tamburlaine marks a
negation of the State. Meander describes him as 'the sturdy Scythian
thief' who 'in your confines with his lawless train / Daily commits uncivil
outrages' (I: I.i.36ff.). The 'confines' of the State are identified with the
Law, eliciting a description of Tamburlaine's actions as 'uncivil' and
'lawless'. For the representatives of Persia, he is a 'fox in the midst of har-
vest-time', which 'doth prey upon my flocks of passengers' (I: I.i.31–2).
Into the domesticated spaces of the civis and farm, Tamburlaine erupts
from without, and can be understood only as the opposite of what these
spaces connote. Tamburlaine's Scythian origins are also significant, since
the association of Scythia with barbarity has itself a long lineage, going
back to Herodotus' *Histories*. That classical retelling of the conflict
between Greece and Persia – the two most powerful state formations of
the ancient Mediterranean world – is crucially framed by its speculations
upon the nomadic barbarians called the Scythians, who live beyond the
pale of civilisation (see Hartog 1988). These threatening people express
an absolute exteriority, their modes of life standing radically outside the
confines of the settled state forms with which Herodotus is familiar.

Consequently, even Tamburlaine's army appears radically different,
its form understandable only in terms of what State armies are not:

Merciless villain, peasant ignorant
Of lawful arms or martial discipline!
Pillage and murder are his usual trades.
The slave usurps the glorious name of war.

(I: IV.i.64–7)

The Sultan of Egypt collapses diverse forms of differentiation internal
to the State in order to define Tamburlaine and render him comprehensible. Class hierarchy ('slave', 'villain', 'peasant'); the distinction
between illegal and legal acts (murder and pillage versus the sanctioned
violence of state armies); discipline against indiscipline: all these oppositions combine to cast Tamburlaine as the negation of what the State
represents.

In fact, the charge of indiscipline and disorder plagues Tamburlaine
throughout, despite his providing much evidence to the contrary. Whereas
State armies are associated with precise formations, ordered ranks, and
honour, Tamburlaine's forces are seen as epitomising dispersal, disorder and greed. Facing the Scythian army, the Persians unknowingly
invert Tamburlaine's own strategy, flinging gold across the battlefield
'to entrap these thieves / That live confounded in disordered troops'.
Meander imagines 'the base-born Tartars' taking up the treasure, while
the Persians 'fighting more for honour than for gold, / Shall massacre
those greedy minded slaves'. Ironically, the plan is meant to ensure that
the gold returns as reward to the royal army: 'And when their scattered
army is subdued, / And you march on their slaughtered carcasses, / Share
equally the gold that bought their lives / And live like gentlemen in Persia'
(I: II.ii.60ff.). The word 'scattered' bears a double weight, referring
both to how Meander envisions the conflict's end (when carcasses will
be strewn randomly across the field) as well as to Tamburlaine's army,
portrayed as the antithesis of the compact Persian formation that hopes
to 'march' over the corpses. Repeatedly in the play Tamburlaine's army
is called a 'swarm'; he himself is characterised as a pack animal ('the
wolf that Themis sent', I: IV.iii.5); identified with the bestial ('savage
Calydonian boar', I: IV.iii.3), the inhuman and uncivil; accused of being
ignorant of the laws of arms, honour, and martial discipline.

The play, however, self-consciously refuses to see Tamburlaine solely
as the State's negation. Rather, his difference from the rulers he subju-
gates marks him as fundamentally outside what the State represents and
demands. Thus, Deleuze and Guattari's description of the Nomad, the
essence of the war machine, seems particularly apt: 'It is not enough',
they suggest,

to affirm that the war machine is external to the apparatus [of the State]. It is necessary to reach the point of conceiving the war machine as itself a pure form of exteriority, whereas the State apparatus constitutes the form of interiority we habitually take as a model, or according to which we are in the habit of thinking. (1987: 354)

This radical exteriority becomes visible in Marlowe's play first and foremost as a short-circuit between the language of description and its referent. For example, Menaphon's portrait of a near divine figure, 'so large of limbs, his joints so strongly knit, / Such breadth of shoulders as might mainly bear / Old Atlas' burden' (I: II.i.9–11), ends in a tautology: 'In every part proportioned like the man / Should make the world subdued to Tamburlaine' (I: II.i.29–30). The truest description of the object turns out to be the object itself (see also the circularity of Cosroe's praise, I: II.i.31–2). Descriptions of Tamburlaine regularly invoke paradoxes, expressing the impossibility of containing him within a consistent representation. Consider the curious ambiguity that dogs Theridamas' recital of his reasons for following Tamburlaine: 'And that made me join with Tamburlaine, / For he is gross and like the massy earth / That moves not upward, nor by princely deeds / Doth mean to soar above the highest sort' (I: II.vii.31–3). It takes several readings to grasp the logic of Theridamas' syntax: the 'he' lines refers not to Tamburlaine but to any person who – unlike Tamburlaine – fails to aspire upwards beyond his earthly station. And yet, the pronoun's contiguity with the name leads us to think that the referent is indeed Tamburlaine. The net effect is that Tamburlaine is characterised through mutually exclusive opposites (earth/heaven, massy/aspiring, below/above, and so on).

It is no surprise therefore that Tamburlaine's actions remain incomprehensible even to his followers: they cannot judge, they can only follow or be swept along in the nomad's movement. When Tamburlaine decides to turn against Cosroe, his erstwhile ally, for the sake of 'novelty' (I: II.v.73) and 'pretty jest' (I: II.v.90), his vexed companion, Theridamas, demurs: 'A jest to charge on twenty thousand men? / I judge the purchase more important far' (I: II.v.91–2). But, as Tamburlaine immediately points out, the end-driven action of 'purchasing' empire or state power is alien to his calculus: 'Judge by thyself, Theridamas, not me' (I: II.v.93).

Indeed, despite his famous speech extolling the 'perfect bliss and sole felicity, / The sweet fruition of an earthly crown' (I: II.vii.28–9), Tamburlaine does not seem to care much for what crowns typically represent; they function for him, rather, as mere objects whose meaning he determines through his encounters with their bearers. When

Tamburlaine crowns his subordinates at the feast preceding the sack of Damascus, the crowns enter as a 'second course', described by the conqueror as the 'cates you [that is, Techelles, Usumcasane and Theridamas] desire to finger' (I: IV.iv.114–15). The play thereby literalises the earlier metaphors of 'ripest fruit' and 'sweet fruition' by transforming the crowns into comestibles. The 'usual' meaning of the word has become something simply to be fingered and consumed.

Tamburlaine's radical exteriority becomes even clearer when we examine space and geography. Beginning with Ethel Seaton's influential study (1924), Marlowe's interest in cartography has been well documented. *Tamburlaine I* delights in place-names, imaginatively reshaping the physical world through maps. However, the conqueror's attitude towards geographic space and cartography have been rather too quickly assimilated to the usual narratives concerning European colonial discovery and appropriation – either as reflection or critique. Let us pursue instead Deleuze and Guattari's suggestion that nomads 'have no history; they only have a geography' (1987: 393). In Tamburlaine's case, history remains hardly more than a place-name, Scythia, coupled with the gesture of a breaking from historical origins in the name of freedom. Thus, he must, he tells Zenocrate, 'maintain [his] life exempt from servitude', casting off 'the weeds' he 'disdains to wear' for the 'complete armour and . . . curtle axe' that 'more beseem' him (I: I.ii.41–3). What defines him consequently is a relationship to space, to geography, announced in the redolence of place-names throughout.

But here, too, the attitude of the Kings and Princes to their domains appears rather different from Tamburlaine's comprehension of spatiality. Cosroe, for instance, is inundated by the names of domains, as he prepares to usurp his brother's throne:

> We here do crown thee [Cosroe] monarch of the East,
> Emperor of Asia and of Persia,
> Great lord of Media and Armenia,
> Duke of Africa and Albania,
> Mesopotamia and of Parthia,
> East India and the late discovered isles,
> Chief lord of all the wide, vast Euxine Sea,
> And of the ever-raging Caspian lake.
>
> (I: I.i.161–7)

In these litanies echo the multiplication of titles by European colonial powers, and in particular, the Iberian monarchs. These moments exemplify how state power is asserted (in theory at least) over closed domains, within and in relation to established structures of sovereign authority. Doubtless, such acquisition of territory demands war, but 'an institutionalised, regulated coded war, with a front, a rear, battles' (Deleuze and Guattari 1987: 353). Tamburlaine embodies a dramatically different principle: rather than being directed at capturing state power, his movement through space is defined by encounters which occur wherever he happens to be, wherever he perceives an obstacle to overcome. (Hence the arbitrariness of his turning against Cosroe, for a 'pretty jest'.) What matters is the dynamic 'of arraying oneself in an open space, of holding space, of maintaining the possibility of springing up at any point; the movement is not from one point to another, but becomes perpetual, without aim or destination, without departure or arrival' (Deleuze and Guattari 1987: 353).

This insight suggests a re-reading of the justly famous moment when Tamburlaine imaginatively remaps the world :

> I will confute those blind geographers
> That make a triple region of the world,
> Excluding regions which I mean to trace,
> And with this pen reduce them to a map,
> Calling the provinces, cities and towns,
> After my name and thine, Zenocrate.
> Here at Damascus will I make the point
> That shall begin the perpendicular.
>
> (I: IV.iv.81–8)

If Tamburlaine here rejects the so-called T-O maps of the past 'that make a triple region of the world', he does not exactly replace them with more up-to-date Ortelian maps, which envision a geometricised space upon which the true geographical location of places can be marked. Nor does he offer the normative colonialist investment in such a map, namely, as an instrument which enables the voyager to delineate routes connecting two fixed points: the places of departure and arrival, the place to buy and the place to sell, home and away. Rather, for Tamburlaine, though the 'points' constitute the paths he takes, they remain strictly subordinated to the lines drawn by his 'pen' which 'traces' the movement, renaming and re-creating places at will. The choice of Damascus, consequently, is entirely contingent: the first meridian will be drawn through that city because he happens to be there; it is the place to which the trajectory of encounters against the State has brought him.

Space thus becomes a matter of flows, following a smooth, un-striated terrain, wherever it leads, overcoming resistances wherever encountered.

If Tamburlaine takes hold of space, it is only to relinquish its actual possession to others (his followers). The hint that such nomadic movement also lay at the heart of European colonial discovery can be discerned in the repeated evocation in its writings and images of the pressures of the material world itself: the winds, the currents, the eddies. But in Abraham Ortelius' famous world map, for example, such nomadic openness has already been implicitly re-coded as colonial domain (through dotted routes and the seals of states). As representation, the mapped world returns to the circuit of the State. By contrast, the redundant, exuberant naming characteristic of Tamburlaine's map denies such coded differentiation, treating space instead as the realm of contingency which can be re-territorialised at any point, for any reason.

It remains to ask what effect the nomad has. This question returns us to the ethical force behind the mighty dualism of Nomad and State. Fredric Jameson's subtle reading of Deleuze and Guattari's *A Thousand Plateaus* allows us to envision what is at stake in *Tamburlaine I*: the production of 'great prophecy'.

> When indeed the ideological is lifted out from its everyday dualistic and ethical space and generalised into the cosmos, it undergoes a dialectical transformation and the unaccustomed voice of great prophecy emerges, in which ethics and ideology, along with the dualism itself, are transfigured. Perhaps it is best to read the opposition between the Nomads and the state in that way: as reterritorialisation by way of the archaic, and as distant thunder . . . of the return of myth and the call of utopian transfiguration. (Jameson 1999: 34)

The clearest signs of this prophetic dimension appear in the play's persistent identification of Tamburlaine with futurity: 'For 'will' and 'shall',' as he himself insists, 'best fitteth Tamburlaine' (I: III.iii.41). What Tamburlaine promises is transfiguration, a new creation out of the destruction of what went before. The connection between reshaping and destroying the world is inescapable, the plays insist. Certainly, this connection can be read as undermining the very ethos Tamburlaine expresses. As Diana Henderson has argued, Marlovian rhetoric confronts the future conditional of lyric promise with the present of a history that always and brutally renders such promise unrealisable (1995: 123). In the first part of Tamburlaine, too, the conqueror's promise to give Zenocrate 'garments . . . of Median silk / Enchased with precious jewels', and 'milk white harts upon an ivory sled' to draw her 'amidst the frozen pools' (I: I.ii.95ff.) is mocked by what he actually gives her: 'Damascus' walls dyed with Egyptian blood', 'Streets strowed with the dissevered joints of men / And wounded bodies gasping yet for life' (I: V.i.321ff.). The fulfilment of promise, the possibility of radical transfiguration, emerges only from its negative side, out of the horrors of revolution.

But such violence nonetheless bespeaks a different ethics, one beyond, as it were, good and evil. Recall, for example, the pitiless killing of the four virgins of Damascus. In considering their fate, it is important not to forget that their being sacrificed has as much to do with the putatively rational politics of state power as with Tamburlaine's brutality. Not only does the First Virgin chide the Governor of Damascus for ignoring 'humble suits or imprecations' (I: V.i.24) 'whiles only danger beat upon our walls' (I: V.i.30), but the Governor himself admits that his obduracy was the product of a rational calculus that 'weighed' 'your honours, liberties and lives' 'in equal care and balance with our own' (I: V.i.40ff.). These explanations may sound reasonable, but we need to recognise, too, that they belong to a different order from Tamburlaine's. He proceeds instead according to an arbitrary, strict semiotic code that exceeds this rational calculus: white for mercy, red for blood and battle, black for death. As the detailed stage directions emphasise, the code must be followed rigorously, but without pleasure in its results: '[Enter] Tamburlaine all in black, and very melancholy'.

No doubt, these colours have their own symbolic associations. Not only does Tamburlaine's messenger explain the sequence, but each colour has its own resonances in the play. For instance, white – ostensibly signifying 'mildness of mind' (I: IV.i.52) – also refers to Zenocrate (as is borne out by the milk-white harts and ivory sleds Tamburlaine gives her). But the significations of colours are never consistent either. So, white is also invoked by Mycetes in a very different way, when he expresses anticipatory delight at seeing his 'milk white steeds . . . / All loaden with the heads of killed men' (I: I.i.77–8). In short, whatever the discrete symbolic associations conveyed by these colours, they are insufficient to explain the rigour of the sequence itself, let alone Tamburlaine's refusal to deviate from the pattern despite Zenocrate's pleas.

What Tamburlaine reveals in such flashes is a transformative drive that exceeds normal frames of representation and their constitutive dualisms: rebel or pervert, atheist or Christian, individual or State, anti-imperialist or proto-colonialist. Neither is his vision oblivious to costs, to the singularity of violence that accompanies transfiguration. And thus it leaves us not with the comfort of having fought and won the right fight, but with the unrelieved ambiguity that only the future can make the judgement (and will, in different and competing ways) by turning the present into history. For us, viewing Tamburlaine's picture in 'this tragic glass', we can only 'applaud his fortunes as we please'. At the same time, the play extracts a response through its rhetorical force, the reverberations of a language that demands response, be it engagement or rejection. For surely this pressure to respond lies at the heart of the play's ethic: so that even when we most forget Marlowe, the 'distant thunder' of Tamburlaine's 'mighty line' harries us into memory, reminding us of tasks too difficult to fulfil and yet too important to ignore.

As I have suggested in Chapter 1, colonialism's material instantiation as a state activity enables a retrospective identification of the colonial dimensions within earlier periods. It is not surprising, then, that the nineteenth century would recognise the driving force and the yearning for an unforeseeable, radically new future so vividly captured by Tamburlaine – and would recognise, too, the presence of that utopian energy in early modern colonial discovery. In *Middlemarch*, the fiery Will Ladislaw, who energetically opposes the injustices of English society, takes Tamburlaine as model. 'I have been making', he tells Casaubon and Dorothea,

> 'a sketch of Marlowe's Tamburlaine Driving the Conquered Kings in his Chariot ... I take Tamburlaine in his chariot for the tremendous course of the world's physical history lashing on the harnessed dynasties. In my opinion, that is a good mythical interpretation.'
> ... 'The sketch must be very grand, if it conveys so much', said Dorothea. 'I should need some explanation even of the meaning you give. Do you intend Tamburlaine to represent earthquakes and volcanoes?'
> 'O yes,' said Will, laughing, 'and migrations of races and clearings of forests – and America and the steam-engine. Everything you can imagine!'
> (Eliot 1965: 245–6)

Much in this 'mythical' description of Marlowe's conquering hero rings true: the unstoppable force of history, sweeping away the detritus of the past, transforming the face of the world. The lines capture the sheer nomadic energy of Marlowe's overreacher. They remind us that the New World was new not only in its never having been seen by Europeans before, but in the promise of transformation it held out for colonialists, many indeed fleeing persecution and emmiseration in the worlds from which they came. It was new also because it would be made anew, and would allow the makers to remake themselves in the process.

And yet, at the same time, Ladislaw construes the forces he evokes in an historically specific way that has its own wide-ranging consequences. For him, not only does the world's 'physical history' exceed the might

of Nature (as Dorothea sees it), but it is represented most fully by the forces of western industrialisation and colonisation. Of those who would be unmade by his remaking of the world there remains no trace. Tamburlaine stands for everything that can be imagined – but only certain things can be imagined at certain times.

And so it is with the 'event' that is Tamburlaine. The nomad ultimately falls to the State, perhaps even becoming the epitome of the State at the height of its power and at its widest reach. Already, in Part II of Marlowe's tragedy, the conqueror's language becomes increasingly similar to that of his competitors; his flights of rhetoric continue but they travel in familiar orbits. The language of geography shifts to emphasise the possession of space rather than the contingency that characterised the nomad's movement. The crowns return as symbols, but this time their 'meaning' is much as we would expect. And the death of the body, when it comes – as come it must – is not an event that shakes the world.

> *Amyras*: Meet heaven and earth, and here let all things end!
> For earth had spent the pride of all her fruit,
> And heaven consumed his choicest living fire.
> Let heaven and earth his timeless death deplore,
> For both their worths will equal him no more.
> *Exeunt* [in procession, with Amyras drawn in the chariot]
>
> (II: V.iii. 250–4)

The imagined end is exhaustion. The fire is consumed, the scorched earth remains.

Primary Works Cited

Bacon, Francis (1854), *The Works*, 3 vols, ed. and trans. Basil Montague, Philadelphia: Parry and Macmillan.

Benzoni, Girolamo (1565), *Historia del Mondo Nuovo*, Venice.

Bodin, Jean [1568] (1924), *Response aux paradoxes de Malestroit touchant l'Encherissment de toute Choses et le Moyen d'y remedier*, in Arthur Eli Monroe (ed.), *Early Economic Thought: Selections from Economic Writing prior to Adam Smith*, Cambridge, MA: Harvard University Press, 121–42.

Bonifacio, Giovanni (1616), *L'Arte de Cenni*, Venice.

Brome, Richard [1640] (1995), *The Antipodes*, in *Three Renaissance Travel Plays*, ed. Anthony Parr, Manchester: Manchester University Press.

Brönte, Charlotte [1847] (1947), *Jane Eyre*, Harlow: Longman.

Camões, Luís Vaz de [1572] (1950), *Os Lusíadas (The Lusiads)*, trans. Leonard Bacon, New York: Hispanic Society of America.

Campion, Edmund [c. 1571] (1633), *The Historie of Ireland*, London.

Casas, Bartolomé de las [1552] (1974), *In Defense of the Indians*, trans. and ed. Stafford Poole, DeKalb: Northern Illinois University Press.

Churchyard, Thomas (1579), *A Generall Rehearsall of Warres* or *Churchyardes Choise*, London.

Columbus, Christopher (1930), *Select Documents Illustrating the Four Voyages of Columbus*, trans. and ed. Cecil Jane, 2 vols, London: Hakluyt Society.

— (1960), *The Journal of Christopher Columbus*, trans. Cecil Jane, London: Hakluyt Society.

Daunce, Edward (1590), *A Briefe Discourse of the Spanish State*, London.

De Bry, Theodore (1595), *Nova alfati effictio*, Frankfurt am Main.

— (1598), *Ander Theil der Orientalischen Indien (India Orientalis II)*, Frankfurt am Main.

— (1628), *II. Pars Indiae Orientalis (India Orientalis II)*, Frankfurt am Main.

De Mendoza, Juan Gonzalez [1585] (1588), *The Historie of the Great and Mightie Kingdome of China*, London.

Dee, John (1577), *General and Rare Memorials Pertayning to the Perfect Arte of Navigation*, London.

Derricke, John (1581), *Image of Irelande*, London.

Donne, John (1967), *The Complete Poetry of John Donne*, ed. John T. Shawcross, New York: Anchor Books.

— (1987), *Selected Prose*, London: Penguin Books.

Dryden, John [1673] (1994), *Amboyna*, in *The Works of John Dryden*, ed. Vinton A. Dearing, Berkeley: University of California Press.

Edelman, Charles, ed. (2005), *The Stukeley Plays*, Manchester: Manchester University Press.

Eden, Richard (1555), *The Decades of the Newe Worlde or West India*, London.

Eliot, George [1874] (1965), *Middlemarch*, London: Penguin Books.

Ercilla y Zuniga, Alonso de [1569–89] (1993), *La Araucana*, ed. Isaías Lerner, Madrid: Ediciones Cátedra.

Faria y Sousa, Manuel (1695), *The Portuguese Asia*, London.

Fernández Retamar, Roberto [1969] (1974), 'Caliban: Notes Toward a Discussion of Culture in Our America', trans. Lynn Garafola et al., *Massachusetts Review* 15.

Fletcher, John [1620–1] (1982), *The Island Princess*, in *The Dramatic Works in the Beaumont and Fletcher Canon*, vol. 5, gen. ed. Fredson Bowers, Cambridge: Cambridge University Press.

Foxe, John (1610), *Actes and Monuments*, 2 vols, London.

Geoffrey of Monmouth [c. 1136] (1966), *The History of the Kings of Britain*, trans. Lewis Thorpe, Harmondsworth: Penguin Books.

Giovio, Paulo (1546), *Short Treatise upon the Turkes Chronicles*, London.

Grafton, Richard (1569), *A Chronicle at Large and Meere History of the Affayres of England*, London.

Hakluyt (the Elder), Richard [c. 1585] (1965), 'Reasons for Colonization', in Louis B. Wright (ed.), *The Elizabethans' America: A Collection of Early Reports by Englishmen on the New World*, London: Edward Arnold.

Hakluyt, Richard [c. 1584] (1993), *A Particuler Discourse . . . Known as the Discourse of Western Planting*, ed. D. B. Quinn, London: Hakluyt Society.

— ed. (1587), *De Orbe Novo Peter Martyris*, Paris.

— (1589), *The Principall Navigations, Voiages and Discoveries of the English Nation*, London.

Hall, Joseph (1605), *Mundus Alter et Idem*, London.

Hariot, Thomas (1590), *A Briefe and True Report of the New Found Land of Virginia*, Frankfurt am Main.

Kemys, Laurence (1596), *A Relation of the Second Voyage to Guiana*, London.

Knolles, Richard (1603), *The Generall Historie of the Turkes*, London.

Lamming, George [1960] (1991), *The Pleasures of Exile*, Ann Arbor: University of Michigan Press.

Le Challeaux, Nicolas (1566), *Discours de l'histoire de la Floride*, Dieppe.

Léry, Jean de [1578] (1990), *History of a Voyage to the Land of Brazil, otherwise called America*, trans. Janet Whatley, Berkeley: University of California Press.

Linschoten, Jan Huygen van [1596] (1598), *Iohn Huighen van Linschoten his Discours of Voyages into ye Easte & West Indies*, London.

Lopes de Castanheda, Fernão (1551), *História do descobrimento e conquista da Índia pelos Portugueses*, Coimbra.

— (1582), *The First Book of the Historie and Discoverie of the Conquest of the East Indies*, trans. N. L[ichefield], London.

Lucretius (1965), *On Nature*, trans. Russel M. Geer, New York: Bobbs-Merrill Co.

Malynes, Gerrard (1601), *A Treatise of the Canker in England's Commonwealth*, London.

Mandeville, John (1968), *Mandeville's Travels*, ed. M. C. Seymour, Oxford: Clarendon Press.

Marlowe, Christopher [c. 1587–8] (1998), *Tamburlaine the Great, Parts I and 2*, in *The Complete Works of Christopher Marlowe*, vol. 5, ed. David Fuller, Oxford: Clarendon Press.

Marvell, Andrew (1972), *The Complete Poems*, ed. Elizabeth Story Donno, London: Penguin Books.

Massinger, Philip [1624] (2010), *The Renegado*, ed. Michael Neill, London: A. and C. Black.

Middleton, Thomas (1964), *The Works of Thomas Middleton*, ed. A. H. Bullen, New York: AMS Press.

Montaigne, Michel de [1580–95] (1958), *The Complete Essays of Montaigne*, trans. Donald Frame, Stanford: Stanford University Press.

Mun, Thomas (1621), *A Discourse of Trade from England to the East Indies*, London.

— (1664), *England's Treasure by Forraign Trade*, London.

Olearius, Adam (1669), *The Voyages and Travells of the Ambassadors sent by Frederick Duke of Holstein to the Great Duke of Muscovey, and the King of Persia*, London.

Oresme, Nicole [c. 1360] (1924), *Traicte de la Premiére Invention des Monnoies*, in Arthur Eli Monroe (ed.), *Early Economic Thought: Selections from Economic Writing prior to Adam Smith*, Cambridge, MA: Harvard University Press, 79–102.

Orta, Garcia da [1563] (1913), *Colloquies on the Simples and Drugs of India by Garcia da Orta*, trans. Sir Clements Markham, London: Hakluyt Society.

Raleigh, Sir Walter [1596] (1848), *The Discoverie of the Large, Rich and Bewtiful Empire of Guiana*, ed. Robert Schomburgk, London: Hakluyt Society.

Robert, Lewes (1641), *The Treasure of Trafficke, or, A Discourse of Forraigne Trade*, London.

Shakespeare, William [c. 1594–6] (1979), *A Midsummer Night's Dream*, ed. Harold F. Brooks, London: The Arden Shakespeare.
— [c. 1596] (2006), *The Merchant of Venice*, ed. Leah S. Marcus, New York: W. W. Norton.
— [c. 1604] (1997), *Othello*, ed. E. A. J. Honigmann, London: The Arden Shakespeare.
— [c. 1611] (1999), *The Tempest*, ed. Virginia Mason Vaughan and Alden T. Vaughan, Walton-on-Thames: Thomas Nelson and Sons.
Spenser, Edmund [I–III, 1590; IV–VI, 1596; VII, 1609] (1978), *The Faerie Queene*, London: Penguin Books.
— [c. 1596] (1970), *A View of the Present State of Ireland*, ed. W. L. Renwick, Oxford: Clarendon Press.
— (1758), *Spenser's Faerie Queene*, ed. John Upton, 2 vols, London.
Staden, Hans [1557] (2008), *Hans Staden's True History: An Account of Cannibal Captivity in Brazil*, trans. and ed. Neil. L. Whitehead and Michael Harbsmeier, Durham, NC: Duke University Press.
Strachey, William [1612] (1953), *The Historie of Travell into Virginia Britannia*, ed. Louis B. Wright and Virginia Freund, London: Hakluyt Society.
Vespucci, Amerigo (1894), *The Letters of Amerigo Vespucci and Other Documents Illustrative of his Career*, trans. Clement R. Markham, London: Hakluyt Society.
Vicente, Gil [c. 1509] (1997), *Auto da Índia*, in *Three Discovery Plays by Gil Vicente*, ed. and trans. Antony Lappin, Warminster: Aris and Phillips.
Wheeler, John (1601), *A Treatise of Commerce*, London.

Secondary Works Cited

Abu-Lughod, Janet (1991), *Before European Hegemony: The World System A.D. 1250–1350*, Oxford: Oxford University Press.

Appiah, Anthony Kwame (1991), 'Is the Post- in Postmodern the Post- in Postcolonial', *Critical Inquiry* 17: 336–57.

Aptekar, Jane (1969), *Icons of Justice: Iconography and Thematic Imagery in Book V of* The Faerie Queene, New York: Columbia University Press.

Archer, John Michael (2001), *Old Worlds: Egypt, Southwest Asia, India, and Russia in Early Modern English Writing*, Stanford: Stanford University Press.

Armitage, David (2000), *The Ideological Origins of the British Empire*, Cambridge: Cambridge University Press.

Aubrey, James R. (1993), 'Race and the Spectacle of the Monstrous in Othello', *CLIO* 22.3: 221–38.

Baker, David J. (1997), 'Where in Ireland is *The Tempest?*', in Mark Thornton Burnett and Ramona Wray (eds), *Shakespeare and Ireland: History, Politics, Culture*, Houndmills: Palgrave Macmillan, 68–88.

Barbour, Richmond (2003), *Before Orientalism: London's Theatre of the East, 1576–1626*, Cambridge: Cambridge University Press.

Barker, Francis and Peter Hulme (1985), 'Nymphs and Reapers Heavily Vanish: The Discursive Con-texts of *The Tempest*', in John Drakakis (ed.), *Alternative Shakespeares 2*, London: Methuen, pp. 191–205.

Barker, Francis, Peter Hulme, Margaret Iverson and Diana Loxley, eds (1985), *Europe and Its Others: Proceedings of the Essex Conference on the Sociology of Literature, July 1984*, 2 vols, Colchester: University of Essex Press.

Baron, Samuel H., ed. and trans. (1967), *The Travels of Olearius in Seventeenth-Century Russia*, Stanford: Stanford University Press.

Bartels, Emily (1993), *Spectacles of Strangeness: Imperialism, Alienation, and Marlowe*, Philadelphia: University of Pennsylvania Press.

— (1997), 'Othello and Africa: Postcolonialism Reconsidered', *William and Mary Quarterly*, 3rd Series, 54.1: 45–64.

— (2009), *Speaking of the Moor: From Alcazar to Othello*, Philadelphia: University of Pennsylvania Press.

Bartlett, Robert (1993), *The Making of Europe: Conquest, Colonization and Cultural Change 950–1350*, New Haven, CT: Yale University Press.

— (2001), 'Medieval and Modern Conceptions of Race and Ethnicity', *Journal of Medieval and Early Modern Studies* 31.1: 39–56.

Bate, Jonathan (1993), *Shakespeare and Ovid*, Oxford: Oxford University Press.

Bauer, Ralph (2003), *The Cultural Geography of Colonial American Literatures: Empire, Travel, Modernity*, Cambridge: Cambridge University Press.

Beekman, E. M. (1996), *Troubled Pleasures: Dutch Colonial Literature from the East Indies 1600–1950*, Cambridge: Cambridge University Press.

Bell, Aubrey F. G. (1922), *Portuguese Literature*, Oxford: Clarendon Press.

Belsey, Catherine (1994), *Desire: Love Stories in Western Culture*, Oxford: Oxford University Press.

— (2008), *Shakespeare in Theory and Practice*, Edinburgh: Edinburgh University Press.

Bhabha, Homi (1994), *The Location of Culture*, London: Routledge.

Biggar, H. P. (1930), *A Collection of Documents Relating to Jacques Cartier and the Sieur de Roberval*, in *Publications of the Public Archive of Canada* 14, Ottawa.

— (1993), *The Voyages of Jacques Cartier*, Toronto: University of Toronto Press.

Bisaha, Nancy (2004), *Creating East and West: Renaissance Humanists and the Ottoman Turks*, Philadelphia: University of Pennsylvania Press.

Blumenberg, Hans (1996), *Shipwreck with Spectator*, Cambridge, MA: MIT Press.

Boxer C. R. (1969), *Four Centuries of Portuguese Expansion, 1415–1825*, Berkeley: University of California Press.

Brading, D. A. (1991), *The First America: The Spanish Monarchy, Creole Patriots, and the Liberal State 1492–1867*, Cambridge: Cambridge University Press.

Brenner, Robert (1993), *Merchants and Revolution: Commercial Change, Political Conflict, and London's Overseas Traders, 1550–1653*, Princeton: Princeton University Press.

Brotton, Jerry (1997), *Trading Territories: Mapping the Early Modern World*, London: Reaktion Books.

— (1998), '"This Tunis, Sir, was Carthage": Contesting Colonialism in *The Tempest*', in Ania Loomba and Martin Orkin (eds), *Post-Colonial Shakespeares*, London: Routledge, 23–42.

Brown, Paul (1985), '"This thing of darkness I acknowledge mine": *The Tempest* and the Discourse of Colonialism', in Jonathan Dollimore and

Alan Sinfield (eds), *Political Shakespeare: Essays in Cultural Materialism*, Ithaca, NY: Cornell University Press, pp. 48–71.

Brummett, Palmira (1994), *Ottoman Seapower and Levantine Diplomacy in the Age of Discovery*, Albany, NY: State University of New York Press.

Bucher, Bernadette (1981), *Icon and Conquest: A Structural Analysis of de Bry's Great Voyages*, Chicago: University of Chicago Press.

Burton, Jonathan (2005), *Traffic and Turning: Islam and English Drama, 1579–1624*, Newark, DE: University of Delaware Press.

Burton, Jonathan and Ania Loomba (2007), *Race in Early Modern England: A Documentary Companion*, New York: Palgrave Macmillan.

Butler, Martin (1984), *Theatre and Crisis 1632–42*, Cambridge: Cambridge University Press.

Campbell, Mary Baine (1999), *Wonder & Science: Imagining Worlds in Early Modern Europe*, Ithaca, NY: Cornell University Press.

Canny, Nicholas P. (1976), *The Elizabethan Conquest of Ireland: A Pattern Established 1565–76*, New York: Barnes & Noble Books.

— (1988), *Kingdom and Colony: Ireland in the Atlantic World 1560–80*, Baltimore: Johns Hopkins University Press.

— (2001), *Making Ireland British 1580–1650*, Oxford: Oxford University Press.

Carroll, Clare (2001), *Circe's Cup: Cultural Transformations in Early Modern Writing about Ireland*, Cork: Cork University Press.

Carroll, Clare and Patricia King, eds (2003), *Ireland and Postcolonial Theory*, Cork: Cork University Press.

Cartelli, Thomas (1991), *Marlowe, Shakespeare, and the Economy of Theatrical Experience*, Philadelphia: University of Pennsylvania Press.

— (1999), *Repositioning Shakespeare: National Formations, Postcolonial Appropriations*, London: Routledge.

Castelo-Branco, Maria dos Remédios (1996), 'Significado do cómico do *Auto da Índia*', *Occidente* LXX.

Cormack, Lesley B. (1997), *Charting an Empire: Geography at the English University, 1580–1620*, Chicago: University of Chicago Press.

Corthell, Ronald (1997), *Ideology and Desire in Renaissance Poetry: The Subject of Donne*, Detroit: Wayne State University Press.

Daston, Lorraine and Katherine Park (1998), *Wonders and the Order of Nature 1150–1750*, New York: Zone Books.

De Certeau, Michel (1980), 'Writing vs. Time: History and Anthropology in the Works of Lafitau', *Yale French Studies* 59: 37–64.

— (1998), *The Writing of History*, New York: Columbia University Press.

De Sousa, Geraldo U. (1999), *Shakespeare's Cross-Cultural Encounters*, New York: Palgrave.

Deleuze, Gilles (1990), *The Logic of Sense*, New York: Columbia University Press.

Deleuze, Gilles and Felix Guattari (1987), *A Thousand Plateaus: Capitalism and Schizophrenia*, Minneapolis: University of Minnesota Press.

Derrida, Jacques (1974), *Of Grammatology*, Baltimore: Johns Hopkins University Press.

— (1985), *The Margins of Philosophy*, Chicago: University of Chicago Press.

Donaldson, Ian (1970), *The World Turned Upside-Down: Comedy from Jonson to Fielding*, Oxford: Clarendon Press.

Dumézil, Georges (1988), *Mitra-Varuna*, New York: Zone Books.

Fanon, Frantz (1967), *Black Skins, White Masks*, New York: Grove Press.

Ferguson, Margaret W. (2003), *Dido's Daughters: Literacy, Gender, and Empire in Early Modern England and France*, Chicago: University of Chicago Press.

Ferreira, Ana Paula (1994), 'Intersecting Historical Performances: Gil Vicente's *Auto da Índia*', *Gestos: Teoria y Practico del Teatro Hispanico* 9.17: 99–113.

Fleming, Juliet (2001), *Graffiti and the Writing Arts in Early Modern England*, Philadelphia: University of Pennsylvania Press.

Floyd-Wilson, Mary (2006), *English Ethnicity and Race in Early Modern Drama*, Cambridge: Cambridge University Press.

Foucault, Michel (1973), *The Order of Things: An Archaeology of the Human Sciences*, New York: Vintage Books.

Freer, Coburn (1996), 'Donne and Elizabethan Economic Theory', *Criticism* 38: 497–520.

French, Milton J. (1934), 'Othello among the Anthropophagi', *PMLA* 49.3: 807–9.

Frey, Charles H. (1979), '*The Tempest* and the New World', *Shakespeare Quarterly* 30: 29–41.

Fuchs, Barbara (1997), 'Conquering Islands: Contextualising *The Tempest*', *Shakespeare Quarterly* 48: 45–62.

— (2001), *Mimesis and Alterity: the New World, Islam, and European Identities*, Cambridge: Cambridge University Press.

— (2009), *Exotic Identities: Maurophilia and the Construction of Early Modern Spain*, Philadelphia: University of Pennsylvania Press.

Fuller, Mary C. (1991), 'Ralegh's Fugitive Gold: Reference and Deferral in *The Discoverie of Guiana*', *Representations* 33: 42–64.

— (2008), *Remembering the Early Modern Voyage: English Narratives in the Age of European Expansion*, New York: Palgrave Macmillan.

Fumerton, Patricia (1991), *Cultural Aesthetics: Renaissance Literature and the Practice of Social Ornament*, Chicago: University of Chicago Press.

Garber, Marjorie (1984), '"Here's Nothing Writ": Scribe, Script, and Circumspections in Marlowe's Plays', *Theatre Journal* 36: 301–20.

Garbero, Maria del Sapio, ed. (2009), *Identity, Otherness and Empire in Shakespeare's Rome*, Burlington, VT: Ashgate.

Gates, Henry Louis Jr. (1986), 'Introduction: Writing "Race" and the

Difference it Makes', in Henry Louis Gates Jr. (ed.), *'Race,' Writing, and Difference*, Chicago: University of Chicago Press.

Gaudio, Michael (2008), *Engraving the Savage: The New World and Techniques of Civilization*, Minneapolis: University of Minnesota Press.

Gil Harris, Jonathan (2004), *Sick Economies: Drama, Mercantilism, and Disease in Shakespeare's England*, Philadelphia: University of Pennsylvania Press.

Gillies, John (1986), 'Shakespeare's Virginian Masque', *English Literary History* 53: 673–707.

Goez, Werner (1958), *Translatio Imperii: Ein Beitrag zur Geschichte des Geschichtsdenkens und der politischen Theorien im Mittel Alter und in der frühen Neuzeit*, Tübingen: J. C. B. Mohr Verlag.

Goffman, Daniel (2002), *The Ottoman Empire and Early Modern Europe*, Cambridge: Cambridge University Press.

Greenblatt, Stephen (1976), 'Learning to Curse: Aspects of Linguistic Colonialism in the Sixteenth Century', in Fredi Chiappelli (ed.), *First Images of America: The Impact of the New World on the Old*, Berkeley: University of California Press.

— (1980), *Renaissance Self-Fashioning from More to Shakespeare*, Chicago: University of Chicago Press.

— (1990), *Learning to Curse: Essays in Early Modern Culture*, New York: Routledge.

— (1991), *Marvelous Possessions: The Wonder of the New World*, Chicago: University of Chicago Press.

Greene, Roland (1999), *Unrequited Conquests: Love and Empire in the Colonial Americas*, Chicago: University of Chicago Press.

Greer, Margaret, Walter Mignolo and Maureen Quilligan, eds (2007), *Rereading the Black Legend: Discourses of Religious and Racial Difference in the Renaissance Empires*, Chicago: University of Chicago Press.

Gregerson, Linda (1995), *The Reformation of the Subject: Spenser, Milton, and the English Protestant Epic*, Cambridge: Cambridge University Press.

Griffiths, Trevor R. (1983), '"This Island's Mine": Caliban and Colonialism', *Yearbook of English Studies* 13: 159–80.

Grove, Richard H. (1995), *Green Imperialism: Colonial Expansion, Tropical Island Edens and the Origins of Environmentalism, 1600–1800*, Delhi: Oxford University Press.

Hadfield, Andrew (1997), *Edmund Spenser's Irish Experience: Wilde Fruit and Salvage Soyl*, Oxford: Clarendon Press.

Hall, Kim (1995), *Things of Darkness: Economies of Race and Gender in Early Modern England*, Ithaca, NY: Cornell University Press.

Hall, Stuart (1986), 'Gramsci's Relevance for the Study of Race and Ethnicity', *Journal of Communication Inquiry* 10: 5–27.

Hardt, Michael and Antonio Negri (2000), *Empire*, Cambridge, MA: Harvard University Press.

Hart, Jonathan (2000), *Representing the New World: The English and French Uses of the Example of Spain*, New York: Palgrave.

Hartog, François (1988), *The Mirror of Herodotus: The Representation of the Other in the Writing of History*, Berkeley: University of California Press.

— (1992), 'Herodotus and the Historiographical Operation', *diacritics* 22.2: 83–93.

Henderson, Diana E. (1995), *Passion Made Public: Elizabethan Lyric, Gender, and Performance*, Urbana-Champaign: University of Illinois Press.

— (2003), '*The Tempest* in Performance' in Richard Dutton and Jean E. Howard (eds), *A Companion to Shakespeare's Works, Volume IV: The Poems, Problem Comedies, Late Plays*, Oxford: Basil Blackwell, 216–39.

Hendricks, Margo and Patricia Parker, eds (1994), *Women, 'Race' and Writing in the Early Modern Period*, London: Routledge.

Highley, Christopher (1997), *Shakespeare, Spenser and the Crisis in Ireland*, Cambridge: Cambridge University Press.

Hopkins, Lisa (2008), *The Cultural Uses of the Caesars on the English Renaissance Stage*, Aldershot: Ashgate Books.

Hulme, Peter (1986), *Colonial Encounters: Europe and the Native Caribbean 1492–1797*, London: Methuen Books.

Hulme, Peter and William Sherman, eds (2000), *'The Tempest' and Its Travels*, London: Reaktion Books.

Hunter, G. K. (1977), 'A Roman Thought: Renaissance Attitudes to History Exemplified in Shakespeare and Jonson', in B. S. Lee (ed.), *An English Miscellany: Presented to W. S. Mackie*, Oxford: Oxford University Press.

Inalcik, Halil (1995), *From Empire to Republic: Essays on Ottoman and Turkish Social History*, Istanbul: Isis Press.

Ivins, William M. Jr. (1969), *Print and Visual Communication*, Cambridge, MA: MIT Press.

James, Heather (1997), *Shakespeare's Troy: Drama, Politics, and the Translation of Empire*, Cambridge: Cambridge University Press.

Jameson, Frederic (1999), 'Marxism and Dualism in Deleuze', in Ian Buchanan (ed.), *A Deleuzian Century?*, Durham, NC: Duke University Press, pp. 13–36.

Judson, Alexander C. (1945), *The Life of Edmund Spenser*, Baltimore: Johns Hopkins University Press.

Kahn, Coppélia (1997), *Roman Shakespeare: Warriors, Wounds, Women*, London: Routledge.

Kastan, David Scott (1999), *Shakespeare After Theory*, New York: Routledge.

Kaye, Joel (1998), *Economy and Nature in the Fourteenth Century: Money, Market Exchange, and the Emergence of Scientific Thought*, Cambridge: Cambridge University Press.

Kermode, Frank (1954), 'Introduction' to New Arden edition of *The Tempest*, London: Methuen Books.

Kosellek, Reinhardt (1979), *Vergangene Zukunft: Zur Semantik geschichtlicher Zeiten*, Frankfurt am Main: Suhrkamp Verlag.

Knapp, Jeffrey (1992), *An Empire Nowhere: England, America, and Literature from 'Utopia' to 'The Tempest'*, Berkeley: University of California Press.

Koebner, Richard (1953), '"The Imperial Crown of the Realm": Henry VIII, Constantine the Great, and Polydore Vergil', *Bulletin of the Institute for Historical Research* XXVI: 29–52.

Lach, Donald (1977), *Asia in the Making of Europe*, 3 vols, Chicago: University of Chicago Press.

Latour, Bruno and Peter Weibel, eds (2005), *Making Things Public: Atmospheres of Democracy*, Cambridge, MA: MIT Press.

Law, John (2001), 'On the Methods of Long Distance Control: Vessels, Navigation, and the Portuguese Route to India', Lancaster: Centre for Science Studies, Lancaster University, at http://www.comp.lancs.ac.uk/sociology/papers/Law-Methods-of-Long-Distance-Control.pdf

Leslie, Marina (1997), 'Antipodal Anxieties: Joseph Hall, Richard Brome, Margaret Cavendish and the Cartographies of Gender', *Genre* 30: 53–80.

Lestringant, Frank (1990), *Le Huguenot et le Sauvage: L'Amérique et la controverse coloniale en France au temps des Guerres de Religion (1555–1589)*, Paris: Klincksieck.

Levin, Harry (1952), *The Overreacher: A Study of Christopher Marlowe*, Cambridge: Cambridge University Press.

Lim, Walter S. H. (1998), *The Arts of Empire: The Poetics of Colonialism from Ralegh to Milton*, Newark, DE: University of Delaware Press.

Linton, Joan Pong (1998), *The Romance of the New World: Gender and the Literary Formations of English Colonialism*, Cambridge: Cambridge University Press.

Livermore, H. V. (1976), *A New History of Portugal*, Cambridge: Cambridge University Press.

Loomba, Ania (1998), *Colonialism/Postcolonialism*, London: Routledge.

— (2002a), *Shakespeare, Race, and Colonialism*, Oxford: Oxford University Press.

— (2002b), '"Break her will, and bruise no bone sir": Colonial and Sexual Mastery in Fletcher's *The Island Princess*', *Journal of Early Modern Cultural Studies* 2.1: 68–108.

Loomba, Ania and Martin Orkin, eds (1998), *Postcolonial Shakespeares*, London: Routledge.

Loomba, Ania, Suvir Kaul, Matti Bunzi et al., eds (2005), *Postcolonial Studies and Beyond*, Durham, NC: Duke University Press.

McCabe, Richard (2002), *Spenser's Monstrous Regiment: Elizabethan Ireland and the Poetics of Difference*, Oxford: Oxford University Press.

McClintock, Anne (1992), 'The Angel of Progress: Pitfalls of the Term "Post-Colonialism"', *Social Text* 31/32: 84–98.

McCulloch, R., ed. (1970), *Early English Tracts on Commerce*, Cambridge: Cambridge University Press.

MacDougall, Hugh A. (1982), *Racial Myth in English History: Trojans, Teutons, and Anglo-Saxons*, Hanover NH: University Press of New England.

MacMillan, Ken (2001), 'Discourse on History, Geography, and Law: John Dee and the Limits of the British Empire, 1576–80', *Canadian Journal of History* 36.1: 1–25.

McMullan, Gordon (1994), *The Politics of Unease in the Plays of John Fletcher*, Amherst: University of Massachusetts Press.

Maley, Willey (1997), *Salvaging Spenser: Colonialism, Culture and Identity*, New York: St Martin's Press.

Malone, Edmond (1808), *An Account of the Incidents from which the Title and Part of the Story of Shakespeare's 'Tempest' were Derived and its True Date Determined*, London: C. and R. Baldwin.

Maltby, William S. (1971), *The Black Legend in England: The Development of Anti-Spanish Sentiment, 1558–1660*, Durham, NC: Duke University Press.

Mannoni, Octave (1956), *Prospero and Caliban: The Psychology of Colonization*, trans. Pamela Powesland, London: Methuen.

Marotti, Arthur (1986), *John Donne, Coterie Poet*, Madison: University of Wisconsin Press.

Matar, Nabil (1998), *Islam in Britain 1558–1685*, Cambridge: Cambridge University Press.

Matthew, H. C. G. and Brian Harrison, eds (2004), *Oxford Dictionary of National Biography*, Oxford: Oxford University Press.

Mignolo, Walter (1995), *The Darker Side of the Renaissance: Literacy, Territoriality, and Colonization*, Ann Arbor: University of Michigan Press.

— (2000), *Local Histories/Global Designs: Coloniality, Subaltern Knowledges, and Border Thinking*, Princeton: Princeton University Press.

Mitchell, W. J. T. (1994), *Picture Theory*, Chicago: University of Chicago Press.

Monroe, Arthur Eli, ed. (1924), *Early Economic Thought: Selections from Economic Literature prior to Adam Smith*, Cambridge, MA: Harvard University Press.

Neely, Carol (1995), 'Circumscriptions and Unhousedness: Othello in the Borderlands', in Deborah Barker and Ivo Kamps (eds), *Shakespeare and Gender: A History*, London: Verso, pp. 302–15.

Neill, Michael (1989), 'Unproper Beds: Race, Adultery and the Hideous in Othello', *Shakespeare Quarterly* 40.4: 383–412.

— (2000), *Putting History to the Question: Power, Politics and Society in the English Renaissance*, New York: Columbia University Press.

Newman, Karen (1987), '"And wash the Ethiop white": Femininity and the

Monstrous in *Othello*', in Jean E. Howard and Marion F. O'Connor (eds), *Shakespeare Reproduced: The Text in History and Ideology*, London: Methuen, pp. 143–62.

Nicolet, Claude (1991), *Space, Geography, and Politics in the Early Roman Empire*, Ann Arbor: University of Michigan Press.

Nixon, Rob (1987), 'Caribbean and African Appropriations of *The Tempest*', *Critical Inquiry* 13: 557–78.

Nocentelli, Carmen (2010), 'Spice Race: *The Island Princess* and the Politics of Transnational Appropriation', *PMLA* 125.3: 572–88.

Orgel, Stephen (1987), 'Introduction', *The Tempest*, Oxford: Oxford University Press.

Pagden, Anthony (1982), *The Fall of Natural Man: The American Indian and the Origins of Comparative Ethnology*, Cambridge: Cambridge University Press.

— (1995), *Lords of All the World: Ideologies of Empire in Spain, Britain and France c. 1500 – c. 1800*, New Haven, CT: Yale University Press.

Parry, J. H. (1940), *The Spanish Theory of Empire in the Sixteenth Century*, Cambridge: Cambridge University Press.

Palmer, Patricia (2001), *Language and Conquest in Early Modern Ireland: English Renaissance Literature and Elizabethan Imperial Expansion*, Cambridge: Cambridge University Press.

Pocock, J. G. A. (1957), *The Ancient Constitution and the Feudal Law: A Study of English Historical Thought in the Seventeenth Century*, Cambridge: Cambridge University Press.

Powell, Timothy, ed. (1999), *Beyond the Binary: Reconstructing Cultural Identity in a Multicultural Context*, New Brunswick, NJ: Rutgers University Press.

Quinn, D. B. (1966), *The Elizabethans and the Irish*, Ithaca, NY: Cornell University Press.

Quint, David (1983), *Origin and Originality in Renaissance Literature: Versions of the Source*, New Haven, CT: Yale University Press.

— (1993), *Epic and Empire*, Princeton: Princeton University Press.

Raman, Shankar (2001a), 'Can't Buy Me Love: Money, Gender, and Colonialism in Donne's Erotic Verse', *Criticism* 43.2: 135–68.

— (2001b), 'Back to the Future: Forging History in Luis de Camões' *Os Lusíadas*' in Ivo Kamps and Jyotsna Singh (eds), *Travel Knowledge: European 'Discoveries' in the Early Modern Period*, New York: Palgrave Macmillan, pp. 127–47.

— (2002), *Framing 'India': The Colonial Imaginary in Early Modern Europe*, Stanford: Stanford University Press.

— (2004), '"The Ship Comes Well-Laden": Court Politics, Colonialism and Cuckoldry in Gil Vicente's *Auto da Índia*', in Balachandran Rajan and Elizabeth Sauer (eds), *Imperialisms: Historical and Literary Investigations 1500–1900*, New York: Palgrave Macmillan, pp. 15–32.

— (2011), 'Learning from De Bry: Lessons in Seeing and Writing the Heathen', *Journal of Medieval and Early Modern Studies*, 41 (1): 13–66.

Riggs, David (2004), *The World of Christopher Marlowe*, New York: Henry Holt and Company.

Robinson, Benedict (2007), *Islam and Early Modern English Literature: The Politics of Romance from Spenser to Milton*, New York: Palgrave Macmillan.

Roig, Adrien (1990), 'Le Theatre de Gil Vicente e le Voyage aux Indes', *Quadrant* 7: 5–23.

Ronan, Clifford (1995), *'Antike Roman': Power Symbology and the Roman Play in Early Modern England, 1585–1635*, Athens, GA: University of Georgia Press.

Said, Edward (1979), *Orientalism*, London: Vintage Books.

— (1993), *Culture and Imperialism*, London: Vintage Books.

Seaton, Ethel (1924), 'Marlowe's Map', *Essays and Studies* X: 13–35.

Shannon, Robert M. (1989), *Visions of the New World in the Drama of Lope de Vega*, New York: Peter Lang.

Sherman, William H. (1995), *John Dee: The Politics of Reading and Writing in the English Renaissance*, Amherst: University of Massachusetts Press.

Shohat, Ella (1992), 'Notes on the "Post-Colonial"' *Social* Text 31/32: 99–113.

Skilliter, S. A. (1977), *William Harborne and the Trade with Turkey, 1578–1582: A Documentary Study of the first Anglo-Ottoman Relations*, Oxford: Oxford University Press.

Subrahmanyam, Sanjay (1993), *The Portuguese Empire in Asia 1500–1700: A Political and Economic History*, London: Longman.

— (2005), 'On World Historians in the Sixteenth Century', *Representations* 91: 26–57.

Tawney, R. H. and Eileen Power, eds (1962), *Tudor Economic Documents*, 3 vols, New York: Barnes and Noble.

Thomaz, Luís Filipe F. R. (1991), 'Factions, Interests, and Messianism: The Politics of Portuguese Expansion in the East, 1500–21', *The Indian Economic and Social History Review* 28: 98–109.

Todorov, Tzvetan (1984), *The Conquest of America: The Question of the Other*, New York: Harper and Row.

Van den Boogaart, Ernest (2004), 'De Bry's Africa', in Susanna Burghartz (ed.), *Inszenierte Welten / Staging New Worlds: De Brys' Illustrated Travel Reports, 1590–1630*, Basel: Schwabe Verlag, pp. 95–149.

Van Groesen, Michiel (2008), *The Representation of the Overseas World in the De Bry Collection of Voyages (1590–1634)*, Leiden: Brill.

Vaughan, Virgina Mason and Alden T. Vaughan (1999), 'Introduction', *The Tempest*, Surrey: Thomas Nelson and Sons.

Vitkus, Daniel (2003), *Turning Turk: English Theater and the Multicultural Mediterranean, 1570–1630*, New York: Palgrave Macmillan.

Wallerstein, Immanuel (1974), *The Modern World System*, vol. 1, New York: Academic Press.

Wey-Gómez, Nicolás (2008), *The Tropics of Empire: Why Columbus Sailed South to the Indies*, Cambridge, MA: MIT Press.

Whitehead, Neil L. (2000), 'Hans Staden and the Cultural Politics of Cannibalism', *Hispanic American Historical Review* 80(4): 721–52.

Williams, Patrick and Laura Chrisman, eds (1994), *Colonial Discourse and Post-Colonial Theory*, New York: Columbia University Press.

Wilson, Bronwen (2005), *The World in Venice: Print, the City, and Early Modern Identity*, Toronto: University of Toronto Press.

Wilson, Richard (1995), 'Visible Bullets: *Tamburlaine the Great* and Ivan the Terrible', *ELH* 62: 47–68.

Yates, Francis Amelia (1975), *Astrae: The Imperial Theme in the Sixteenth Century*, London: Routledge.

Young, Robert (1990), *White Mythologies: Writing History and the West*, London: Routledge.

Further Reading

Armitage, David (2000), *The Ideological Origins of the British Empire*, Cambridge: Cambridge University Press. Persuasive intellectual and political history reintegrating Britain's domestic history with its extraterritorial expansion.

Bartels, Emily (1993), *Spectacles of Strangeness: Imperialism, Alienation, and Marlowe*, Philadelphia: University of Pennsylvania Press. Full-length study of Christopher Marlowe, showing the centrality of colonialism to his *oeuvre*.

Bhabha, Homi (1994), *The Location of Culture*, London: Routledge. A collection that includes his oft-cited essays on hybridity and mimicry.

Bisaha, Nancy (2004), *Creating East and West: Renaissance Humanists and the Ottoman Turks*, Philadelphia: University of Pennsylvania Press. Lucid account of how Europeans responded to the Ottoman empire after Constantinople's fall to the Turks in 1453.

Burton, Jonathan (2005), *Traffic and Turning: Islam and English Drama, 1579–1624*, Newark, DE: University of Delaware Press. Balanced study of England's relationship to Islamic kingdoms, especially interesting for drawing non-European sources into the conversation.

Burton, Jonathan and Ania Loomba (2007), *Race in Early Modern England: A Documentary Companion*, New York: Palgrave Macmillan. Wide-ranging compendium of primary sources, though the unavoidable brevity of extracts sometimes makes it difficult to place them in the larger context of the works from which they have been excerpted.

Canny, Nicholas P. (1976), *The Elizabethan Conquest of Ireland: A Pattern Established 1565–76*, New York: Barnes & Noble. Good historical analysis of the engagement with Ireland during a crucial period in the consolidation of England's extraterritorial ambitions.

Ferguson, Margaret W. (2003), *Dido's Daughters: Literacy, Gender and Empire in Early Modern England and France*, Chicago: University of Chicago Press. Nuanced treatment of literacy as a site of social contest, through which ideologies of gender and empire were articulated.

Fuller, Mary C. (2008), *Remembering the Early Modern Voyage: English Narratives in the Age of European Expansion*, New York: Palgrave Macmillan. Elegant discussion of colonial memory and forgetting using English travel narratives drawn from Hakluyt's *The Principal Navigations*.

Greenblatt, Stephen (1991), *Marvelous Possessions: The Wonder of the New World*, Chicago: University of Chicago Press. Beautifully written, influential examination of the uses of wonder in early modern responses to the Americas.

Greer, Margaret R., Walter D. Mignolo and Margaret W. Ferguson, eds (2008), *Rereading the Black Legend: The Discourses of Religion and Racial Difference in the Renaissance Empires*, Chicago: University of Chicago Press. Though a little heavily focused on Spanish texts, this collection offers good comparative analyses of early modern practices of racialised discrimination. Especially notable are essays by Pierce, Nirenberg, Lomana and Gravatt.

Hadfield, Andrew (1997), *Edmund Spenser's Irish Experience: Wilde Fruit and Salvage Soyl*, Oxford: Clarendon Press. Perhaps the best of a number of recent studies on England's colonisation of Ireland, focusing on Spenser's ambivalent position between poet of nation and of empire.

Hardt, Michael and Antonio Negri (2000), *Empire*, Cambridge, MA: Harvard University Press. Provocative theoretical re-interpretation that uncovers a genealogy of imperialism leading to neo-imperial forms of contemporary globalisation.

Hart, Jonathan (2000), *Representing the New World: The English and French Uses of the Example of Spain*, New York: Palgrave. Useful comparativist account of how English and French colonialism was shaped by Spanish precedents.

Helgerson, Richard (1992), *Forms of Nationhood: The Elizabethan Writing of England*, Chicago: University of Chicago Press. Well-regarded, wide-ranging study of the sixteenth-century English search for a national identity. The chapters on mapping England and Hakluyt's *Principal Navigations* are especially pertinent.

Hendricks, Margo and Patricia Parker, eds (1994), *Women, 'Race' and Writing in the Early Modern Period*, London: Routledge. Combining feminist criticism with postcolonial and cultural studies, this collection examines the intersections among gendered, racialised and colonial systems of discrimination.

Hulme, Peter (1986), *Colonial Encounters: Europe and the Native Caribbean* 1492–1797, London: Methuen Books. Among the best books to trace the diverse semantic networks underpinning the New World's 'discovery'.

Israel, Jonathan I. (1989), *Dutch Primacy in World Trade, 1585–1640*, Oxford: Clarendon Press. Excellent historical account of the rise of Netherlands' colonial empire.

Kamps, Ivo and Jyotsna Singh, eds (2001), *Travel Knowledge: European 'Discoveries' in the Early Modern Period*, New York: Palgrave. Combining primary sources with critical readings, this collection introduces multiple sites of colonial 'discovery' (from the Levant to Africa). A limitation is its heavy weighting towards English accounts.

Lloyd, David (2003), 'After History: Historicism and Irish Postcolonial Studies', in Clare Carroll (ed.), *Ireland and Postcolonial Theory*, Cork: Cork University Press, pp. 46–62. Though focused on Ireland's colonial status, this superb essay offers a rich discussion of postcolonial studies and its aims.

Loomba, Ania (1998), *Colonialism/Postcolonialism*, London: Routledge. A useful survey of the main issues, contexts, and concepts.

Loomba, Ania, Suvir Kaul, Matti Bunzi et al., eds (2005), *Postcolonial Studies and Beyond*, Durham, NC: Duke University Press. A wide-ranging interdisciplinary collection which examines the state of postcolonial studies and speculates on its future directions.

Mignolo, Walter (1995), *The Darker Side of the Renaissance: Literacy, Territoriality, and Colonization*, Ann Arbor: University of Michigan Press. A study of Spanish, Latin American and Amerindian cultural histories exploring how the rebirth of the classical tradition served also to justify colonial expansion.

Nicolet, Claude (1991), *Space, Geography, and Politics in the Early Roman Empire*, Ann Arbor: University of Michigan Press. Although focused on a much earlier period, this book has significant implications for early modern Europe as well, given the continuing importance of Rome as a colonial model.

Nixon, Rob (1987), 'Caribbean and African Appropriations of *The Tempest*', *Critical Inquiry* 13: 557–78. A strong essay on how Shakespeare's late play became as it were a postcolonial text.

Pagden, Anthony (1982), *The Fall of Natural Man: The American Indian and the Origins of Comparative Ethnology*, Cambridge: Cambridge University Press. Careful reconstruction of the complicated intellectual histories informing Spanish debates over the status of New World natives.

Pincus, Steven C. A. (1992), *Protestantism and Patriotism: Ideologies and the Making of English Foreign Policy, 1650–1688*, Cambridge: Cambridge University Press. Perhaps the best historical account of mid-seventeenth-century conflicts between the rising commercial empires of England and the Netherlands. Focuses on the importance of religion to mercantile competition and foreign policy.

Quint, David (1993), *Epic and Empire*, Princeton: Princeton University Press. Excellent study of the relationship between imperial ideologies and epic as a literary form, from Virgil's *Aeneid* to Milton's *Paradise Lost*.

Raman, Shankar (2002), *Framing 'India': The Colonial Imaginary in Early Modern Europe*, Stanford: Stanford University Press. Contexualises the figures of 'India' and 'the East' to show how they helped produce patterns of thought and behaviour distinctive to European colonialism.

Said, Edward (1979), *Orientalism*, London: Vintage Books. The classic book that set the field going, and still has much to offer.

— (1993), *Culture and Imperialism*, London: Vintage Books. A more open-ended investigation into the cultural repercussions of imperialism, with important interpretations of nineteenth-century novels.

Van Groesen, Michiel (2008), *The Representation of the Overseas World in the De Bry Collection of Voyages (1590–1634)*, Leiden: Brill. Although a little dryly historicist, a comprehensive account of Theodore de Bry's multi-volume compendia, perhaps the most important travel collections for late sixteenth- and seventeenth-century Europe.

Williams, Patrick and Laura Chrisman, eds (1994), *Colonial Discourse and Post-Colonial Theory*, New York: Columbia University Press. Useful compilation of theoretical contributions to postcolonial studies from a variety of perspectives.

Young, Robert (2004), *White Mythologies*, 2nd edn, London: Routledge. Good overview of prominent postcolonial theoretical positions (including those of Jameson, Said, Bhabha and Spivak). Better for its analyses of others' positions than for its own theoretical contributions, however.

Index

Note: page numbers in *italics* refer to illustrations.